MONEY LAUNDERING
AND ILLICIT FINANCIAL FLOWS

Money Laundering
and
Illicit Financial Flows

Following the Money and Value Trails

John A. Cassara

"The love of money is a root of all kinds of evil"

(1 Timothy 6:10)

Contents_i

About the Author

JOHN CASSARA RETIRED AFTER A 26-year career in the federal government intelligence and law enforcement communities. He is considered an expert in anti-money laundering and counterterrorist finance, with particular expertise in the growing threat of alternative remittance systems and forms of trade-based money laundering and value transfer. He invented the concept of international "Trade Transparency Units," an innovative countermeasure to entrenched forms of trade-based money laundering and value transfer. A large part of his career was spent overseas. He is one of the very few to have been both a clandestine operations officer in the U.S. CIA and a special agent for the Department of Treasury.

His last position was as a special agent detailee to the Department of Treasury's Office of Terrorism Finance and Financial Intelligence (TFI). His parent Treasury agency was the Financial Crimes Enforcement Network (FinCEN). Mr. Cassara was also detailed to the U.S. Department of State's Bureau of International Narcotics and Law Enforcement Affairs (INL) Anti-Money Laundering Section to help coordinate U.S. interagency international anti-terrorist finance training and technical assistance efforts.

While working as an investigative Special Agent for U.S. Customs Service, Mr. Cassara conducted a large number of money laundering, fraud, intellectual property rights, smuggling, and diversion of weapons and high technology investigations in Africa, the Middle East, and Europe. He also served two years as an undercover arms dealer. He began his career with Treasury as a special agent assigned to the Washington D.C. field office of the U.S. Secret Service.

Since his retirement, he has lectured in the United States and around the world on a variety transnational crime issues. Mr. Cassara has testified six times as an expert witness before various Congressional committees on matters related to money laundering and terror finance. He is on the Board of Directors of Global Financial Integrity. Mr. Cassara has authored or co-authored several articles and books on money laundering, terror finance, and transnational crime. For additional information or for contact, see www.JohnCassara.com

Preface

"WE ARE GOING TO ASSIGN you to the anti-money laundering section." Those words were spoken to me by Clark Settles, the Division Chief of the Smuggling Division at U.S. Customs headquarters. The year was 1989.

The assignment marked the beginning of my career in anti-money laundering (AML). I was worried. I had only been with Customs for a few years and most of that time was as an undercover arms dealer. I didn't know much about money laundering, but I was willing to learn. I soon discovered a broad, fascinating, and vitally important area of investigation and study. Even though my investigative days are over, I'm still learning.

After I "retired" from a 26-year career in the U.S. intelligence and law enforcement communities, I tried to draw attention to the intertwined threats of money laundering and terrorist finance. I wrote three nonfiction books: Hide & Seek: Intelligence, Law Enforcement and the Stalled War on Terror Finance (Washington, D.C.: Potomac Books, 2006), On the Trail of Terror Finance: What Law Enforcement and Intelligence Officers Need to Know (Washington, D.C.: Red Cell IG, 2010), and Trade-Based Money Laundering: The Next Frontier in International Money Laundering Enforcement (Hoboken, New Jersey, Wiley, 2016). Realizing that some readers are not enthusiastic about whitepapers and PowerPoint presentations, I wrote Demons of Gadara (CreateSpace, 2013) — the first novel to focus on threat finance and underground value transfer. I tried to teach by telling a story. I continued my efforts by writing articles, consulting, speaking before various industry and government groups, and testifying before Congressional committees. Thirty years of investigating, studying, writing, and talking about anti-money laundering and counter-terrorist finance (AML/CFT) and illicit financial flows (IFF) has given me some perspective and rather strong views. This book is a natural sequitur.

The last three decades of AML have witnessed many changes. When I began my career in money laundering enforcement, the investigative focus was on large amounts of drug money sloshing around western banks. The financial transactions environment focused almost solely on formal financial institutions. Transactions were slow, cumbersome, paper-driven, and expensive. Real time transaction processing was barely feasible. Banks were only beginning to put AML safeguards in place — and only with government pressure. Today, there is an explosion in processing speed, efficiency, digitalized data, and advanced analytics. In the United States and many advanced areas of the world, robust AML compliance standards and norms are now the accepted way of doing business. Almost instantaneous financial transparency and corresponding alerts are achievable. In addition to banks, there has been an explosion in the number of non-bank financial institutions, money service businesses (MSBs) and related financial services and corresponding AML protocols.

In 1989, the Financial Action Task Force (FATF) was in its infancy and the FATF 40 recommendations to combat money laundering did not exist. The United States had recently become the first country in the world to make money laundering a crime and enacted a law that is still one of the most powerful in the world, Title 18, U.S. Code Section 1956 (also known as the Money Laundering Control Act). Today we have a wealth of AML/CFT laws, rules, and enabling regulations. Years ago, it was still relatively commonplace for money launderers in the United States to walk into banks with bags filled with cash. The money would more than likely be accepted for deposit with no questions asked and no financial intelligence reports filed.

Thirty years ago, we had some financial intelligence — Currency Transaction Reports (CTRs) and Currency Monetary Instrument Reports (CMIRs) — but there were few attempts to systematically analyze the information. The IRS 8300 form that mandates reporting of cash transactions over $10,000 was in its early stages and the information generated stayed within the IRS and was used primarily for tax enforcement purposes. Suspicious Activity Reports (SARs) did not exist. The first nascent discussions about the establishment of what is now known as the Financial Crimes Enforcement Network (FinCEN) were beginning at Main Treasury, Customs and the IRS. FinCEN is the world's first financial intelligence unit (FIU). Thirty years later there are over 160 FIUs around the world.

In 1989 Treasury's Customs was credited with headline cases such as Operation C-Chase, one of the most successful undercover operations in history that led to the indictment of several individuals associated with the seventh largest privately held bank in the world and eventually the conviction of Panamanian strongman, Manuel Noriega. Thirty years later some international financial institutions abetted by non-transparent offshore companies and financial secrecy havens persist in activities that threaten the integrity of the international financial system. With the creation of the Department of Homeland Security, U.S. Customs no longer exists. Its important work has been diluted with Immigration and Customs Enforcement (ICE's) dual mission. Outside of the IRS (its primary mission is tax enforcement), the Department of Treasury no longer has the capability of investigating financial crimes.

Trade-based money laundering and underground financial systems have been operating around the world for hundreds of years. When I started my anti-money laundering career, they were simply not recognized by law enforcement. Thirty years later, I believe trade-based money laundering in all its varied forms is the largest money laundering methodology in the world. Nevertheless, it is still the least recognized, understood and enforced major money laundering methodology.

Latin American narco-trafficking and money laundering cartels have been a constant. They have received nearly continuous government and media attention. The United States has spent tens of billions of dollars to help combat narco-regimes in Colombia, Mexico, and elsewhere in the region. Despite a tremendous twenty year investment in blood and treasure, Afghanistan remains the primary supplier of opium to the world.

Today, I believe China is the most pervasive and menacing global money laundering threat. Yet the international community looks the other way.

Thirty years ago, cyber banking, e-currencies and mobile payments did not exist. Today, despite their incredible benefits, new payment methods (NPMs) pose increasing challenges for law enforcement.

The study of illicit financial flows (IFFs) emerged in the 1990s. Originally it was mostly an academic exercise and the studies were initially associated with capital flight. Over the years, many non-profits and non-governmental organizations have adopted the analysis of IFFs. Today IFFs now generally refers to cross-border movement of capital and money associated with a variety of illegal activity. IFFs primary impact is the hemorrhage of much needed capital from the developing world and the associated human costs. IFFs exacerbate human suffering and social and political instability.

In short, over the last thirty years I have been both a player in the arena, and I have also had a front row seat observing slow and steady changes in the world of money laundering and illicit financial flows enforcement. This book will discuss what I believe are the most important developments. We will discuss what works and what does not. I candidly posit lessons learned. With the perspective of time and experience, readily acknowledging my many shortcomings, limitations, and lack of expertise in certain areas, I will advance recommendations and steps forward.

Bank compliance officers are well aware of AML "look-backs." A look-back might result after a period of lax compliance and repeated warnings by regulators triggered perhaps by evidence of suspicious transactions not reported or internal procedures not followed. This type of reactive look-back is inherently negative. A proactive look-back, on the other hand, is positive. Undertaken in response to self-initiative, a look-back can identify issues that need to be corrected and recommend positive action. That is exactly what my goal is for this book. It is a roughly 30 year proactive look-back on money laundering methodologies and our AML policies and actions. I can't cover everything. I'm selecting topics of particular concern. But the book is designed to be a candid proactive appraisal that will result in recommendations and steps forward. I promise to tell it "like it is."

How This Book Is Organized

Money laundering and illicit financial flows are very broad topics. The ways to launder money are only limited by criminals' imaginations. So I am going to include money laundering methodologies, case examples and issues that are representative of the challenges we face; I selected topics that have at least some recognized data, and I chose subjects that, frankly, interest me and/or where, for the most part, I have first-hand knowledge and experience. This book is a mix of facts, straight-forward explanations, examples, and case studies. I sometimes include personal experiences, views and commentary.

Chapter 1 makes the argument that our anti-money laundering efforts are essential. Yet Chapter 2 uses publicly available official statistics and bottom line metrics to show that our AML efforts both in the United States and internationally have failed. While I assume most readers of this book already have a solid grasp of money laundering and its countermeasures, for those that do not and before proceeding further, Chapter 3 provides a very brief overview of the subject. A broad understanding of basic anti-money laundering countermeasures and terminology is a prerequisite for issues that will be discussed in the rest of the book. Likewise, Chapter 4 is a very brief primer on illicit financial flows.

The following chapters discuss specific money laundering methodologies such as bulk cash smuggling, trade-based money laundering, underground financial systems, and many others. We will use
examples and data to demonstrate some success stories but also
our inadequate countermeasures. The later chapters discuss money
laundering enablers and new threats. While most of the individual
methodology chapters include recommendations, the final chapter
views our AML stratagem from a holistic perspective and argues
for an AML paradigm shift. It includes additional steps forward.

In order to simplify things for the reader, I added a glossary.
Unfortunately, there are a lot of acronyms and jargon in AML field.
I try to keep them to a minimum, but readers need to understand
essential terms.

Style and Sourcing

This is not an academic book. I am writing primarily from my background in law enforcement. While topics are presented in a factual
and objective style, I purposefully tried to make much of the narrative informal and conversational in tone. Some chapters are quite
short and others lengthy. I borrowed some themes and content
(with updates) from my previous writings and Congressional testi-
monies. But most of the material is completely new. Everything is
sourced accordingly with chapter endnotes.

I am not including charts or other graphics. I am purposefully
keeping the narrative and formatting straight forward and easy to
read. I have been underwhelmed with my experience with traditional publishing. So, this book is self-published. I want this book
to be easily accessible. I am pleased with the final results. I hope
the reader will be as well.

A Note to Friends and Colleagues

I've been blessed with a wonderful career with incredible adven-
tures as both a Case Officer for the CIA and a Special Agent for

Treasury. I've traveled extensively within the United States and around the world. Outside of government service, I've had a healthy exposure to industry, journalism, and academia. Late in life, I discovered how much I enjoy teaching and mentoring. The most gratifying part of the journey has been making friends along the way. I have never ceased to be amazed at the talented, dedicated, smart, and patriotic people I have had the pleasure to work with. There are so many — in government, industry, and non-profits — that serve our country and the greater good with little recognition or monetary reward. AML professionals certainly don't have all the answers but we keep trying. The challenges manifest themselves all around us. The issues involved are too important for us to fail. It has been an exciting, worthwhile, and principled journey.

Thank you!

CHAPTER 1
Why Money Laundering Matters

OUTSIDE CRIMES OF PASSION, FOR example, murder committed in a jealous rage, criminals, criminal organizations, kleptocrats, and some businesses and corporations are typically motivated by greed. In Christianity, greed — sometimes called avarice — is labeled as one of the seven deadly sins. It is an intrinsic part of the human condition. In today's increasingly interconnected world, the manifestations of unfettered material acquisitions impact all of us — politically, socially, economically, and culturally. Its effects are pernicious.

Around the world people see the results of greed in their communities. In the United States, the opioid, methamphetamine, heroin, and cocaine epidemics are devastating. Gang violence, financial fraud, the proliferation of counterfeit goods, fraud in government contracting, corruption, identity theft, social benefits fraud, Internet scams and ransomware attacks, and a plethora of other crimes affect our daily lives. Individual human costs are staggering. Manifestations are also often found in the disintegration of families. Collectively, it is taking a massive toll on societal values and norms.

By most measures the range and magnitude of organized criminal activity that generates illicit financial flows are increasing. For example, human trafficking, wildlife trafficking, environmental and natural resource degradation and exploitation are all unfortunate indicators of greed that are facilitated by our increasingly borderless world. The trade in illicit tobacco has existed for generations. It affects every country in the world. So does customs fraud.

Financial crimes and abusive tax evasion practiced by elites contribute to the deterioration of social compacts. Worldwide, distrust in the privileged class has seemingly reached epidemic proportions[1] coupled with (if not driven by) a corresponding absence of accountability.[2] Anger and inequality are common themes in both the developed and developing world.

Some countries are also confronted by the uncertainties caused by currency controls and failed economic policies. Hyper-inflation, high taxes, value-added tax (VAT) fraud, unexpected currency devaluations, and poor fiscal management cause citizens to lose faith in their governments. Underground economies, the black market, and informal value transfer systems outside of government control often result. Corruption is the great facilitator.

Law enforcement, policymakers, and the media get distracted with the immediacy of criminal behavior. We watch two minute video clips on the evening news — sex trafficking, a family torn apart by drugs, gang violence. Producers demand ever more shocking visuals. Citizens and politicians become alarmed. Law enforcement reacts and cracks down. But the criminal organizations regroup and move on. It's a vicious cycle.

The criminals themselves, common sense, and criminal science all tell us that the aim of these activities is not the crime itself — but the proceeds of crime. Criminals and criminal organizations do not traffic in narcotics, people, and weapons for the sake of the criminal act. They do not engage in scams and fraud to make innocents suffer. They engage in illegal behavior because of the money the criminal actions generate.

Scholars, researchers, politicians, and even some in law enforcement have all questioned the efficacy of the "War on Drugs." But why don't we acknowledge that our inability to follow the money, stop the laundering, and seize the proceeds fuels the greed behind the drug trade?

When notorious bank robber, Willie Sutton, was asked why he pursued his chosen career, he reportedly replied, "I rob banks because that's where the money is." The same is true for organized crime groups. They engage in crime for the money. It's a simple truism, but it is often overlooked.

Unfortunately, the last thirty years have demonstrated that our anti-money laundering (AML) countermeasures for the most part have been proven ineffective. And the outlook going forward is not promising due to our continued inability to effectively combat old-fashioned money laundering methodologies. Until criminals learn that a particular laundering technique is no longer viable, they will continue to use it.

The future holds even greater challenges because of ever new technologies. Techniques such as the use of cell phones and cyber currencies will increasingly be exploited by criminals and criminal organizations. Quantum encryption in the cloud is going to revolutionize business but also criminal activity. Global commercial and informational connectivity increasingly permit a lucrative criminal economy. Social media is being used by criminal organizations. The current rate of data creation has us doubling the world's data every two years. By 2025 it is estimated the amount of data will double every 12 hours![3] There is a concurrent revolution in advanced analytics. In other words, we should cheer these incredible technological developments but be fully aware they are likewise being exploited by criminals and other nefarious actors.

The last few decades have seen a shift from large, easily targeted hierarchical organizations spanning multiple countries. These are most easily characterized by the international drug trade (e.g. Colombia's Medellin and Cali cartels, and the Sinaloa cartel in Mexico). The drug cartels still exist, but transnational criminal organizations of all sorts are on the ascendency. Violent criminal gangs and cooperative alliances between loose-knit criminal networks are growing. China's involvement in transnational crime deserves immediate scrutiny.

On November 9, 1989 the Berlin Wall fell. The collapse of communism in Russia and other Soviet states followed. Incredible wealth and kleptocratic fortunes hemorrhaged out of the former Soviet bloc. Much was routed into the West for secret safekeeping. When Berkeley economist, Gabriel Zucman, studied the problem in 2015, he found that 52 percent of Russia's wealth resided outside the country.[4] Kleptocrats and government officials around the world have always looted their countries' coffers and accumulated bribes. But over the last 30 years the globalization of banking and offshore havens has made the export and laundering of their illicit proceeds far more efficient, convenient, and hidden. This, of course, inspires more crime, looting, and laundering.

As in the Russian case, much of this plundered wealth finds its way to the United States. New York, Los Angeles, and Miami have joined London as the world's most desired destinations for laundered money. This boom has enriched American elites who have enabled it — and, in the process, has degraded the nation's political and social mores.

Greed will always be with us. Nevertheless, there is reason for hope. Hard won lessons point the way forward. There is more AML/CFT and financial crimes expertise than ever before. We can benefit from increasing data, transparency, and incredible advances in technology. By successfully shifting the traditional AML paradigm, following the money and value trails could truly be an effective countermeasure against many of the pressing economic and societal ills faced today. We can do a much better job holding individuals, criminal organizations, businesses and even countries that cheat and engage in illicit activity accountable. We must do better at limiting the hemorrhaging of scarce capital from the developing world that exacerbates social/political/economic tensions. By making progress in taking away the proceeds of crime, we simultaneously help to diminish rising anger and the feelings of helplessness, injustice, and inequality. What could matter more?

NOTES

1 Cheryl Hall, "You Won't Believe the Level of Distrust that People Have in Everything, Edelman Survey Shows," The Dallas Morning News, January 24, 2017; https://www.dallasnews.com/business/business/2017/01/24/trust-drops-power-people-grows-edelman-survey-shows

2 Roger Cohen, "The Age of Distrust," The New York Times, September 19, 2016; https://www.nytimes.com/2016/09/20/opinion/the-age-of-distrust.html

3 Barry Libert and Megan Beck, "Leaders Need AI to Keep Pace with The Data Explosion," Forbes, March 26, 2019; https://www.forbes.com/sites/barrylibert/2019/03/26/leaders-need-ai-to-keep-pace-with-data/#ee4d6a1691e0

4 Gabriel Zucman, The Hidden Wealth of Nations, University of Chicago Press, 2015

CHAPTER 2

Sobering Statistics

WHEN I WAS A SMALL boy, I loved the Danish fairy tale written by Hans Christian Andersen "The Emperor Wears No Clothes." The story describes how townspeople wildly praised the magnificent clothes of the emperor, afraid to admit that they could not see them. Finally, a small child said: "But he has nothing on!"

The metaphor could also be used to describe our efforts to combat international money laundering. The overwhelming majority of observers are unwilling to see what is obvious. Perhaps they personally benefit from the status quo. Maybe they just don't want to speak out. Possibly government agencies and departments involved are embarrassed to tell the truth. So, let me mimic the boy in the fairy tale, "The emperor wears no clothes!" In other words, very simply, directly, and loudly, "AML countermeasures don't work!"

July 2019 marked the 30th anniversary of the creation of the Financial Action Task Force (FATF) — the international AML/CFT policy making-body. In the thirty years I have been involved with combatting international money laundering, I have witnessed the FATF, successive U.S. administrations, as well as periodic pronouncements from the Departments of Justice and Treasury tout our successes. And it is true that we have had many tactical wins. But what is not openly discussed is that the government's and non-government organizations' own numbers conclusively demonstrate overall failure. It was apparent years ago. I have been publicly saying this for at least the last 15 years.

I think there are two primary reasons for the inability to admit what should be obvious: 1. It is politically embarrassing on multi-levels to admit failure. 2. There are vested interests in both govern-ment and industry — particularly the AML compliance industry and associations — that financially benefit from the status quo. They work hand-in-hand. We will discuss some of these vested interests later in the book.

Magnitude of the Global Problem

In order to logically examine the problem, we must first ask, "How much money is being laundered?" Unfortunately, there aren't many reliable estimates and the few available are admittedly imprecise. The FATF states, "Due to the illegal nature of the transactions, pre-cise statistics are not available and it is therefore impossible to pro-duce a definitive estimate of the amount of money that is globally laundered every year."[1] With that caveat in mind, the International Monetary Fund (IMF) has estimated that money laundering com-prises approximately 2 to 5 percent of the world's gross domestic product (GDP) each year.[2] According to the World Bank, in 2018 the world GDP was approximately $85 trillion.[3] In other words, in a very round and imprecise number, money laundering is approximately $4 trillion per year!

Another comparison is that the amount of global money laun-dering is approximately three times the amount of currency notes in circulation in the United States![4] Similarly, the United Nations Office on Drugs and Crime (UNODC) conducted a study to determine the magnitude of illicit funds. According to the UNODC, criminal proceeds in 2009 amounted to 3.6 percent of global GDP, roughly $2.7 trillion.[5] Eleven years later I think it is probably fair to add another trillion or two.

In another estimate by the United Nations, criminal funds equal about 2.7 percent of global gross domestic product that are laun-dered annually through the world's financial system.[6] Note that this estimate is only the formal financial system — i.e. through recognized financial institutions. So roughly, according to the United Nations, approximately $2.4 trillion is laundered just through banks every year. That does not count many other methodologies we will cover in this book such as bulk cash smuggling, forms of trade-based value transfer, new payment methods, etc.

What is not counted is important. For example, there is an international movement to recognize tax evasion as a predicate offense to charge money laundering. [7] Is capital flight considered money laundering? It might not be considered money laundering for the United States. But over the last decade, an estimated $3.8 trillion in capital has left China.[8] Undoubtedly, some illicit funds are "mixed" or "co-mingled" with the funds fleeing China. Moreover, much of the money exodus violates internal Chinese capital controls. The same holds true for many other countries such as Iran, Venezuela, Pakistan, etc. A strong case could be made the techniques employed to move, hide, and invest capital involve money laundering.

What about hidden cash? A study by Tax Justice Network estimated that in 2010, between $21 and $32 trillion was hiding in more than 80 international tax havens. The study also found that privileged elites in 139 lower-and middle-income countries had $7.3 to $9.3 trillion in unrecorded offshore wealth; while at the same time, most of the governments of the countries involved were borrowing themselves into bankruptcy and other economic dangers.[9]

The 2016 release of the "Panama Papers" offers additional evidence of the scope of the problem, showing how one Panamanian law firm created a network of over 200,000 non-transparent entities, allowing criminals, corrupt government officials, taxpayers, and others to hide their income and wealth. Similar outrages were reported with the recent release of the "Paradise Papers." The leaks provide a glimpse into the opaque practices of business formation and the placement and layering and integration of funds that facilitate a myriad of financial crimes, tax evasion, and avoiding of sanctions.

Global Financial Integrity estimates that the developing world loses over $1 trillion in illicit outflows every year, largely through abusive trade misinvoicing. This practice is a form of trade-based money laundering (TBML). Trade misinvoicing is also a common tactic in customs fraud and tax evasion.[10] We will have specific examples of TBML and value transfer in Chapter 6.

Further complicating reliable estimates on the magnitude of international money laundering is the enormity of "black" and "grey" markets around the world. Underground, informal, parallel, and cash-based economies can comprise a substantial portion of a country's GDP. For example, in the economies of countries as diverse as India and Mexico, the underground or informal economies are estimated at approximately 30 to 50 percent of GDP. Much economic activity in the developing world takes place in the informal sector, with many transactions, even those of legitimate businesses, carried out in cash (often in U.S. dollars). International grey markets often include barter trade and forms of cyber payments — two common money laundering methodologies on opposite ends of the tech spectrum — that are generally impervious to financial transparency reporting requirements, taxes, and law enforcement countermeasures. We will talk much more about "underground" financial systems in Chapter 7.

During the late 1990s the Director of the Financial Crimes Enforcement Network (FinCEN) hired an economist to come up with a knowledgeable estimate regarding the magnitude of money laundering. The FATF couldn't do it, so FinCEN thought it would try. After about two years the economist gave up. There were just too many variables, issues, lack of data and questions about the data that did exist. Suffice it to say the total is in the multi-trillions of dollars every year. We will have to leave it at that.

Bottom-Line Metrics

So out of the multi-trillions of dollars that are laundered how much of the proceeds of crime are actually seized and frozen? According to the UNODC, the answer is less than one percent.[11] Please let that sink in. It bears repeating. . . Our success rate is less than one percent! And, according to the UNODC, that is money that is just frozen not forfeited. Much of that frozen money is ultimately released.

In addition to forfeitures, the other bottom-line metric that matters is the number of successful investigations, prosecutions, and convictions. While statistics of this nature vary markedly from country to country, are open to question, and sometimes do not include the money laundering activities of criminals convicted on other charges, the sobering fact is that for a money launderer to be caught and convicted today, he or she has to be either very stupid or very unlucky.

The number of money laundering cases filed worldwide is miniscule. For example, the Philippines has a large economy and is increasingly recognized as an important regional financial center. According to 2016 data, only 49 anti-money laundering cases have been filed since 2001. As of 2016 there had not been a single successful prosecution or conviction.[12] Probably due to embarrassment related to lack of enforcement and some major money laundering cases that made international news, the Government of the Philippines has recently ramped up enforcement action. In 2018, there were 10 reported convictions for money laundering.[13]

The British Virgin Islands is advertised as the world's leading offshore center, with more offshore companies than any other country. In 2014, there was one prosecution for money laundering.[14]

According to the Angolan Central Bank, approximately $17 billion has been siphoned from the Angolan economy in the last five years alone — several orders of magnitude above foreign direct investment into the country. The origin of this money is unclear. Additional value is transferred out of the country through abusive trade misinvoicing. Widespread corruption in government and commerce facilitates money laundering. There are few — if any — prosecutions or convictions for money laundering.[15]

In Japan, the numbers of investigations, prosecutions, and convictions for money laundering are so low that they are not even publicly released.[16]

The list goes on and on. The annual State Department International Narcotics Control Strategy Report (INCSR), which tracks countries' anti-money laundering efforts around the world, reinforces this conclusion. While there have been many positive developments, a comprehensive and objective reading of the report's statistics on prosecutions and convictions is sobering and does not inspire confidence in the effectiveness of the current AML program.

Money laundering is international in scope. Criminals and criminal organizations are attracted to the weak link. The lack of AML/CFT enforcement in one country can affect many others.

While tremendous work has been done to enact AML/CFT regimes around the world that on paper adhere to the FATF 40 AML/CFT recommendations, the results as measured by illicit money seized and money launderers convicted can only be accurately described as abysmal. That is the primary reason why the FATF revamped its evaluation procedures in 2012 to place more emphasis on enforcement results. There has not been much improvement.

Situation in the United States

The United States has the world's most effective 20th century anti-money laundering regime; it is expensive and extensive, but for the most part remains unequipped to deal with 21st century laundering and illicit financial flows. When I started my anti-money laundering career in the late 1980s, the U.S. AML system was primarily designed to stop the money laundering of a Miami "cocaine cowboy" where large amounts of drug money were sloshing around in western financial institutions. Our anti-money laundering regime was not engineered to combat the diverse threats of the present day transnational money launderer. Some of the methodologies used today were simply not known thirty years ago.

The total amount of money laundered in the United States is conservatively estimated in the hundreds of billions of dollars every year. The U.S. Treasury National Money Laundering Risk Assessment of 2015 estimates the amount of money laundered in the United

States at approximately $300 billion but also acknowledges little certainty. Fraud and drug trafficking comprise the majority of the illicit proceeds.[17] I personally believe the total approaches close to $1 trillion or more a year. Once again, it depends what is included in the count. According to the Internal Revenue Service, tax evasion is also skyrocketing, and the IRS believes that "money laundering is in effect tax evasion in progress."[18] While tax evasion is not yet considered to be a specified unlawful activity for money launder-ing in the U.S., related crimes are. For example, identity theft con-nected to tax fraud is rampant. We will discuss other predicate offenses and money laundering methodologies that inflate the total estimate in later chapters. For example, the U.S. Treasury has never systematically examined trade-based money laundering, but academic evidence suggests trade fraud in all its forms (a predicate offense) could easily be in the hundreds of billions of dollars a year.

While the magnitude of money laundering in the United States is difficult to measure, we do have some statistics regarding how much illicit money is seized and forfeited.

In 2014 the U.S. "confiscated" approximately $4.4 billion.[19] While this sounds like an impressive total, it is not certain what percentage was actually forfeited instead of ultimately released. Let us approxi-mate $3 billion. The UNODC estimated proceeds from all forms of financial crime in the U.S., excluding tax evasion, was $300 billion in 2010 (about 2 percent of the U.S. economy).[20] If we use the UNODC estimate (I believe a more accurate estimate is at least triple that amount), that means we are actually recovering less than 1 percent of the illicit money generated by criminal activity every year!

Using 2019 data, C2-iBrief estimates that there were approxi-mately $2.3 billion in government AML/CFT fines and penalties.[21] Therefore, if you add the approximately $2 billion from AML and BSA penalties to the approximate $4 billion "confiscated" (remem-ber the actual forfeitures were probably much less than that) from USG regulatory and enforcement actions, that totals $6 billion. We can slice and dice the numbers further, but the bottom line is that our combined success rate of actually recovering (including both forfeiting and fining) dirty money from criminals and culpable businesses and institutions is once again somewhere in the neighborhood of 1 percent!

The $6 billion or so that we recover from all of our AML "enforcement" actions is dwarfed by the multi-tens of billions of dollars the federal government and industry annually pays for the AML countermeasures. We will discuss these expenditures later.

It is important to note that the U.S. has the best AML enforcement in the world. So, the logical question — which nobody asks — what's the "success rate" elsewhere? It varies by country but I can assure you the numbers are not good.

We can drill down even further for specific examples. As we will discuss in Chapter 5 on Bulk Cash Smuggling, a few years ago it was estimated that up to $39 billion of illicit proceeds were smuggled annually across our southern border in the form of bulk cash.[22]

Yet that simple statistic does not tell the whole story. The long-term consequences of our failure to effectively combat money laundering are far worse than the above estimates thanks to the "miracle of compounding." We often forget about the money made on the money that is successfully laundered. According to a domain practitioner's 2011 assessment[23] looking at compound interest, assuming the $39 billion is accurate and the cartels simply invest the illicit proceeds at a 5 percent annualized rate of return, after 20 years just that one year has mushroomed into a $1.7 trillion problem!

The above is a simplistic example, but compound interest works not only in IRAs and 401ks, but in the cartels' favor as well. And that is just one example of AML failure, representing just the southwest border, for one year, and for just one comparatively straight-forward asset class.

If we take Chapter 6's estimates that billions of dollars are laundered annually in the United States via the misuse of trade, the compounded interest over time is truly staggering.

Remember that the other money laundering metric that matters is the amount of convictions. Some apologists will have you believe that AML is all about "disruption," or "deterrence" or the number of "FIUs created" or the number of suspicious activity reports or "SARS filed." I have heard them all. These platitudes are ridiculous. Our AML efforts ultimately all come down to enforcement. Once again, I emphasize that the United States has the best and most robust law enforcement in the world. Yet dated information suggests that, in the United States, money launderers face a less than five percent risk of conviction (some plead to lesser charges). Currently, there are about 1,200 money laundering convictions a year at the federal level.[24] That seems like a large number, but — divided into the amount of criminal activity and factoring in the multi-hundreds of billions of illicit proceeds generated — it is not.

Raymond Baker, a longtime financial crime expert and the Founding President of Global Financial Integrity, stated, "Total failure is just a decimal point away."[25] His catchphrase regarding the success rate of our AML efforts succinctly sums up both the problem and our challenge. Einstein reportedly defined "insanity" as "doing the same thing over and over again expecting a different result." Are we going to spend another thirty years combatting money laundering using countermeasures that are not effective? I'm certain we can do better. But before we can discuss steps forward, we need first to understand the basic concepts of money laundering and some of the primary methodologies.

NOTES

1 Financial Action Task Force, "What is Money Laundering?" accessed November 17, 2017; http://www.fatf-gafi.org/faq/moneylaundering/

2 Ibid

3 "World GDP Ranking 2018;" https://knoema.com/nwnfkne/ world-gdp-ranking-2018-gdp-by-country-data-and-charts

4 Federal Reserve Bank of San Francisco; https://www.frbsf.org/cash/ cash-lifecycle/cash-circulation-infographic/

5 United Nations Office on Drugs and Crime, "Estimating illicit financial flows resulting from drug trafficking and other transnational organized crimes," October 2011; http://www.unodc.org/documents/ data-and-analysis/Studies/Illicit_financial_flows_2011_web.pdf

6 Jeanne Whalen, "To combat dirty money, Britain asks: How did you pay for that mansion?" The Washington Post, December 14, 2018; https://www.washingtonpost.com/business/economy/ to-combat-dirty-money-britain-asks-how-did-you-pay-for-that-mansion/2018/12/14/33062c5e-ec38-11e8-baac-2a674e91502b_story.html?utm_term=.c117fd798ab7

7 International Monetary Fund, "Revisions to the Financial Action Task Force (FATF) Standard—Information Note to the Executive Board," July 17, 2012; https://www.imf.org/external/np/pp/ eng/2012/071712a.pdf

8 Frank R. Guntner, "Why China Lost About $3.8 Trillion To Capital Flight In The Last Decade," Forbes, February 22, 2017; www.forbes.com/sites/insideasia/2017/02/22/ china-capital-flight-migration/#4f5111da4a37

9 James Henry, "The Price of Offshore Revisited," Tax Justice Network, July 2012; https://www.taxjustice.net/cms/upload/pdf/Price_of_ Offshore_Revisited_120722.pdf

10 Dev Kar and Joseph Spanjers, "Illicit Financial Flows from Developing Countries: 2004-2013," Global Financial Integrity, December 8,

2015; http://www.gfintegrity.org/wp-content/uploads/2015/12/IFF-Update_2015-Final-1.pdf

11 United Nations Office on Drugs and Crime, "Estimating illicit financial flows resulting from drug trafficking and other transnational organized crimes, United Nations Office on Drugs and Crime," October 2011; https://www.unodc.org/documents/data-and-analysis/Studies/Illicit_financial_flows_2011_web.pdf

12 Author's knowledge. See also: John Chalmers and Karen Lema, "For bank heist hackers, the Philippines was a handy black hole," Reuters, March, 21, 2016; http://www.reuters.com/article/us-usa-fed-bangladesh-philippines-idUSKCN0WM13B

13 U.S. Department of State, International Narcotics Control Report Volume II on Money Laundering, March 2019, page 159; https://www.state.gov/wp-content/uploads/2019/03/INCSR-Vol-INCSR-Vol.-2-pdf.pdf

14 U.S. Department of State, "Countries/Jurisdictions of Primary Concern - British Virgin Islands," 2015 International Narcotics Control Strategy Report, March 2015

15 U.S. Department of State, 2016 International Narcotics Control Strategy Report, March 2016; https://www.state.gov/j/inl/rls/nrcrpt/2016/; see also Ricardo Soares De Oliveira, "Cash-rich Angola comes to cash-strapped Portugal," Politico, October 2, 2015; http://www.politico.eu/article/cash-rich-angola-comes-to-cash-strapped-portugal-colony-oil-santos-luanda-lisbon/

16 U.S. Department of State, "Countries/Jurisdictions of Primary Concern – Japan," 2016 International Narcotics Control Strategy Report, March 2016; https://www.state.gov/j/inl/rls/nrcrpt/2016/

17 U.S. Treasury National Money Laundering Risk Assessment, U.S. Department of Treasury, 2015, page 2; https://www.treasury.gov/resource-center/terrorist-illicit-finance/Documents/National%20Money%20Laundering%20Risk%20Assessment%20%E2%80%93%2006-12-2015.pdf

18 U.S. Internal Revenue Service, "Overview - Money Laundering," March 2, 2017; https://www.irs.gov/uac/overview-money-laundering

19 Financial Action Task Force, "Anti-money laundering and counter-terrorist financing measures: United States: Mutual Evaluation Report," December 2016, page 8; http://www.fatf-gafi.org/media/fatf/documents/reports/mer4/MER-United-States-2016.pdf

20 Ibid, page 5

21 Joseph Hanvey, C2-I Brief, February 20, 2020 email exchanges with the author

22 Julianne Stanford, "More drug profits slipping into Mexico as border seizures plummet," Arizona Daily Star

January 26, 2017; http://tucson.com/news/local/border/more-drug-profits-slipping-into-mexico-as-border-seizures-plummet/article_4642d8bf-9bee-5e4e-906b-f2d24fb2eff8.html

23 Information given to the author by Leveraged Outcomes, LLC. via email on November 10, 2017

24 Financial Action Task Force, "Anti-money laundering and counter-terrorist financing measures: United States: Mutual Evaluation Report," December 2016, page 4; http://www.fatf-gafi.org/media/fatf/documents/reports/mer4/MER-United-States-2016.pdf

25 Raymond Baker, Capitalism's Achilles Heel, Wiley & Sons Publishing, Hoboken, New Jersey, 2005; page 173

CHAPTER 3

Money Laundering Basics

BEFORE WE GO FURTHER, WE need to have a baseline of money laundering and AML knowledge. This chapter is not comprehensive. Admittedly, it is not very exciting. But for those readers that feel they need an introduction or a quick review, let's discuss some money laundering basics.

There are lots of definitions of money laundering. Mine is very simple: money laundering is the hiding or the disguising of the proceeds of *any* form of illegal activity.

The key word in the definition is *any*. When I began my anti-money laundering career, there was a sometimes heated debate between the DEA and Customs that revolved around the "predicate offense" or "specified unlawful activity" to charge money laundering. At the time, the United States' and most international anti-money laundering efforts were focused on narcotics trafficking. The DEA insisted that the battle against money laundering was synonymous to the "War on Drugs." However, criminal investigators at Treasury (which at that time included Customs, the Secret Service, the Bureau of Alcohol Tobacco and Firearms as well as the IRS) felt strongly that concealing the proceeds from almost all forms of serious criminal activity should be considered money laundering. Over the years, the United States and the rest of the world adopted Treasury's original and more inclusive view of money laundering. Today, at the federal level, the United States recognizes hundreds of predicate offenses for money laundering including drug trafficking, racketeering, fraud, smuggling, etc. The international standard as championed by the FATF is that "all serious crimes" should trigger money laundering charges. In 2012, the FATF also stated that countries should ensure that "tax crimes" are predicate offenses.[1] (FYI: In the United States, there are some preliminary discussions on Capitol Hill about making "all serious crimes" including tax evasion the governing factor in charging money laundering. We will discuss this a bit more in the final chapter.)

Nobody knows the origin of the term "money laundering," but in the United States it is thought to have originated in the 1920s or 1930s during the era of Al Capone, Meyer Lansky, and other infamous gangsters. They took illicit cash that originated from a variety of criminal enterprises such as gambling, prostitution, and Prohibition era alcohol sales, and "mixed" or "co-mingled" it with clean money in cash-intensive businesses such as laundromats and restaurants. In other words, they tried to wash their dirty money and make it appear clean and legitimate.[2]

Money laundering gained more prominence in the 1960s with the proliferation of the sale of illegal narcotics. In the early 1970's, the term received additional notoriety during the Watergate investigation in which suitcases of cash played a role in the eventual resignation of President Richard Nixon. The pithy and memorable term "follow the money" was reportedly coined by the "Deep Throat" informant that helped investigative journalists and others unravel the scandal.

Financial Intelligence

Ironically, it was the same President Nixon who declared the "War on Drugs." In order to give criminal investigators tools so they could follow the narcotic money trails, in 1970 Congress started passing a series of laws later augmented by rules and regulations that collectively is known as the Bank Secrecy Act or BSA. I have always thought that the BSA was a misnomer. The BSA isn't secrecy. It actually means financial transparency.

Although money laundering had been around for a long time, the BSA was the first legislation that systematically tried to control the growing problem. The BSA mandated a series of reporting and record keeping requirements. The data is now commonly called "financial intelligence." It is also sometimes referred to as "financial transparency reporting requirements" or simply "BSA data." Today, Treasury's Financial Crimes Enforcement Network (FinCEN) acts as the designated administrator of the BSA.

There are various types of financial intelligence. The original BSA required the first three recordkeeping requirements listed below. Over the years, additional types of financial intelligence have been created.

Currency Transaction Reports

Banks and other financial institutions are required to report currency transactions (deposits or withdrawals) of $10,000 or more by or on behalf of the same person on the same business day. There are exemptions to the filing requirements for these large transactions if they are between domestic banks and for transactions conducted with certain retail cash-intensive businesses and government agencies.

The form used is popularly called the Currency Transaction Report or CTR; although a few years ago it was changed to the FinCEN Form 104. Today financial institutions must use the new FinCEN report (FinCEN CTR Form 112) which is available only electronically through the BSA E-Filing System. FinCEN no longer accepts legacy reports.[3]

Unlike the Suspicious Activity Reports described below, generally a client is informed about the obligation to file a CTR. Sometimes money launderers try to "structure" transactions to avoid the reporting requirement by depositing smaller sums of money under the reporting threshold. Runners, sometimes known as "smurfs," are also recruited by professional money launderers to deposit small sums of illicit money in multiple financial institutions in an effort to evade reporting requirements. We will talk more about that later.

Approximately 150 data fields are included in the CTR form. The information (name, address, account data, etc.) represent a wealth of information for law enforcement professionals tracking financial and other crimes. The CTR represents the largest volume of BSA data filed; approximately 14 million CTRs are filed with Treasury's FinCEN every year. More information about financial intelligence, forms, and filing can be found on the FinCEN website (www.fincen.gov).

Currency and Monetary Instrument Report

A customs report must be filed by individuals or entities that transport $10,000 or more in cash (including in foreign currencies) or negotiable monetary instruments into or out of the United States. These entities include banks and armored car companies.

For example, if the reader flies into or out of the United States via John F. Kennedy Airport or any other international airport, he or she must be notified or given forms inquiring whether the passenger is transporting $10,000 or more. The same holds true for those crossing a land border by foot or vehicle or those entering or departing the United States by sea. It is not illegal to transport money in large amounts across the border. In fact, the government encourages foreigners to bring money to spend! The only obligation is that a form must be filed.

At the time of the BSA, the original cross-border currency declaration form was known as a "Report of International Transaction of Currency or Monetary Instruments," commonly known as a CMIR. Today, the official designation for a CMIR is the FinCEN Form 105. Hundreds of thousands of these forms are filed every year. Each form has approximately 70 data fields containing useful identifying information and financial intelligence.

Report of Foreign Bank and Financial Accounts (FBAR)

Citizens and resident aliens of the United States are required to file a report with the IRS if they maintain a financial interest or a signature authority over a foreign bank account, brokerage account, or other type of foreign account that exceeds certain thresholds. Originally, the report was filed on IRS Form 90–22–1 and was known as a "Foreign Bank Account Report" or FBAR. It is known today as the FinCEN Form 114.

Form 8300 (Cash Over $10,000 Received in Trade or Business)

This is an IRS form and is required for cash transactions over $10,000 by a trade or business not otherwise covered by BSA reporting such as real estate agencies, car dealerships, and jewelers and dealers in precious metals and stones. The form must be filed when a covered business receives more than $10,000 in cash in one transaction or in two or more related transactions.

Similar to other types of financial intelligence, Form 8300 has detailed identifying information, including the customer's name, address, the amount of cash received, and the date and nature of the transaction, etc. Generally, the customer is not notified when the form is filed. In addition to submitting the forms to the Department of Treasury, businesses must maintain associated records for at least five years.

Form 8300 was originally used for tax purposes. Similar to other tax reports, the release of the data to law enforcement outside of IRS was restricted. Over the past few years, 8300 data has become more available and is increasingly used for a wider variety of investigations.

Suspicious Activity Reports

Suspicious Activity Reports (SARs) were initiated in the United States in 1996. They were modeled in part after the Suspicious

Transaction Report (STR) disclosure system that was already in existence in many European countries.

Financial institutions (FIs), money service businesses (MSBs), and designated non-financial businesses and professions (DNFBPs) should file a SAR if a transaction is inconsistent with normal account activity or otherwise appears suspicious. Banks are obligated to "know your customer" (KYC) and practice due diligence. As a result, banks and increasingly non-bank financial institutions have compliance programs that help spot suspicious transactions. The numbers vary, but in recent years approximately 2.3 million SARs are filed annually in the United States. The total fillings are very roughly divided between SARS filed by banks and those filed by MSBs such as currency exchangers, gold and jewelry dealers, and money remitters.[4] Today, SARs are filed electronically with FinCEN.

The information on SAR filings has proven very helpful for law enforcement. In addition to the identifying data, SARs also provide a narrative field for the filers to include their observations and reasons why they feel the transaction is suspicious in nature. Some of the narratives are short, perhaps only a few sentences. Others are quite lengthy and provide detailed information and an explanation as to why the transaction is suspicious. Banks and other institutions that file SARs are also required to maintain supporting documentation for the reports and make it available upon request.

The SAR form also contains a field in which the filing institutions can indicate the type of suspicious activity encountered. Categories include money laundering (structuring), counterfeit financial instruments, false statements, mortgage loan fraud, identity theft, check fraud, counterfeit currency, terrorism financing, and others. Investigators can tailor their data queries by specifying the type of SARs they are interested in by date, geographic location, and categories of suspicious transactions.

How Is Financial Intelligence Used?

The tens of millions of financial intelligence reports that are produced in the United States and other countries (see discussion of the Egmont Group below) every year have proven to be a tremendous resource to help criminal investigators follow the money trails. The information is not classified, but it is considered law enforcement sensitive. There are strict protocols regarding the access and dissemination of BSA reports.

The financial data is valuable not only in money laundering investigations but also in providing some financial transparency in other types of criminal activity. Querying a subject's name in the financial databases may disclose further identifying information, including an address, telephone number, or business association that might be the vital key to the investigation. The intelligence might also provide some insight or at least a snapshot of the suspect's financial transaction, which could be very valuable to investigators. However, financial intelligence alone rarely "makes a case." Generally, law enforcement will have to combine the financial intelligence with information from other data bases (for example: criminal databases, immigration databases, customs databases, commercially available information about businesses, social network sites, etc.). By connecting the dots between individuals, companies, bank accounts, etc., a picture of financial relationships and money flows begins to develop.

Most commonly, financial data is used "reactively" by law enforcement. In a reactive case, a crime has occurred and a criminal investigator is assigned to solve the crime through a variety of investigative techniques, including interviews, developing informants, performing surveillance, and conducting an undercover investigation, etc. Financial intelligence can help in developing identifying data, establishing networks, and constructing a paper trail.

Financial crimes investigations can also be "proactive" in nature. In these situations, a criminal violation has not yet occurred. Instead, law enforcement examines financial intelligence (CTRs, CMIRs. SARs, etc.) and tries to identify anomalies, suspect patterns, and trends. The information is then used to intercept criminal activity in progress and take appropriate countermeasures.

Availability of Financial Intelligence

Financial institutions, including banks and non-bank financial institutions, MSBs, and DNFBPs, are required to have policies and procedures that generate financial intelligence and include key AML requirements based on the BSA. At a minimum, the institution must establish a system of internal controls to ensure ongoing compliance; conduct AML compliance training for appropriate personnel; provide for independent testing of BSA compliance — such as periodically testing transactions for adherence to recordkeeping and reporting requirements; designate a person or persons responsible for managing BSA compliance; and establish risk-based customer due diligence procedures.[5]

Treasury's FinCEN is responsible for the collection, warehousing, analysis, and dissemination of financial information in the United States. It is the country's Financial Intelligence Unit (FIU). In theory, official consumers of financial intelligence at the federal, state, and local levels can contact FinCEN and ask for appropriate queries to be made of the financial databases. There are various programs and platforms for these official inquiries. Queries should be as specific as possible and include known identifying information. Of course, FinCEN only has access to financial intelligence that has a nexus or link to the United States. FinCEN also grants certain law enforcement entities such as the FBI direct bulk downloads of financial information.

Law enforcement consumers can also request financial intelligence from an appropriate interagency/departmental task force. A representative from the Department of Treasury (FinCEN or the IRS) or the Department of Homeland Security (Immigration and Customs Enforcement) should have direct access to most of the same financial databases. Generally, non-Treasury and DHS enforcement agencies are limited in their abilities to make direct queries.

Law enforcement can also gain access to financial intelligence through regional federal, state, and local task forces; these include Joint Terrorism Task Forces (JTTFs), High Intensity Financial Crime Areas (HIFCAs), and U.S. Attorney SAR Review Teams.

In 1995, FinCEN was a founding member of the Egmont Group of Financial Intelligence Units. In plain language, a FIU is a foreign FinCEN. The idea behind Egmont was for member countries around the world to obtain, warehouse, analyze, and disclose financial intelligence. The FIU's focus is to support host-country law enforcement and other officials, but Egmont Group members also support official requests for information from other Egmont Group members. In 2020, approximately 160 FIUs are officially accredited to the Egmont Group. Although there are different FIU models (judicial, law enforcement, administrative, and hybrid), and different countries have various types of financial intelligence and reporting thresholds, all have the equivalent of SARs — also frequently known as Suspicious Transaction Reports (STRs).

Legislation

In 1986, the United States became the first country in the world to make money laundering a crime and enacted a law that is still one of the most powerful in the world (Title 18, US Code Section 1956, also known as the Money Laundering Control Act). It provided federal agents and prosecutors the necessary tools to fight money laundering and made several significant amendments to the BSA, including criminalizing structuring (cash deposits under reporting thresholds) to evade BSA requirements and increasing civil and criminal penalties for money laundering. An amendment to the Right to Financial Privacy Act made it easier for banks to furnish suspicious transaction data to federal enforcement agencies without the risk of being sued by clients.[6]

The law also has an extraterritorial reach if at least part of the offense takes place in the United States or even if money is only transferred through the United States. As a result, the United States

can insert itself into dollar-based transactions or U.S. dollar transfers that are settled through correspondent bank accounts in the
United States.

The Money Laundering Control Act was followed by other legislation over the years that strengthened the United States' AML/CFT
regime. Noteworthy laws include the Anti-Drug Abuse Act of 1988,
the Annunzio-Wylie Anti-Money Laundering Act of 1992, the Money
Laundering Suppression Act of 1994, and the Money Laundering
and Financial Crimes Strategy Act of 1998.

Following the September 11 terror attacks, Congress passed the
Uniting and Strengthening America by Providing Appropriate Tools
Required to Intercept and Obstruct Terrorism Act, better known
as the USA PATRIOT Act. The PATRIOT Act requires more kinds of
companies to monitor and report suspicious activity. Check cashers and currency exchanges, along with registered broker/dealers
and traders of precious metals, stones, and jewels were required
to comply with FinCEN's reporting requirements.

Stages of Money Laundering

The U.S. intelligence and law enforcement communities agree that
dirty money is laundered in three recognizable stages: placement,
layering, and integration.

In the placement stage, illicit cash must somehow be deposited
into financial institutions. Criminal organizations attempt to put
their money in banks for the simple reason that they want to be
able to spend it and protect it. Because large amounts of cash are
involved, law enforcement feels that criminals are at their most vulnerable when they try to deposit or place illegally obtained funds directly into a bank account. It is a tremendous challenge for criminal
organizations to deposit that much cash into banks in ways that do
not raise suspicions. One common way this is done is by smuggling
the dirty money out of the country to destinations where the cash
will be readily accepted. For example, billions of dollars of bulk cash
representing the proceeds of narcotics sales are smuggled across

the southern U.S. border into Mexico every year. We will elaborate on this in Chapter 5. Another common placement technique used by money launderers is to use runners, couriers, or "smurfs" that deposit small amounts of money in financial institutions in ways that do not trigger mandatory currency reporting requirements imposed by the BSA. This technique is called "structuring" transactions.

During the layering stage, criminals and criminal organizations attempt to separate the source of the funds by way of complex transactions such as wiring funds to multiple accounts in multiple jurisdictions and to secrecy havens that do not have beneficial ownership information. Criminals do this in order to make it difficult for law enforcement to follow the money trail.

Finally, in the integration stage, criminals try to create the appearance of legitimacy by, for example, investing the placed and layered funds in tangible goods such as property, businesses, or even investing in the stock market.

Law enforcement has found that money launderers are at their most vulnerable at the placement stage. They have to take more risks placing dirty money into financial institutions then layering or integrating the funds. While it is theoretically possible for investigators to work "backwards," e.g. try to determine if a suspect shopping center or high rise residential tower was constructed or purchased with tainted funding, it is much easier to initiate a successful investigation by starting with the dirty money itself and link it to a specified unlawful activity.

Money Laundering Methodologies

Per our discussion in the Preface, in 1989 the G-7 created the FATF. The international anti-money laundering policy-making body championed 40 recommendations for countries and jurisdictions around the world aimed at the establishment of AML and after September 11 CFT countermeasures. These include the passage of AML/CFT laws, the creation of financial intelligence, "know your customer" or KYC compliance programs for financial institutions and money service businesses, the creation of FIUs, and other safeguards. Over the years, FATF-style regional bodies (FSRBs) have spread around the world. The FATF and FSRBs conduct mutual evaluations, support member countries in formulating AML/CFT regimes, and periodically conduct studies on money laundering threats and methodologies. Since 1990 over 205 countries and jurisdictions have signed up to implement the FATF's 40 recommendations, a commitment repeatedly reaffirmed at international meetings.[7]

As of 2018 the level of country compliance with the FATF 40 recommendations rests at just 32 percent across countries most recently assessed.[8] That's not good. But as discussed in Chapter 2, metrics like this are completely dependent on what is included in the count. If a comparatively high level of effectiveness means that there still aren't many convictions and forfeitures in comparison to the amount of money laundered then one must question how "effective" the AML procedures and enforcement really are.

According to the FATF, the three primary methods of laundering money are:[9]

1. Via financial institutions and non-bank financial institutions. This includes the placement and structuring of deposits of tainted money into banks, wiring or layering the dirty money to multiple accounts to multiple banks in multiple jurisdictions to confuse the paper trail, and then using the laundered money by integrating it into the economy by way of purchasing high value properties and goods.

2. Bulk cash smuggling or the physical smuggling of illicit cash from one country or jurisdiction to another where it will be more readily accepted for deposit.

3. Trade-based money laundering and value transfer in all its varied forms.

Of course, there are a myriad of other money laundering methodologies and techniques. Although not currently included in the FATF "top three" money laundering methodologies, concerned international observers are increasingly calling attention to "new payment methods" or NPMs. They are also sometimes called "e-money" or "digital cash." Examples include Internet payment services, cyber currency, stored value cards, prepaid calling and credit cards, digital precious metals, mobile payments or "m-payments," or the use of cell phones to send/receive/transfer money and digital value.

The use of "shell corporations" that lack transparent beneficial ownership information is not necessarily considered a money laundering methodology. However, the use of such phantom companies is extensive in various money laundering schemes.

Criminals often mix or use many of the above methodologies and techniques in combination, thereby increasing the difficulty of following the money, digital-cyber, or trade-based value trails. And criminal and terrorist organizations are adept at exploiting vulnerabilities in our global AML/CFT countermeasures and the challenges posed by differing venues, jurisdiction, and lack of expertise. They are also attracted to countries that have weak enforcement or lack the political will to enforce their laws. Global AML/CFT is only as strong as the weakest link. We will discuss some of the above methodologies and related issues such as shell companies and other enablers during the course of the book.

Efforts to Evade

Over the last thirty years, law enforcement in the United States and around the world has been strengthened by a succession of laws, rules, and regulations designed to better combat international money laundering. But during the same time frame, money launderers have reacted with new and innovative techniques enabling them to stay one step ahead of investigators. It is a game of cat and mouse. Law enforcement applies pressure to criminal activity in one area. Criminals react. Another way of looking at it is "squeezing the balloon." Law enforcement observes how pressure applied in one area causes criminal activity to inflate in another. In other words, if we put a barrier in front of criminal organizations, should we be surprised when they react and/or simply go around it?

For example, in the 1970s and 1980s money launderers knew that repeated large currency deposits into South Florida financial institutions did not trigger government inquiries. When Customs' Operation Greenback began to investigate the cash deposits, the criminals' tactics changed. Some started to recruit "smurfs" or "runners" to purchase cashier's checks, money orders, and other financial instruments in attempts to evade the $10,000 reporting threshold. When investigators and financial institutions caught on to that tactic, many reacted by simply smuggling huge amounts of bulk cash out of the United States for deposit into other jurisdictions where few questions were asked. Bulk cash smuggling remains a major challenge for customs and law enforcement to this day.

During the era of coordinated crack downs on smurfing and currency smuggling operations, the launderers began to use legitimate businesses to place, layer, and integrate illicit funds. For example, in the late 1980s Operation Polar Cap targeted the misuse of the international gold trade to dispose of over $1 billion in currency. The misuse of gold and various corollary systems involved with trade-based money laundering continue to be heavily used by money launderers around the world.

The evasive tactics used by money launderers continue to present challenges to financial institutions, particularly in the development and implementation of BSA compliance programs. The turning point came in 1985 when the Bank of Boston pled guilty to violating currency reporting requirements and was fined $500,000[10] (almost insignificant by today's standards). It wasn't the fine that caused banks around the country to begin to scramble to implement compliance. Rather, it was the resulting negative publicity and the hit to revenue. Congressional hearings were held. The law was strengthened to impose harsher penalties and fines for noncompliance. New concepts were adopted. Financial institutions started to promote standards such as "know your customer," and "know your customer's customer." AML/CFT software was designed to provide "red flags" to alert compliance officers of possible suspicious activity. Today, AML/CFT compliance costs in the United States and Canada are estimated to be approximately $31.5 billion per year. [11]

Yet despite tremendous progress implementing compliance programs and banks' overwhelming cooperation with law enforcement, problems still remain. Since the end of 2009, U.S. regulators have levied more than $16 billion in fines for AML compliance failings.[12] For example, in 2012 HSBC paid a then record $1.92 billion in fines to U.S. authorities for allowing itself to be used to launder almost $900 billion of drug money flowing out of Mexico and other banking lapses.[13] In 2014, BNP Paribas was fined $8.9 billion after admitting that it "willfully and knowingly structured, conducted, and concealed U.S. dollar transactions using the U.S. financial system on behalf of banks and other entities" located in or controlled by Sudan, Iran, and Cuba. The bank deliberately falsified transaction data by stripping information from wire transfers, so they would pass through the U.S. financial system undetected.[14] One of China's largest banks is currently embroiled in allegations that it knowingly facilitated the laundering of 1.2 billion euros of criminal proceeds out of Spain and into China.[15] Citibank, Wachovia, and Deutsche Bank are other examples of large banks that have received multi-million dollar penalties.[16]

Today's criminals continue to innovate in order to evade AML countermeasures. We will elaborate in this book by using examples of bulk cash smuggling, trade-based money laundering (TBML), international gold trade misuse, underground financial systems, mobile payments, and others. The rise of cryptocurrencies, particularly Bitcoin, is another illustration. Criminal organizations have found that cryptocurrencies are able to bypass banks, financial intelligence reporting requirements, and international borders in an instant. As recently as a few years ago, it seemed that anyone could buy or sell anything with Bitcoin and never be tracked or prosecuted if they broke the law. "It's totally anonymous," was how one commenter put it in Bitcoin's forums in June 2013. "The FBI does not have a prayer of a chance of finding out who is who."[17]

Once again law enforcement reacted to criminals' attempts to evade. Bitcoins do leave a trail that can be audited. Bitcoins are values associated with addresses, unique strings of letters and numbers that can be followed. When investigators followed the crypto trails, criminal elements then started to use Bitcoin "mixing" services. The idea is to protect the anonymity of transactions exchanging people's Bitcoin reserves with each other, as in a shell game. The forensic trail shows the money going in, but then goes cold because it is impossible to know which Bitcoins belong to whom on the other end of the "mix." But in the cat and mouse game of crypto-detection, law enforcement found that even mixing has weaknesses that forensic investigators can exploit.[18]

Bitcoins and other cyber-currencies are sexy. They receive a lot of media attention. But from an AML perspective, the numbers involved do not come close to old-fashioned methods used successfully by money launderers such as bulk cash smuggling or trade-based money laundering. According to 2017 remarks in front of the Senate Judiciary Committee, the Deputy Assistant Secretary for Terrorist Financing and Financial Crimes at the U.S. Department of the Treasury, Jennifer Fowler, explained the currency of choice for criminals is still the old-fashioned U.S. dollar. She notes: "Although virtual currencies are used for illicit transactions, the volume is small compared to the volume of illicit activity through traditional financial services."[19] Or as I said at the same hearing in response to a question regarding the transition from cash to digital cash, "I think if you look at the metrics, today's numbers suggest that digital currencies are a small fraction of the threat that we face. That may not be the case 5 to 10 years from now. We are at a crossroads, and it's going to be very, very interesting to see what goes forward."[20]

Constructing a National AML Regime

Not long after September 11, I was detailed from FinCEN to the Department of State's Bureau of International Narcotics and Law Enforcement Affairs (INL) and assigned to the Money Laundering Section. Congress had given INL and State's Office of the Coordinator for Counterterrorism (S/CT) a special appropriation dedicated to counter-terrorist finance by providing training and technical assistance. My primary responsibility was to develop an interagency implementation plan for countries around the world that were deemed most at risk and that had requested U.S. assistance. Training modules were developed and special interagency teams deployed overseas to help countries construct an AML/CFT regime that conformed to international standards. When I retired from active U.S. government employment, I continued my involvement with international AML/CFT training efforts as a contractor with Treasury's Office of Technical Assistance (OTA) and other federal agencies and departments. Considerable effort and resources were expended to assess countries' needs and help them develop effective AML/CFT regimes. While this assistance can be considered "foreign aid," it more accurately was done in the United States' and international community's interest to safeguard the international financial system.

Every country is different. A "cookie cutter approach" to establish AML/CFT infrastructure, programs, and policies is not appropriate. Yet in conjunction with the FATF guidelines and other internationally accepted norms, we urged countries to put in place an effective AML regime supported by two pillars: 1. prevention and 2. enforcement.

Simplifying and abbreviating a complex process, the prevention pillar supports reporting entities such as financial institutions, MSBs, and DNFBPs as they forward financial intelligence to the FIU. Reporting is accomplished under strict regulatory oversight. Central banks and other supervisory agencies should provide needed training to both government and mandated reporting industries. The FIU receives, analyzes, and discloses the information to appropriate law enforcement entities. Per international norms, the FIU should also establish appropriate channels for sharing financial intelligence with foreign counterparts.

The enforcement pillar uses financial intelligence and other law enforcement techniques to investigate and prosecute. Depending on the country, intelligence agencies, customs, and other special services might assist. Assistance may also be provided by international partners. International cooperation and information sharing agreements are essential. Finally, if the case has merit, the prosecutor or investigating magistrate brings charges. A well-trained team of prosecutors and judges familiar with financial crime should be formed. The goals are a criminal conviction and forfeiture of any criminally derived or tainted assets. All of the above must follow and adhere to the country's AML/CFT legal framework and enabling regulations.

Vulnerabilities

On paper, the above outline is logical and, in some locations, has proven effective. However, all too often it simply doesn't work in practice. I've been to many countries — primarily in the developing world — helping them establish an AML/CFT regime. The following (in no particular order of precedence) are common roadblocks. There are many more.

- Some countries put in place an AML regime that looks good on paper and more or less adheres to FATF guidelines, but their efforts are simply for cosmetic purposes. The boxes are checked on a FATF or FATF-style regional body mutual evaluation but there is little political will, expertise, initiative, talent, funding, or heart to meaningfully implement the plan.

- The FATF 40 Recommendations were originally constructed with a western perspective. They are still over-weighted to focus on money laundering via financial institutions. That sometimes doesn't translate well in cash-based economies. TBML — the largest and most pervasive money laundering methodology — remains virtually ignored.

- In many instances there is too much financial intelligence being filed. For example, in the United States, around 19 million pieces of financial intelligence are filed every year with FinCEN including approximately two million SARs. The following is admittedly very simplistic: There are perhaps 20 analysts at FinCEN that actually work with SARs every day. That means each analyst is responsible for roughly 100,000 SARs. If each analyst works roughly 200 days a year, that means the analyst would have to review approximately 500 SARs a day or about 75 SARS an hour or more than one SAR a minute! And if anybody thinks that technology and advanced analytics are force multipliers, they have never worked at FinCEN! Of course, the above illustration is silly, but hopefully it proves the point that SARs produced at massive cost by industry, are not being adequately exploited by the government.

- In most countries there is an overemphasis on SARs to generate cases. A SAR by itself will not magically make a case. The U.S. and other countries that successfully combat money laundering generally use financial intelligence to buttress or add additional information to their investigations. SARs and other types of financial intelligence are but one tool (albeit sometimes an important one) in the investigator's toolbox.

- There is weak financial crimes enforcement across the board. Countries often find that it is comparatively simple (and inexpensive) to pass AML legislation and regulations. But the rubber meets the road with enforcement. Effective enforcement can be hard, tedious, time-consuming, and resource intensive. There are economic and political obstacles and policy push-backs to making that kind of investment.

- There is a lack of capacity, expertise, and knowledge in financial crimes enforcement and prosecution as well as little understanding of money laundering methodologies, countermeasures, and available resources and tools.

- Corruption is the great facilitator for money laundering. It is no accident that countries that rank well in the annual Transparency International Corruption Perception Index[21] generally have strong AML/CFT regimes, and those that score poorly fail at the meaningful AML metrics.

- There is a lack of bureaucratic initiative. Often countries (for example the Gulf countries of the Middle East) will respond to an outside request for investigative assistance into a criminal network operating in their territory. On their own, however, they will not initiate an investigation into that same network.

- There are interagency and inter-departmental rivalries, turf wars, and bureaucratic stovepipes. Information is hoarded and not shared.

- Western ideals, linear logic, and the rule of law often do not translate elsewhere.

- There can be undue political interference. I have been repeatedly told by foreign law enforcement colleagues that they begin money laundering investigations only to be told by higher ups to shut them down once they get too close to a powerful political figure, influential businessman, or ruling family member.

- Personnel are policy. It is a universal bureaucratic truism that the wrong person in a position of importance can wreak havoc on programs and policies.

- There is little meaningful cooperation and "partnership" between law enforcement and industry.

- Insufficient resources — both personnel and financial — are very real obstacles in our AML efforts.

- Many countries are not adequately collecting, analyzing, and sharing data — even within their own governments.

Most of the above roadblocks can be overcome. Experience has shown us that constructing an effective AML regime is often a multi-generational process. For example, in 1990 I was assigned to the U.S. Embassy in Rome to head up the first-ever truly international money laundering task force to combat Italian-American organized crime (or the mafia). The task force was a partnership between the U.S. Customs Service and the Italian Guardia di Finanza or fiscal police. We called the task force Operation Primo Passo or "first step." It was the first step because, at the time, the Italians had a very rudimentary knowledge of anti-money laundering measures and few legislative and procedural tools for law enforcement. Yet in a relatively short time, the Italians made remarkable progress. They supplied the resources and successive governments provided the political will. Today, Italy has one of the top AML/CFT regimes in the world.

So, while there are examples of excellence, for the most part the status quo isn't working as advertised. The roadblocks are big, powerful, and resistant to change. As Ron Pol, a respected anti-money laundering researcher said, "Anti-money laundering [legislation] is the least effective of any anti-crime measure, anywhere."[22] That's a powerful statement and, unfortunately, one I believe is quite true.

NOTES

1 Financial Action Task Force, "FATF steps up the fight against money laundering and terrorist financing," February 16, 2012; http://www.fatf-gafi.org/publications/fatfrecommendations/documents/fatf-stepsupthefightagainstmoneylaunderingandterroristfinancing.html

2 Much of the material in this section comes from the author's knowledge. Background texts that were helpful include:

John Cassara and Avi Jorisch, On the Trail of Terror Finance: What Law Enforcement and Intelligence Officers Need to Know, Red Cell Publishing, Red Cell Publishing, 2010; see Chapter 2 on Sources of Financial Information.

John Cassara, Strategic Financial Intelligence: A Primer on Middle Eastern and South Asian Value Transfer Techniques, Lockheed, Washington, DC Lockheed, 2008; see Chapter 1, "An Overview of Financial Intelligence."

Robert E. Powis, The Money Launderers, Probus Publishing, Chicago, 1992; see Prologue

John A. Cassara, Trade-Based Money Laundering: The Next Frontier in International Money Laundering Enforcement; Wiley, Hoboken, New Jersey, 2016; much of the text originated from Appendix A "Money Laundering Primer"

3 More information on current BSA filing requirements is available on the FinCEN website, https://www.fincen.gov/resources/filing-information

4 See FinCEN "SAR Stats;" https://www.fincen.gov

5 "Countering Illicit Finance and Trade," General Accountability Office, December 29, 2019; https://www.gao.gov/products/gao-20-314r

6 Powis, p. xii

7 Dr. Ron Pol, "How governments can enable the anti-money laundering system to have a real impact on serious, profit-motivated crime,"

The Mandarin, March 2, 2020; https://www.themandarin.com.
au/126375-how-governments-can-enable-the-anti-money-laun-
dering-system-to-have-a-real-impact-on-serious-profit-motivated-
crime/

8 "Stopping Dirty Money – The Global Effective Meters,"
Transparency International, December 13, 2017;
https://www.transparency.org/news/feature/
stopping_dirty_money_the_global_effective_o_meter

9 Financial Action Task Force, "Trade Based Money Laundering," June
23, 2006, page 1; http://www.fatf-gafi.org/publications/method-
sandtrends/documents/trade-basedmoneylaundering.html

10 Powis, p. 9

11 "Increase AML compliance efficiencies and lower costs," Lexis-Nexis,
2019; https://risk.lexisnexis.com/insights-resources/research/2019-
true-cost-of-aml-compliance-study-for-united-states-and-canada

12 Ibid

13 Aruna Viswanatha and Brett Wolf, "HSBC to pay $1.9 billion U.S. fine
in money laundering case," Reuters, December 11, 2012; https://
www.reuters.com/article/us-hsbc-probe/hsbc-to-pay-1-9-billion-u-
s-fine-in-money-laundering-case-idUSBRE8BA05M20121211

14 Anne Eberhardt, "History and Enforcement of Anti-Money
Laundering Laws in the U.S.," Claims Journal, January 8, 2018;
https://www.claimsjournal.com/news/national/2018/01/08/282388.
htm

15 Angus Berwick and David Lague, "How China's biggest bank became
ensnared in a sprawling money laundering probe," Reuters, July
31, 2017; https://www.reuters.com/investigates/special-report/
icbc-spain/

16 Louise Shelley, Dark Commerce, Princeton University Press, 2018, p.
144

17 John Bohannon, "Why criminals can't hide behind Bitcoin," Science,
March 9, 2016; http://www.sciencemag.org/news/2016/03/
why-criminals-cant-hide-behind-bitcoin

18 Ibid

19 Jeff Francis, "The Dollar Far Outstrips Cryptocurrency in Illicit Activity Usage," Bitcoinist, January 3, 2018; http://bitcoinist.com/the-dollar-far-outstrips-cryptocurrency-in-illicit-activity-spending/

20 Jamie Redman, "Proposed U.S. Legislation May Criminalize Those Who Conceal Bitcoin," Bitcoin.com, December 2, 2017; https://news.bitcoin.com/proposed-u-s-legislation-may-criminalize-those-who-conceal-bitcoin/

21 Additional information is available at the Transparency International website - https://www.transparency.org/research/cpi

22 Ron Pol cited in: Hamish Fletcher, "Dirty cash: The fight against money laundering – should NZ do more?" The New Zealand Herald, September 10, 2015; http://www.nzherald.co.nz/business/news/article.cfm?c_id=3&objectid=11510931

CHAPTER 4
Illicit Financial Flows

ANOTHER WAY OF EXAMINING INTERNATIONAL money laundering is by studying illicit financial flows (IFFs) and sources of dirty money. Compared to the study of money laundering, IFFs is a comparatively recent field. The term is not generally used by law enforcement or for that matter those involved with AML compliance. Over the last twenty years, the study of IFFs has been made popular by academics, non-profits, think tanks, and international organizations such as the World Bank.

There is no widely agreed-upon definition or agreement of which specific forms of capital movement constitute IFFs. According to the World Bank, IFFs "generally refers to cross-border movement of capital associated with illegal activity or more explicitly, money that is illegally earned, transferred or used that crosses borders."[1]

IFFs have three primary elements:[2]

- Criminal activity (e.g., corruption, tax evasion)

- The illicit funds are the results of illegal acts (e.g. fraud, narcotics trafficking)

- The funds are used for illegal purposes (e.g., the support of organized crime)

In economics, IFFs are generally considered a form of illegal capital flight; for example, when capital is illegally earned, transferred, or spent and disappears from the country of origin. Earnings on IFFs do not return to the originating country.

Capital flight occurs when money (and value) leaves primarily developing countries. Traditional thought is the onus to solve the problem is on the developing country or the country exporting the capital. The study of IFFs makes the case that the country that receives or imports the capital is also involved and bears responsibility.

Compounding the challenge, IFFs can be generated in a variety of ways that are not part of the official national record such as those associated with the underground economy, bulk cash movements, smuggling, informal value transfer systems, trade-based value transfer, etc.

As we will discuss further in the book, IFFs are facilitated by offshore financial centers and secrecy havens; they can destabilize the global financial system, and IFFs are exploited to finance international organized crime, instability, and terrorist activities. Thus, over the last decade or so, world leaders, international organizations, some academics and non-profits consider IFFs to be a major global problem which necessitate urgent collective action.[3]

There are many examples of IFFs: An Argentine importer using trade misinvoicing to evade customs duties, value added tax (VAT), or income taxes; Hezbollah using trade-based money laundering techniques to mix legal money from the sale of used cars with illegal money from drug sales; an African kleptocrat using an international labyrinth of shell companies and secrecy havens to hide kickbacks from a Chinese business consortium; a Russian organized crime group wiring money to Dubai for the purchase of high-end properties.

There is disagreement among those that follow IFFs regarding whether or not tax avoidance should be considered part of IFFs. Basically, tax avoidance is legal while tax evasion is not. Businesses get into trouble with tax authorities when they intentionally evade taxes. Yet many business practices such as international transfer pricing that lower tax liability are perfectly legal. We are not talking about moral business practice — only what is legal and what is not. Recall from our earlier discussion that we are trending to equate tax evasion with money laundering.

For example, profit shifting by multinational corporations (transfer pricing) has drained billions of dollars from developing countries. In 2019, the IMF's Director of the IMF, Christine Lagarde, noted that developing countries "collectively lose about $200 billion in revenue a year, or about 1.3 percent of gross domestic product" due to the manipulation of profits by huge global companies.[4]

IFFs have seen increasing scrutiny in large part because of the important work done by Global Financial Integrity (GFI).[5] Tom Cardamone, President and CEO of GFI, has taken a lead role in heightening the awareness of IFFs. A conservative estimate by GFI finds the developing world is losing over $1 trillion every year in IFFs! A 2013 GFI report examining Africa found that even after accounting for both legitimate and illegitimate financial flows — including investment, remittances, debt forgiveness, and natural resource export — Africa is a net creditor to the world.[6] This finding flies in the face of traditional thinking.

We will examine trade misinvoicing — a form of trade-based money laundering — in Chapter 6. Trade misinvoicing is the major component of IFFs — perhaps accounting up to 80 percent of IFFs that can be measured using available data.[7] GFI has examined official government trade data reported to the United Nations to estimate the magnitude of trade misinvoicing between and among 135 developing countries and 36 advanced economies. GFI uses partner-country analysis to compare and contrast the reported data differences or anomalies between any set of two countries. For example, if Costa Rica reported exporting $30 million in bananas to the United States in 2016, but the U.S. reported having imported only $20 million in bananas from Costa Rica that year, this would reflect a mismatch, or value gap, of $10 million in the reported trade of this particular product between the two trading partners for that year. By conducting this type of analysis, GFI found that there was a $8.7 trillion value gap in trade between 135 developing countries and 36 advanced economies over the ten-year period 2008-2017; in 2017 alone the value gap was $817.6 billion.[8]

We can drill down further and show specific impacts of trade misinvoicing. For example, 2018 GFI analysis of South Africa trade misinvoicing for the four year period 2010 — 2014 shows that the potential average loss of revenue to the government was approximately $7.4 billion per year or $37 billion during the period studied.[9] GFI analysis of trade misinvoicing in Nigeria shows that the potential loss of revenue to the government was approximately $2.2 billion in 2014 alone. To put this number in context, this amount represents 4 percent of total annual government revenue as reported to the International Monetary Fund.[10] In another example, in 2019 GFI released a study on the level of trade misinvoicing in Egypt that estimated potential tax revenue losses to the Egyptian government in 2016 was approximately $1.6 billion or approximately 4.1 percent of the value of Egypt's total government revenue collections.[11]

As we recall from the last chapter, in the United States there are hundreds of predicate offenses or specified unlawful activities to charge money laundering. The international standard is all serious crimes. Hence it stands to reason that if we examine the crimes that generate some of the highest totals of illicit proceeds, we can get a much better picture of the enormity of international money laundering. This is because most of these proceeds must be laundered or hidden in some fashion.

GFI did precisely that in a 2017 study on "Transnational Crime and the Developing World."[12] GFI found that globally the business of transnational crime is valued at an average of $1.7 trillion to $2.3 trillion annually. The study evaluates the magnitude of criminal markets in 11 categories:

Counterfeiting (IPR)	$923 billion to $1.13 trillion
Drug trafficking	$426 billion to $652 billion
Illegal logging	$52 billion to $157 billion
Human trafficking	$150 billion
Illicit tobacco	$40 to 60 billion
Illegal mining	$12 billion to $48 billion

Illegal fishing	$15.5 billion to $36.4 billion
Illegal wildlife trade	$5 billion to $12 billion
Organ trafficking	$840 million to $1.7 billion
Cultural property	$1.2 billion to $1.6 billion
Total	$1.7 trillion to $2.3 trillion

Of course, the above just reflects ongoing transnational criminal enterprises. It does not reflect other large predicates for money laundering such as trade fraud and government program fraud. It also does not include tax evasion or capital flight. Adding these and others into the total, and we would easily double or triple the above total and surely reach the conservative estimates of 2 to 5 percent of world GDP discussed in Chapter 2.

I think focusing on IFFs is valuable addition to the study of international money laundering because it provides added perspective by breaking down quantifiable criminal offenses and examining their effects. It looks at both ends of the money and value transfer equation: sender and receiver. IFFs have a destabilizing impact on governments and society. Individuals suffer. IFFs nurture corruption, undermine governance, and reduce tax revenues. Some of the crimes behind the illicit flows of cash undermine economies, destroy the environment, and jeopardize the health and well-being of the public. Other negative consequences of IFFs include:

- Retards development

- Promotes unemployment

- Diverts scarce resources

- Fosters unfair competition

- Abrogates the rule of law

- Catalyst for social and political instability/unrest

- Exacerbates societal rivalries and competition between the haves vs. have-nots

Even more important, Thomas Pogge, Director of the Global Justice Program and President of Academics Stand Against Poverty (ASAP), has estimated that 18 million people die each year of economic deprivation and related causes.[13] That breaks down to about 50,000 people per day every day of the year. As we pondered in closing Chapter 1, "What could matter more?"

NOTES

1 Illicit Financial Flows, The World Bank, July 7, 2017; http://
    www.worldbank.org/en/topic/financialsector/brief/
    illicit-financial-flows-iffs

2 Ibid

3 "Illicit Financial Flows via Trade Misinvoicing, World Customs
    Organization, 2018, page 7; http://www.wcoomd.org/-/me-
    dia/wco/public/global/pdf/media/newsroom/reports/2018/
    wco-study-report-on-iffs_tm.pdf?la=en

4 Tom Cardamone, "Need Funds for the SDG's? Tackle Trade
    Fraud," Global Financial Integrity, July 9, 2019; https://
    gfintegrity.org/need-funds-for-the-sdgs-tackle-trade-
    fraud/?utm_source=hs_email&utm_medium=email&utm_con-
    tent=75260487&_hsenc=p2ANqtz-8nMFvBx43DMfZWIwB-
    bEVMFr-vSWLW4m6C0WUmQFCjiAcGpAtNzpm8Ee-x2_QB_
    DA5sB_0auFbgq9UTIGy0KE1Okr0Glg&_hsmi=75260487

5 Full disclosure, I am on the Board of Directors of Global Financial
    Integrity (GFI)

6 For an excellent GFI overview of IFFs including some of the data
    used in this section see: https://www.gfintegrity.org/issue/
    illicit-financial-flows/

7 See Chapter 6 quote by Raymond Baker, a worldwide authority on
    financial crime and Founding President of GFI, "Trade misinvoicing
    – a prevalent form of TBML – accounts for nearly 80 percent of all
    illicit financial outflows (IFFs) that can be measured by using avail-
    able data."

8 "Trade-Related Illicit Financial Flows in 135 Developing Countries:
    2008-2017," Global Financial Integrity, March 3, 2020; https://
    gfintegrity.org/report/trade-related-illicit-financial-flows-ir
    135-developing-countries-2008-2017/?utm_source=hs_er
    medium=email&utm_content=84332160&_hsenc=p2A'

kFB0I6X3cuCrGcnm4aJt_rAhL3-sQjLWcIUyMNAvb66Otj0Zztbzcou-ONFYLIOHc4VxoCdc5l4hOrUuSXXLKA&_hsmi=84332160

9 "Global Financial Integrity Releases New Study on Trade Misinvoicing in South Africa," Global Financial Integrity, November 13, 2018; https://www.gfintegrity.org/press-release/global-financial-integri-ty-releases-new-study-on-trade-misinvoicing-in-south-africa/

10 "Global Financial Integrity Releases New Study on Trade Misinvoicing in Nigeria," Global Financial Integrity, October 31, 2018; https://www.gfintegrity.org/press-release/global-financial-integrity-re-leases-new-study-on-trade-misinvoicing-in-nigeria/

11 "Egypt: Potential Revenue Losses Associated with Trade Misinvoicing," Global Financial Integrity, June 26, 2019; https://gfintegrity.org/report/egypt-potential-revenue-losses-associated-with-trade-misinvoicing/

12 Channing Mavrellis, "Transnational Crime and the Developing World," March 27, 2017; https://www.gfintegrity.org/report/transnational-crime-and-the-developing-world/

13 Raymond Baker, "Orders of Magnitude and the Human Cost of Illicit Financial Flows," November 25, 2014; https://www.gfintegrity.org/orders-magnitude-human-cost-illicit-financial-flows/

CHAPTER 5
Bulk Cash Smuggling

ACCORDING TO THE FATF, BULK cash smuggling is one of the top three money laundering methodologies in the world. The other two major methodologies are laundering via financial institutions and trade-based laundering and value transfer.[1]

Bulk cash refers to the large amounts of currency notes that criminals accumulate as a result of various types of criminal activity. "Smuggling," in the context of bulk cash, refers to criminals' subsequent attempts to physically transport the money from one country to another. Bulk cash smuggling is particularly common when and where criminal organizations need to launder large amounts of narcotics proceeds.[2]

U.S. law enforcement learned early on during the "War on Drugs" that "placing" drug proceeds into traditional financial institutions posed a tremendous logistical challenge for traffickers. Estimates vary widely, but narcotics sales in the United States annually generate between $50 to $100 billion and more. Using the conservative $50 billion figure, that generates approximately 10 million pounds of currency every year. Put another way, a money launderer attempting to deposit $1 million in $100 bills could not simply walk into a bank carrying a briefcase full of cash — a stack of that many bills would stand five feet high and weigh more than 20 pounds![3] Smaller denominations would make the transaction even more absurd. As per our discussion on financial intelligence reporting in Chapter 3, large deposits of bulk cash will also trigger CTR and perhaps SAR reporting.

As a result, money launderers frequently attempt to move cash to foreign jurisdictions with less stringent currency controls (or with corrupt banking officials willing to accept the funds). In other words, they physically smuggle the currency out of the United States so that it can be more readily deposited into international banking networks. In the context of money laundering in the United States, this means most bulk cash is often smuggled from the United States across our southern border into Mexico. The magnitude of the problem has lessened in recent years, as Mexico has tightened up its enforcement and compliance programs. Nevertheless, the smuggling continues. Media attention is focused on drugs and people smuggled north. We too often forget about money smuggled south — which is the reason the cartels are engaged in illegal activity.

Bulk cash smuggling also exists in other areas of the world and consistently involves transnational organized crime groups; for example, there is reporting that Mexican cartels increasingly seek to bypass their home country when moving money that will be reinvested in paying for more cocaine. They smuggle the cash into Colombia and Ecuador. Sometimes the cartels use international criminal groups based in Russia and China as smugglers.[4] Bulk cash smuggling has also been well documented in troublesome areas in Asia, the Middle East and elsewhere.

U.S. Cross Border Currency Reporting Requirements

Per our discussion in Chapter 3, the United States created international cross-border currency reporting requirements as part of the Bank Secrecy Act (BSA) of 1970. These requirements were intended to provide a paper trail for the movement of currency and serve as a mechanism to seize unreported/smuggled cash. Specifically, the law mandates the filing of a Cross Border Currency or Monetary Instrument Report (CMIR) — now known as FinCEN Form 105 — when $10,000 or more of currency or negotiable monetary instruments are being transported across the border or via international mail. It should be emphasized that transporting bulk cash is not illegal. The law simply requires that a form be filled out and filed with Customs and Border Protection (CBP, formerly known as the U.S. Customs Service).

The CMIR form has approximately 70 different data fields including name, address, passport identification number, residence, and more.[5] This information provides excellent financial intelligence for criminal investigators. Although hundreds of thousands of CMIR forms are filed every year, only a small percentage of individuals who transport large amounts of cash actually declare and fill out a form. This is particularly true of outbound cash because there is much less monitoring of outbound travelers than inbound.

After the September 11 attacks, the USA PATRIOT Act updated the BSA reporting requirements for the international transportation of bulk cash. The legislation formally defined cash smuggling as follows:

> Whoever...knowingly conceals more than $10,000 in currency or other monetary instruments on the person of such individual or in any conveyance, article of luggage, merchandise, or other container, and transports or transfers or attempts to transport or transfer such currency or monetary instruments from a place within the United States to a place outside of the United States, or from a place outside the United States to a place within the United States, shall be guilty of a currency smuggling offense.[6]

Of course, there are other forms of "monetary instruments" that are used by money launderers. A primary example is the use of value-loaded gift cards and other "stored-value" or "pre-paid cards." The use of these cards has grown steadily in recent years. According to the Mercator Advisory Group, in 2015 more than $623 billion was loaded on to prepaid cards and gift cards.[7] The prepaid card volume is expected to reach $3,653 billion by 2022.[8] An unknown portion of money used to purchase the cards comes from drug trafficking and other illegal activities. Law enforcement believes the percentage could be substantial.

In a simplistic and hypothetical example, narcotics trafficking organizations use runners to purchase gift cards at Walmart stores located in the United States. The cards can be purchased in amounts ranging in various amounts up to $500. The cards are then transported into Mexico. Currently, this type of monetary instrument is not subject to cross-border currency reporting requirements. Once in Mexico they can be sold on the black market in mass for dollars or pesos at a discount or easily redeemed at Walmart stores throughout Mexico.

The IRS has declared prepaid cards "the currency of criminals."[9] Stored value cards are also commonly used in various tax fraud scams. While FinCEN has weighed proposals that would include prepaid cards under the definition of monetary instruments for purposes of cross-border reporting, so far industry pushback has prevailed.

Enforcement

Customs and Border Protection (CBP) and Immigration and Customs Enforcement (ICE) have been given primary responsibility for cross-border currency enforcement. These agencies — part of the Department of Homeland Security — are the designated "competent authorities" vested with the power to stop, search, seize, compel forfeiture, and make arrests related to cross-border crimes, with or without a search warrant. This power extends to "any vehicle, vessel, aircraft, or other conveyance, any envelope or other container, and any person" entering or departing the United States via any point.[10]

The Fourth Amendment to the Constitution does not require warrants or probable cause for routine border stops and searches because it is within the power of the federal government to protect the country by inspecting persons and property entering and leaving. Government authorities also have the right of "extended border search." This means customs and border officials may conduct a warrantless search beyond the border or its functional equivalent if 1) they believe there is a "high degree of probability" that a border was crossed; 2) they also have reasonable certainty that no change in the object of the search has occurred between the time of the border crossing and the search; and 3) they have "reasonable suspicion" that criminal activity was occurring.[11] In other words, if a suspect is kept under constant surveillance after crossing the border into the United States, he or she can be stopped and subjected to a warrantless search even hundreds of miles away from the border.

Other law enforcement officers at the federal, state, and local levels also intercept bulk cash smugglers during routine police work. Chicago, Phoenix, Seattle, Los Angles, Atlanta and other major cities are interstate hubs for drug trafficking. For example, trucks carrying contraband from the Atlanta area can reach more than 80 percent of the U.S. population within two days; in addition, cash often moves in the opposite direction. The bulk cash from street drug sales usually arrives at central counting centers located in major transportation hubs. The smaller bills are converted to $100 or $50 bills. This is done primarily to reduce the bulk of the cash and make it easier to conceal. Often the cash is then vacuum sealed to further reduce the bulk.

Currency Smuggling

Currency smuggling generally follows the same routes as drugs but in reverse. The criminal organizations frequently use the same personnel and transport infrastructure. The most popular route with drug traffickers is crossing the Mexico-United States border. The land border between the United States and Mexico is approximately 2,000 miles long. There are 48 Mexico-United States border crossings, hundreds more official points of entry (land, air, sea), and numerous "unofficial" border crossings. The points of entry/

egress vary in size. Some are comparatively remote, and others are located in major urban areas.

The San Ysidro Port of Entry in San Diego is the busiest land port in the Western Hemisphere. Every day, approximately 70,000 northbound vehicle passengers and 20,000 pedestrians are processed. The flow is nonstop, 24 hours a day. Officials estimate the volume of the southbound flow is similar.[12] The volume of traffic across the border is the primary challenge for customs and law enforcement to spot the occasional smuggler as well as the varied and extended transportation routes. As a former U.S. Ambassador to Mexico said, "Over a million people cross the border every day; over $1 billion worth of legitimate trade crosses the border every day. The border does not just follow a river as it courses between El Paso and Ciudad Juárez. The border has one end at a strawberry field in Guanajuato and the other end in the produce market at a Costco in Kansas City and includes everyone in the process."[13]

Generally, bulk currency is smuggled across the border via cars and trucks. Sometimes it is simply boxed and placed in a trunk or covered truck bed. It can also be concealed in car panels, spare tires, gasoline tanks/containers, seat cushions, floorboards, dashboards, inside the engine compartment, and other spots. Tanker trucks or similar vehicles may have altered gasoline or water tanks with false bottoms, so the cash is hidden inside these compartments. Many times the cash is concealed in the same trucks and other vehicles that that bring contraband north.

The narco-trafficking organizations use several tactics in an attempt to minimize the impact of potential seizures by authorities. For example, the cash transport vehicles are rotated often to minimize suspicion. Most shipments range from $150,000 to $500,000. If any one vehicle is stopped, the loss of currency is not as significant and does not disrupt operations. Typically multiple vehicles/couriers are involved with each carrying a relatively small percentage of any given cash shipment.[14]

In addition to smuggling in vehicles, cash smugglers use a wide variety of techniques and conveyances. The methods are only limited by the imagination! A comprehensive list is impossible. The following are typical cash smuggling techniques:

- Currency can be concealed in air and ocean cargo shipping containers, whether freely or hidden inside other items.

- Many couriers tape currency on their bodies or use special smuggling vests, girdles, belts, and even pantyhose. Using large-denomination notes, it is possible to smuggle hundreds of thousands of dollars in this manner.

- Cash can be hidden in body cavities, as is often done with narcotics. For example, smugglers can swallow or insert condoms filled with tightly rolled cash.

- Various types of machines, air compressors, tools, furniture, sports equipment, household appliances, toys, stuffed animals, games, flowers, produce, and foodstuffs have all been found with concealed cash.

- Bulk cash is frequently found in passengers' luggage, duffel bags, briefcases, and so forth.

- Cash is sometimes sewn in the lining of coats and other garments.

- Mail services such as FedEx, DHS, and UPS have also proven popular with smugglers because of the web tracking features they offer. Traditional mail services are also used to ship currency across borders.

International Standards

For many years, the United States was the only major country that mandated cross-border currency reporting. In 2004, the

FATF sought to change the situation by issuing FATF "Special Recommendation IX" covering cross-border currency reporting. The FATF Recommendations were reviewed and updated; in 2012 the FATF released its current international AML/CFT guidelines. FATF Recommendation #32 now covers bulk cash smuggling countermeasures.[15] The international norm to combat bulk cash smuggling reads:

> Countries should have measures in place to detect the physical cross-border transportation of currency and bearer negotiable instruments, including through a declaration system and/or disclosure system. Countries should ensure that their competent authorities have the legal authority to stop or restrain currency or bearer negotiable instruments that are suspected to be related to terrorist financing, money laundering or predicate offences, or that are falsely declared or disclosed. Countries should ensure that effective, proportionate and dissuasive sanctions are available to deal with persons who make false declaration(s) or disclosure(s). In cases where the currency or bearer negotiable instruments are related to terrorist financing, money laundering or predicate offences, countries should also adopt measures, including legislative ones consistent with Recommendation 4, which would enable the confiscation of such currency or instruments.

From the interpretive note accompanying the recommendation, bulk cash smuggling includes the following modes of transportation: 1) physical transportation by a natural person, or in that person's accompanying luggage or vehicle; 2) shipment of currency or [monetary instrument] through containerized cargo or 3) the mailing of currency by a natural or legal person. FATF also urges that the declarations be both inbound and outbound. FATF also suggests the reports be forwarded to the country's FIU.

To meet the recommendation, the FATF encourages countries to implement either a "declaration" or a "disclosure" system for incoming and outgoing money. Countries need not use the same system for both situations. Customs officials strongly prefer the declaration model, in large part because of the paper trails it creates. In a declaration system, individuals transporting currency or bearer negotiable instruments are required to submit a declaration form to the relevant government agency if the amount exceeds a certain threshold. Although reporting levels vary, FATF has encouraged countries to implement a threshold of USD/EUR 15,000 or less.

In a disclosure system, individuals do not need to declare any funds they are carrying unless asked to do so by the authorities. According to FATF, countries that choose this system should ensure that they empower authorities to make such inquiries based on "intelligence, suspicion or on a random basis."[16] In practice, however, disclosure systems are simply not effective. It is also unfortunate that too many countries do not keep records on currency seizures even though FATF Recommendation #33 specifically urges that countries "should maintain comprehensive statistics on matters relevant to the effectiveness" of their AML/CFT countermeasures.[17]

Case Examples

The following three cases are examples of the varied nature of bulk cash smuggling:

Operation Dragon

The law enforcement community hit the jackpot on March 16, 2007, when "Operation Dragon" netted more than $207 million in seized drug proceeds in Mexico City.[18] The U.S. government called it "the largest single drug cash seizure the world has ever seen."[19]

Surprisingly, the money did not belong to a Mexican drug cartel, nor did it represent profits from traditional drug sales such as Colombian cocaine, Mexican marijuana, or black-tar heroin. Rather, Mexican police working with U.S. Drug Enforcement Administration (DEA) agents seized the money from a broker who supplied chemicals to Mexican cartels specializing in methamphetamine — most of which was destined for the United States. According to law enforcement officials, many drug traffickers believe that "meth" has major advantages over drugs like cocaine — it is a highly addictive, it can be made at home and smuggled easily, and it can produce huge profits.[20]

Zhenli Ye Gon, a naturalized Mexican citizen from Shanghai, China, ran a pharmaceuticals front company responsible for one of the Western Hemisphere's largest pseudoephedrine networks, the primary ingredient in meth.[21] The Operation Dragon bust took place at his home in Lomas de Chapultepec, one of Mexico City's most exclusive neighborhoods. Along with the cash (mostly $100 bills hidden in walls, closets, and suitcases), police seized eight luxury vehicles, seven weapons, and a machine to make pills. Seven people were arrested — but not Gon himself.[22] He was not captured until July 2007, in a suburb of Washington, D.C.[23]

In the U.S. district court affidavit, federal authorities alleged that between December 2005 and August 2006, Gon's company, Unimed Pharm Chem de Mexico, illegally imported 86 metric tons of restricted chemicals into Mexico "for the express purpose of manufacturing pseudoephedrine/ephedrine." The affidavit claimed that the imported chemicals were enough to produce 36,568 kilograms of meth, with a street value of approximately $724 million.[24]

Border Patrol Arrests Duo for Bulk Cash Smuggling

In 2016, U.S. Border Patrol agents arrested two men for smuggling more than $3 million dollars that were being transported in separate vehicles traveling near San Diego. The Border Patrol agents noticed that two cars — a Kia Forte and a Volkswagen Passat — were driving suspiciously and in tandem. At the scene of a vehicle stop off Interstate 15, a Border Patrol K-9 alerted agents. They searched the Kia Forte, resulting in the discovery of eight vacuum-sealed bundles containing $33,880 that was stashed in the center console. A 53-year-old male U.S. citizen was arrested upon the discovery. The Volkswagen Passat was found abandoned at a cul-de-sac located in a residential area within close proximity of the vehicle stop. The agents then found the vehicle's driver, a 41-year-old male Mexican national, hiding in some brush nearby and arrested him for suspicion of currency smuggling. Agents searched the vehicle and seized $3,018,000 that was found inside eight boxes located in the trunk of the Passat.[25]

Bulk Cash Smuggling Using Stuffed Toy Animals

Jeanette Barraza-Galindo, 33, of Monterrey, Mexico, was a passenger aboard a bus stopped by Customs and Border Protection at the Hidalgo, Texas, Port of Entry. The bus was heading southbound toward Mexico. CBP officers explained the currency-reporting requirements to all passengers. When the CBP officers asked Barraza if she had more than $10,000 in cash to declare, Barraza gave a negative declaration even though she knew that she was carrying more than $10,000 in cash. The CBP officers searched two teddy bears and two pillows that Barraza had with her and found a total of $277,556 in cash in the stuffed toys. Barraza was later convicted, and as part of a plea agreement, forfeited the $277,556 in currency to the United States.[26]

The Metrics

As we noted at the outset of this book, lost in the discussion about transnational crime is the fact that criminal organizations are motivated by greed. Cartels do not traffic in drugs for the sake of drugs. The objective is to make money. And trafficking drugs is highly profitable.

The estimates of U.S. narcotics sales vary widely. A 2010 White House study pegged the number at $109 billion annually.[27] In a 2014 report, the Office of National Drug Control Policy (ONDCP) estimated that over the 2000-2010 decade, Americans spent approximately $100 billion annually on the four major illegal drugs, i.e. heroin, cocaine, methamphetamine and marijuana. This amount does not include what Americans spend on other illegal plant-based and synthetic drugs.[28]

Analysts believe much of the money is laundered in the U.S. through a variety of methods such as the use of banks and MSBs in order to place illegal drug proceeds into the financial system. Trade-based money laundering, crypto currencies and online payment systems, underground financial systems and other methodologies that we will discuss in this book are also used.

As we have seen, narcotics trafficking organizations also smuggle bulk cash into jurisdictions such as Mexico where "placing" their ill-gotten gains into financial networks is much easier. Once again, estimates vary, but a few years ago the National Drug Intelligence Center (NDIC) estimated that approximately $18 billion to $39 billion in bulk cash is smuggled annually across our southern border.[29]

So how have we done? Per the above discussion, a variety of law enforcement agencies play a role in detecting and intercepting bulk cash smuggling, but ICE and CBP are most active. From 2005 to 2016, CBP officers reportedly seized a total of $211 million along the southern border.[30] Between fiscal years 2003 and 2016, ICE bulk cash smuggling investigations led to the arrest of more than 4,000 individuals and seizures of more than $769.2 million.[31]

Using the above DHS generated numbers, ICE and CBP together seize an average of about $80 million a year in bulk cash. Of course, additional cash is being seized by other federal, state, and local law enforcement agencies sometimes in the interior of the country. In addition, Mexican law enforcement also confiscates bulk cash on its side of the border. A very rough estimate would be that $100 million of bulk cash is seized every year. But that number represents what is initially seized — not forfeited. It also includes all enforcement areas of operation and not just the southern border with Mexico.

For example, significant amounts of bulk cash are generated from the U.S. sale of Canada-produced drugs that cross the U.S.-Canada border into Canada. Canada-based drug trafficking organizations, primarily Asian, generate tens of billions of dollars annually from drug sales in the United States which is very likely smuggled across the U.S.-Canada border. The Akwesasne Territory, in upstate New York which straddles the U.S.-Canada border, is one of the most important corridors for bulk cash smuggling.[32] Moreover, much more bulk cash is smuggled out of the United States via air and sea. Data for these seizures are not available.

The best data we have comes from our southern border with Mexico. So if we use a generous seizure/forfeiture number of $100 million on average a year out of a total of approximately $25 billion on average that is smuggled across our southern border, our success rate is less than 1 percent! This dovetails with a 2011 GAO study that estimates we are seizing less than 1 percent of the multi-billion in drug-trafficking proceeds smuggled across the border.[33] Another study suggests a success rate of .0025 percent or that $99.75 of every $100 the cartels ship south is getting through.[34]

Think of it this way: We seize a George Washington 25 cent coin out of a $100 Benjamin Franklin currency note!

These statistics are even more sobering because bulk cash smuggling is the most straightforward of money laundering investigations. We are not talking about complex money trails layered via off shore havens, tracking trade-based laundering schemes, or tracing virtual currencies in cyber space. At its core, bulk cash is a physical commodity (money) that generally moves from point A (U.S. side of the border) to point B (Mexican side of the border). The cash shipments are hidden, but the methodology is not complicated.

U.S. and Mexican officials admit that their governments are getting only a small fraction of the money that flows across the border. They also understand how much remains unquantifiable in any meaningful way.[35]

Consequences

The consequences of bulk cash smuggling are devastating. The uncontrolled hemorrhage of billions of dollars of untaxed drug proceeds that flow into the coffers of organized criminal organizations directly fuels massive crime, corruption, and violence in Mexico that is spreading to parts of the United States. In the United States, the murder carnage in Chicago and many other cities exemplifies our failure. Our inability to put a dent in bulk cash smuggling is not only a glaring failure of law enforcement, but it is also a national embarrassment.

It gets worse. Using an earlier example, let's use the above $39 billion estimate of drug money smuggled out of the United States each year. If the cartels invest their illicit proceeds at a 5 percent annualized rate of return, after 20 years just that one year has mushroomed into a $1.7 trillion dollar problem![36] And that represents just one year, using one methodology, in one geographic sector.

Countermeasures

Despite valiant efforts by our law enforcement professionals to stem the bulk cash smuggling tide, buttressed by new initiatives such as regional task forces and Homeland Security Investigations' National Bulk Cash Smuggling Center,[37] the above metrics prove the bottom line is not good. The U.S. government is fully aware of the bulk cash smuggling problem. In fact, bulk cash smuggling was prominently featured in our last (2007) National Money Laundering Strategy.[38] The "action items" in the report, centered on traditional law enforcement countermeasures such as increased intelligence, coordination, border inspections, etc., have proved wholly inadequate. In 2013, the U.S. Senate Drug Caucus released an excellent report on improving U.S. anti-money laundering practices. The report notes that bulk cash smuggling continues to be a primary money laundering technique and that our counter-measures have been ineffectual.[39]

Law enforcement officials have long observed that if we put a barrier (in all its varied forms) in front of criminals, they will try going around it.

For example, after the Mexican government restricted the deposit of U.S. dollars in Mexican banks and currency exchange houses in 2010, law enforcement witnessed the money launderers using "funnel accounts" in conjunction with trade-based money laundering to move money and value across the border.[40] FinCEN describes funnel accounts as having "an individual or business account in one geographic area that receives multiple cash deposits, often in amounts below the cash reporting threshold, and from which the funds are withdrawn in a different geographic area with little time elapsing between the deposits and withdrawals." [41] Sometimes funnel accounts are used to purchase goods involved in a TBML scheme. Sometimes multiple funnel accounts have been observed to transfer funds into a single consolidated account from where the funds are subsequently withdrawn. Some observers feel a recent drop of cash seizures could also be the result of new ways of moving money across the border such as prepaid cards or even cyber currencies. And, of course, criminals will try to go around, under, and over a border wall. Therefore, countermeasures must take the above into consideration.

Proposal

Taking the politics out of arguments for or against the construction of a border "wall," I believe a physical border wall will assist in thwarting contraband and human trafficking. But in designing the wall, we should have stopping bulk cash on the northern side of the border in mind as well as thwarting drugs and illegal immigrants coming from the south. The construction and placement of the physical wall should be done in such a way as will "funnel" currency smugglers to border crossings that will be heavily controlled and monitored. In other words, just like a successful tactical military maneuver, we should use terrain, barriers, and deploy our resources (technology and personnel) to force smugglers to use routes and border crossings we want them to use.

There will never be enough law enforcement personnel and customs inspectors in the fight against bulk cash smuggling. But better use of data and technology can be a modern day force multiplier. Over the last few years, there have been tremendous advances in the amount and variety of data collected. Financial intelligence, travel and trade records, motor vehicle data, and criminal intelligence reports are just a few examples of big data sets available to law enforcement agencies. Predictive analytics, financial fraud frameworks and social network analytics are new capabilities that can help law enforcers more efficiently target their efforts.

There are exciting developments in an emerging breed of software that can explore and analyze data to help uncover unknown patterns, links, opportunities and insights that can drive proactive, cause-based decisions. Often referred to as "predictive analytics," it is now available to help law enforcement sort through large volumes of data to predict the likelihood of targeted activity. A limited pilot program has proved very successful in intercepting narcotics flowing north from Mexico into the United States. I believe this same technology could revolutionize law enforcement decision-making at the border by increasing our odds of identifying, intercepting, and seizing bulk cash.[42]

If we could increase our bulk cash seizure rate from approximately 1 percent to 5 percent, within twenty years we could pay for the new "wall" along our southern border. All of the above countermeasures and others included in this book are entirely doable. Not only do these approaches to combatting criminality adhere to our already-articulated inter-departmental bi-partisan national anti-money laundering strategy, but they should be acceptable as they are self-funding and provide reasonable political cover for all sides in the debate about funding for "the wall." Who could object if we use cartel money to buttress law enforcement techniques that recovers illicit proceeds of crime?

NOTES

1 "Trade Based Money Laundering," The FATF, 2006; http://www.fatf-gafi.org/publications/methodsandtrends/documents/trade-based-moneylaundering.html

2 Some of the material in this chapter quotes material from John A. Cassara and Avi Jorisch, On the Trail of Terror Finance: What Law Enforcement and Intelligence Officers Need to Know, Red Cell Publishing, Arlington, Virginia, 201, Chapter 3 on Bulk Cash Smuggling, pages 39- 55.

3 Mary Lee Warren, deputy assistant attorney-general, Criminal Division, U.S. Justice Department, testimony before the Judiciary Subcommittee on Crime, House of Representatives, 105th Congress (July 24, 1997).

4 James Bargent, "Ecuador Bulk Cash Smuggling Reflects New Laundering Trend," Insight Crime, April 11, 2013; https://www.insightcrime.org/news/analysis/rise-in-ecuador-cash-smuggling-reflects-wider-crime-trends/

5 For more information about the FinCEN 105 and other financial intelligence forms visit the FinCEN website at www.FinCEN.gov

6 See Section 371 of the Patriot Act (31 USC 5332). See also 18 USC 5332.

7 "Treasury Department Cracking Down on Prepaid Cards," Get.com; https://www.get.com/news/treasury-department-cracking-down-prepaid-cards/

8 "Prepaid Card Market Outlook," Allied Market Research; https://www.alliedmarketresearch.com/prepaid-card-market

9 "Prepaid Cards are the 'Currency of Criminals', IRS Chief Tells 60 Minutes," ECredit Daily, September 22, 2015; http://ecreditdaily.com/2014/09/prepaid-cards-are-currency-of-criminals-irs-chief-tells-60-minutes/

10 See 19 USC 1595, 31 USC 5316, and 31 USC 5317. CBP and ICE also have the authority to stop or restrain unreported or falsely reported currency for a reasonable time (31 USC 5316, 31 USC 5217, and 31 USC 5332).

11 "Reasonable certainty" in this context has been defined as a standard that requires more than probable cause, but less than proof beyond a reasonable doubt. See, for example, United States v. Cardenas and United States v. Delgado. In the Delgado case, smugglers used a footbridge to transfer narcotics to delivery trucks on a farm near El Paso, Texas. The court upheld an extended border search conducted on a farm road near and leading from the border but otherwise away from the official border checkpoint.

12 Sandra Dibble, "Long waits a painful routine for San Ysidro border commuters," San Diego Union, July 12, 2016; http://www.sandiegouniontribune.com/news/border-baja-california/sdut-commuter-wait-and-san-ysidro-port-entry-2016jul12-story.html and Sandra Dibble, "Tijuana detour: Southbound lanes at San Ysidro border crossing to be closed for 57 hours," Los Angeles Times, September 8, 2017; http://www.latimes.com/local/lanow/la-me-border-closure-20170908-story.html

13 Juan Aguilar, "Ambassador: U.S. & Mexico seize only 3-5% of drug money," The Tucson Sentinel, August 12, 2010; http://www.tucsonsentinel.com/nationworld/report/081210_us_mexico/ambassador-us-mexico-seize-only-3-5-drug-money/

14 Douglas Farah, "Money Laundering and Bulk Cash Smuggling – Challenges for the Merida Initiative," The Wilson Center, August 4, 2010, page 147; http://www.wilsoncenter.org/sites/default/files/Chapter%205-Money%20Laundering%20and%20Bulk%20Cash%20Smuggling%20Challenges%20for%20the%20Merida%20Initiative.pdf

15 See FATF 40 Recommendations; http://www.fatf-gafi.org/media/fatf/documents/recommendations/pdfs/FATF%20Recommendations%202012.pdf

16 See FATF, "Interpretative Notes to the 9 Special Recommendations on Terrorist Financing," Interpretative

Note to Special Recommendation IX, n.d. Available online; http://
www.fatf-gafi.org/media/fatf/documents/reports/FATF%20
Standards%20-%20IX%20Special%20Recommendations%20
and%20IN%20rc.pdf

17 See FATF 40 Recommendations.

18 The amount included $205.6 million in U.S. dollars, 200,000 in eu-
ros, and 17.3 million in pesos. "Mexico: World's Largest Drug Cash
Seizure Is Larger Than Originally Announced," Associated Press,
March 22, 2007; http://www.iht.com/articles/ap/2007/03/22/ameri-
ca/LA-GEN-Mexico-Drug-Money.php

19 U.S. Justice Department, "Statement by Administrator Karen P.
Tandy on Two Hundred and Seven Million in Drug Money Seized
in Mexico City," March 20, 2007; http://www.usdoj.gov/dea/pubs/
pressrel/pr032007.html

20 See Laurence Iliff, "Meth Production Flourishes South of the
Border," Dallas Morning News, April 28, 2007; http://www.fox11az.
com/sharedcontent/dws/news/dmn/stories/042807dnintmexme
th.3794852.html; Mexican trafficking organizations operating on
both sides of the border are the source of at least 80 percent of the
meth consumed in the United States.

21 Ibid. Gon's citizenship became official in 2002. See Mark Stevenson
and Michael Rubinkam, "Biggest Cash Seizure in History—$205M—
in Mexico City," Associated Press, July 2, 2007; http://seattletimes.
nwsource.com/html/nationworld/2003771087_webmillions02.html

22 "Mexico: World's Largest Drug Cash Seizure." See also Paul Duggan
and Ernesto Londoño, "Not Your Average Drug Bust," Washington
Post, July 25, 2007; http://www.washingtonpost.com/wp-dyn/
content/article/2007/07/24/AR2007072400150.html. See also Iliff,
"Meth Production Flourishes."

23 Duggan and Londoño, "Not Your Average Drug Bust."

24 U.S. Department of Justice, "Affidavit in Support of Complaint and
Arrest Warrant For Zhenli Ye Gon;" http://www.washingtonpost.
com/wp-srv/metro/gon-affidavit.pdf

25 "Border Patrol Arrests Duo for Bulk Cash Smuggling," U.S. Customs and Border Protection Press Release, August 26, 2016; https://www.cbp.gov/newsroom/local-media-release/border-patrol-arrests-duo-bulk-cash-smuggling

26 "Mexican woman convicted of bulk-cash smuggling using stuffed toy animals," ICE Press Release, June 30, 2011; https://www.ice.gov/news/releases/mexican-woman-convicted-bulk-cash-smuggling-using-stuffed-toy-animals

27 Christopher Woody, "NARCONOMICS: 'The real drugs millionaires are right here in the United States,"Business Insider, March 16, 2016; http://www.businessinsider.com/where-drug-money-goes-2016-3

28 See Drug Enforcement Administration website. (https://www.dea.gov/ops/money.shtml)

29 See "Illicit Finance," National Drug Intelligence Center; https://www.justice.gov/archive/ndic/pubs31/31379/finance.htm

30 Julianne Stanford, "More drug profits slipping into Mexico as border seizures plummet," Arizona Dailey Star, January 26, 2017; http://tucson.com/news/local/border/more-drug-profits-slipping-into-mexico-as-border-seizures-plummet/article_4642d8bf-9bee-5e4e-906b-f2d24fb2eff8.html

31 See Bulk Cash Smuggling Center; https://www.ice.gov/bulk-cash-smuggling-center

32 National Drug Intelligence Center

33 Statement of Richard M. Stana, Director Homeland and Security Issues Before the Senate Caucus on International Narcotics Control, "MOVING ILLEGAL PROCEEDS: Opportunities Exist for Strengthening the Federal Government's Efforts to Stem Cross-Border Currency Smuggling," GAO Report, March 19, 2011; https://www.gao.gov/new.items/d11407t.pdf

34 "U.S. Drug Cartel Crackdown Misses the Money," Associated Press, December 17, 2009; http://www.nbcnews.com/id/34466436/ns/world_news-americas/t/us-drug-cartel-crackdown-misses-money/#.WmC-DZJy7Y9

35 Farah, "Money Laundering and Bulk Cash Smuggling," p. 154

36 Example provided to the author by J.R. Helmig

37 For more information see the BCS website; https://www.ice.gov/bulk-cash-smuggling-center

38 See 2007 National Anti-Money Laundering Strategy Report; https://www.treasury.gov/resource-center/terrorist-illicit-finance/Documents/nmls.pdf

39 "The Buck Stops Here: U.S. Anti-Money Laundering Practices," United States Senate Caucus on International Narcotics Control, April 25, 2013; https://www.drugcaucus.senate.gov/content/buck-stops-here-us-anti-money-laundering-practices

40 Julianne Stanford, "More Drug Profits"

41 "Update on U.S. Currency Restrictions in Mexico: Funnel Accounts and TBML," FinCEN Advisory FIN-2014-A005, May 28, 2014; https://www.fincen.gov/resources/advisories/fincen-advisory-fin-2014-a005

42 The author explored the use of technology to help combat bulk cash smuggling in two articles and an internal "white paper" distributed to some Congressional members. See John A. Cassara, "How Big Data Could Help Law Enforcement Catch Bulk Cash Smugglers," NextGov, April 7, 2014; http://www.nextgov.com/ideas/2014/04/how-big-data-could-help-law-enforcement-catch-bulk-cash-smugglers/82048/) and John A. Cassara, "Bulk Cash Pays for the Wall," American Thinker, April 25, 2017; http://www.americanthinker.com/articles/2017/04/bulk_cash_pays_for_the_wall.html

CHAPTER 6

Trade-Based Money Laundering

NOT LONG AFTER THE SEPTEMBER 11 attacks, I had a conversation with a Pakistani entrepreneur. The businessman could generously be described as being involved in international grey markets and illicit finance. We discussed many of the money laundering subjects addressed in Chapters 6 and 7 including trade-based value transfer, hawala, fictitious invoicing, and counter-valuation. At the end of the discussion, he looked at me and said, "Mr. John, don't you know that your adversaries are transferring money and value right under your noses? But the West doesn't see it. Your enemies are laughing at you."[1]

The conversation made a profound impact on me. I knew he was right. At the time of our conversation, the U.S. government and the international community had not focused attention or resources on the misuse of international trade to launder money, transfer value, avoid taxes, commit commercial fraud, and finance terror. Our adversaries – terrorists, criminals, kleptocrats, and fraudsters – were operating in these areas with almost total impunity. The methodology was completely under our radar screen. And unfortunately, many years later and after the tremendous expenditure of resources to counter illicit finance, trade-based money laundering and value transfer are still not recognized as significant threats. Perhaps as the Pakistani businessman inferred, it is because the subterfuges are "hiding in plain sight."

As noted, the FATF has declared that there are three broad categories for the purpose of hiding illicit funds and introducing them into the formal economy. The first is via the use of financial institutions; the second is to physically smuggle bulk cash from one country or jurisdiction to another; and the third is the transfer of value via trade aka trade-based money laundering or TBML.[2] The United States and the international community have devoted attention, countermeasures, and resources to the first two categories. In my opinion, TBML is the largest money laundering methodology. However, for the most part it has been ignored. This oversight has contributed in large part to our AML efforts being "a decimal point away" from failure.

The FATF defines TBML as "the process of disguising the proceeds of crime and moving value through the use of trade transactions in an attempt to legitimize their illicit origins."[3] The key word in the definition is value. Instead of following the money trail via bulk cash or the electronic bits and bytes of a bank-to-bank wire transfer, with TBML we examine the shipments of commodities and trade goods. Their sale and transfer — real and fictitious — can launder money, evade taxes and tariffs, and transfer value between cooperating parties in the transaction(s).

Magnitude of the Problem

TBML is a very broad topic. Unfortunately, there are no known official estimates on the global or domestic magnitude of TBML. Since the issue impacts national security, law enforcement, and the collection of national revenue, it is remarkable that TBML has never been systematically examined by the U.S. government. (The final chapter discussing "steps forward" will explain some of the bureaucratic reasons why TBML has been overlooked.) As a result, there are few available metrics. And as with other topics involving money laundering, the magnitude of TBML depends on what is included in the count. Nevertheless, the following few examples are staggering:

According to the World Trade Organization (WTO), the amount of global merchandise trade varies annually but averages approximately $20 trillion.[4] In "traditional" money laundering, the kind that the FATF has emphasized, money launderers mix or "co-mingle" illicit funds with the overwhelming percentage of legitimate money sloshing around and through the world's financial institutions. The same holds true with international trade. It is very easy to hide the occasional suspect or illicit trade transaction in the tens of trillions of dollars of annual global merchandise trade.

As noted in Chapter 4 and discussed further below, according to some estimates, 80 percent of the world's illicit money flow stems from trade-related activities.[5]

Dr. John Zdanowicz, an academic and early pioneer in the field of TBML, analyzed 2013 U.S. trade data obtained from the U.S. Census Bureau. By examining under-valued exports ($124,116,420,714) and over-valued imports ($94,796,135,280), Dr. Zdanowicz found that $218,912,555,994 was moved out of the United States in the form of value transfer! That figure represents 5.69 percent of U.S. trade. Reviewing over-valued exports ($68,332,594,940) and under-valued imports ($272,753,571,621), Dr. Zdanowicz calculated that $341,086,166,561 was moved into the United States! That figure represents 8.87 percent of U.S. trade in 2013.[6]

Trends are accelerating. Examining 2017 data, Dr. Zdanowicz found that nearly $400 billion was moved into the U.S. via over-valued exports and under-valued imports. Approximately $250 billion was moved out of the U.S. via undervalued exports and over-valued imports.[7]

In my opinion, the United States has the most professional and vigorous customs enforcement service in the world. Thus if almost 6 to 9 percent of our trade is tainted by customs fraud and perhaps trade-based money laundering, what does that mean for the rest of the world, in particular countries with weak governance and high corruption?

If we extrapolate the above globally using a fair estimate that 10 percent of worldwide trade is infected with customs fraud, using the WTO estimate an argument could be made that there is about $2 trillion in TBML annually! And that number is only based on customs fraud. TBML is much more than that. (Note: this is why I noted in Chapter 2 that the magnitude of money laundering is probably far greater than what is officially estimated. It depends on what is included in the count. As far as I can tell, TBML is not included in the generally accepted IMF estimate of global money laundering at 2 to 5 percent of world GDP.)

The above TBML estimate is buttressed by Global Financial Integrity (GFI) studies. According to Raymond Baker, a worldwide authority on financial crime, "Trade misinvoicing — a prevalent form of TBML — accounts for nearly 80 percent of all illicit financial outflows (IFFs) that can be measured by using available data."[8] According to a 2017 study by GFI, illicit financial flows from developing and emerging economies totaled approximately $1 trillion in 2014. The study finds that over the period between 2005 and 2014, IFFs likely accounted for between about 14.1 percent and 24.0 percent of total developing country trade, on average, with outflows estimated at 4.6 percent to 7.2 percent of total trade and inflows between 9.5 percent to 16.8 percent. By just focusing on developing economies, cumulative illicit outflows were approximately $7.8 trillion between 2004 and 2013.[9]

TBML is found in every country in the world — both developed and developing. But the massive transfer of wealth offshore through abusive trade misinvoicing is particularly harmful to countries with weak economies, high corruption, and little adherence to the rule of law. The developmental, human and societal costs are staggering.

Trade-based value transfer has existed long before the advent of modern "Western" banking. Settling accounts via trade has occurred for millennia. In areas where our adversaries operate, trade-based value transfer is part of a way of life. It is part of their culture; a way of doing business.

While this book does not focus on terror finance, TBML does play a role. In just one example of TBML and terrorist financing, a Pakistani madrassa — a fundamentalist Islamic religious school

— was linked to radical jihadist groups. The madrassa received large amounts of money from foreign sources. It was engaged in a side business dealing in animal hides. In order to justify the large inflow of funds, the madrassa claimed to sell a large number of hides to foreign customers at grossly inflated prices. This ruse allowed the extremists to "legitimize" the inflow of funds which were then passed to terrorists.[10]

TBML is also intertwined with the misuse of the Afghan Transit Trade, Iran/Dubai commercial connections, the Tri-Border region in South America, suspect international Lebanese/Hezbollah trading syndicates, non-banked lawless regimes such those in Somalia and Libya, territory controlled by Islamic extremists in Syria and Iraq, Iranian sanctions busting, and many more. As we will see in Chapter 7, historically and culturally trade-based value transfer is also used in "counter-valuation" between hawaladars — an alternative remittance system unfortunately linked to terrorists.

By examining other forms of TBML the magnitude of the problem increases further. For example, TBML is also involved with customs fraud, tax evasion, export incentive fraud, VAT fraud, capital flight or the transfer of wealth offshore, evading capital controls, barter trade, underground financial systems such as fei-chien — the Chinese "flying money system, the black market peso exchange (BMPE), and commercial trade-based money laundering such as trade diversion, transfer pricing, and abusive trade misinvoicing.

Including all its varied forms, I believe the argument can be made that TBML and value transfer is the largest and most pervasive money laundering methodology in the world. Conversely, it is also the least understood, recognized, and enforced. In comparison to the annual volume of tens of trillions of dollars in international general merchandise trade, successful enforcement efforts are practically nil. Despite being one of the FATF's top three money laundering methodologies, by examining available metrics it is obvious that once again our AML/CFT countermeasures are not effective.

How Does TBML Work?

In its primary form, TBML revolves around invoice fraud and associated manipulation of supporting documents. When a buyer and seller work together, the price of goods (or services) can be whatever the parties want it to be. There is no invoice police! As Raymond Baker, Founding President of Global Financial Integrity, succinctly notes, "Anything that can be priced can be mispriced. False pricing is done every day, in every country, on a large percentage of import and export transactions. This is the most commonly used technique for generating and transferring dirty money." [11]

I wish I could say there are just one or two techniques involved with TBML. Unfortunately, trade-based money laundering often involves multi, varied, and sometimes elaborate schemes employed by fraudsters and criminal organizations to ensure their trades appear legitimate or unsuspicious. It is important to understand that the primary techniques involve invoice fraud and manipulation. They include:

- Over- and under-invoicing of goods and services

- Multiple invoicing of goods and services

- Falsely described goods and services

Other common techniques related to the above include:

- Short shipping: this occurs when the exporter ships fewer goods than the invoiced quantity of goods thus misrepresenting the true value of the goods in the documentation. The effect of this technique is similar to over-invoicing.

- Over shipping: the exporter ships more goods than what is invoiced thus misrepresenting the true value of the goods in the documentation. The effect is similar to under-invoicing.

- Phantom shipping: No goods are actually shipped. The fraudulent documentation generated is used to justify payment abroad.

Invoice Fraud

Money laundering and value transfer through the over- and under-invoicing of goods and services is a common practice around the world. The key element of this technique is the misrepresentation of trade goods to transfer value between the importer and exporter or settle debts/balance accounts between the trading parties. The shipment (real or fictitious) of goods and the accompanying documentation provide cover for the transfer of money. Invoice fraud is generally considered customs fraud. Moreover, customs fraud is the primary predicate offense or specified unlawful activity in TBML cases.

What are the most common invoice scams? First, by under-invoicing goods below their fair market price, an exporter is able to transfer value to an importer while avoiding the scrutiny associated with more direct forms of money transfer. The value the importer receives when selling (directly or indirectly) the goods on the open market is considerably greater than the amount he or she paid the exporter.

For example, Company A located in the United States ships one million widgets worth $2 each to Company B based in Mexico. On the invoice, however, Company A lists the widgets at a price of only $1 each, and the Mexican importer pays the U.S. exporter only $1 million for them. Thus, extra value has been transferred to Mexico where the importer can sell (directly or indirectly) the widgets on the open market for a total of $2 million. The Mexican company then has several options: it can keep the profits; transfer some of them to a bank account outside the country where the proceeds can be further laundered via layering and integration; share the proceeds with the U.S. exporter (depending on the nature of their relationship); or even transfer them to a criminal organization that may be the power behind the business transactions.

To transfer value in the opposite direction, an exporter can over-invoice goods above their fair market price. In this manner, the exporter receives value from the importer because the latter's payment is higher than the goods' actual value on the open market.

Invoice Manipulation Made Simple

To move money/value out:

- Import goods at overvalued prices or export goods at un-dervalued prices

To move money/value in:

- Import goods at undervalued prices or export goods at over-valued prices

There are incredible examples of trade-mispricing. For example, Dr. John Zdanowicz conducted a study analyzing U.S. trade data.[12] He found plastic buckets from the Czech Republic imported with the declared price of $972 per bucket! Toilet tissue from China is imported at the price of over $4,000 per kilogram. Bulldozers are being shipped to Colombia at $1.74 each! Of course, there are various reasons why the prices could be abnormal. For example, there could simply be a data "input" or "classification" error. However, recalling the above explanation of over-and under-invoicing, the abnormal prices could also represent attempts to transfer value in or out of the United States in the form of trade goods. At the very least, the prices should be considered suspicious. Only analysis and investigation will reveal the true reasons for such large discrepancies between market price and declared price. Unfortunately, that rarely happens.

Trade misinvoicing is widespread. It happens in every country in the world countless times every day. To paraphrase the Pakistani entrepreneur I quoted at the outset of this chapter, our adversaries are "laughing" at us. According to GFI's Raymond Baker, "The practice of trade misinvoicing has become normalized in many categories of international trade. It is a major contributor to poverty, inequality, and insecurity in emerging markets and developing economies. The social cost attendant to trade misinvoicing undermines sustainable growth in living standards and exacerbates inequities and social divisions."[13]

Trade misinvoicing should be a tremendous global concern. It is one of the largest money laundering methodologies in the world. Yet over the last thirty years the AML/CFT community has concentrated almost exclusively on money laundering through financial institutions. I can say with absolute certainty that until we systematically focus on trade misinvoicing and TBML in all its varied forms our AML/CFT efforts will continue to fail.

Time out! Service-based Money Laundering (SBML)

Service-based money laundering is similarly almost unknown in anti-laundering enforcement. Like TBML, SBML revolves around invoice fraud and manipulation. But instead of laundering money or transferring value through trade goods, services are used. Common service-based laundering scams include accounting, legal, marketing, and natural resource exploration fees. Fraudulent construction costs, such as is common with the Italian mafia and those uncovered in Brazil's "Operation Car Wash" that spotlighted official corruption, is a common tactic.[14] Software development, marketing surveys, consulting, product promotion, etc., are other common "service" ruses.

The State Department's 2015 global anti-money laundering review cites one example of SBML where "offshore companies send fictitious bills to a Montenegrin company (for market research, consulting, software, leasing, etc.) for the purpose of extracting money from the company's account in Montenegro, so funds can be sent abroad." [15] Fraudulent invoices generated from supposed concert promotions or other services that are difficult to quantify can be used to move illicit funds. Technical fees, such as writing computer code, add complexity to SMBL schemes, and require investigators with specialized expertise.

Stopping SBML is no easy task. Pricing for trade goods is objective. There are sometimes fluctuations but prices for goods and commodities generally adhere to world pricing norms. When investigating TBML, authorities can often track an item or a commodity, following a physical trail. For example, when a product is manufactured and sent from country A to country B, import and export data exist. Shipping information exists even if it is routed through country C. Through analytics, authorities can discover anomalies that indicate customs fraud. SBML, by contrast, leaves no physical commodity trail, and the value of the service on the invoice is almost always subjective presenting many opportunities for manipulation and fraud.

Illicit Trade

Illicit trade is distinct from TBML. Somewhat similar to the parallels between money laundering and illicit financial flows, illicit trade operates in the shadow of the global economy. Increasingly sophisticated transnational criminal organizations traffic narcotics, people, arms, wildlife, illicit tobacco, counterfeit goods, forest products and other natural resources, and manipulate sports and gaming.

While precise measurements of the magnitude of these criminal activities are difficult to obtain because of the clandestine nature of illicit transactions, one estimate puts the profits of international organized crime as high as 1.5 percent of global GDP.[16] Per our discussion in Chapters 2 and 3 about estimating the global magnitude of money laundering, think of the above criminal actions in illicit trade as predicate offenses. As a result, the difference between illicit trade and TBML is that illicit trade is comprised of specified unlawful products or actions that are traded internationally while TBML comprises a variety of trade fraud and trade-related techniques and methodologies used to launder illicit proceeds.

Illicit trade and illicit financial flows are a growing global security concern. Their convergence presents threats to communities and societies as a whole: threatening the health and safety of people with narcotics or consumers with substandard products and counterfeits such as fake medicines, food, alcohol and defective automotive and aircraft parts; bringing endangered wildlife closer to the brink of extinction; endangering our rainforests and planet through illegal logging, illicit fishing, and other environmental crimes; exploiting our most vulnerable and desperate into forced labor or trafficking humans across borders into slavery; and enabling lucrative illicit empires that finance acts of criminality and terrorism and create greater instability and violence around the world."[17]

In Chapter 11 we will examine illicit trade in more detail by using China as a case example. Examining the list of illicit trade offenses, the one common denominator is China. I'm getting ahead of myself, but the metrics will show that China is the biggest money laundering threat in the world today.

Commercial TBML

In Chapter 4, we discussed illicit financial flows. According to Global Financial Integrity, trade misinvoicing is the largest component of IFFs that the non-profit organization is able to measure.[18] Trade misinvoicing is related to TBML but is not exactly the same. Accordingly to our introductory explanation, there are a number of reasons to engage in TBML: money laundering, evading taxes and duties, tax incentives, and avoiding capital controls. With trade misinvoicing, commercial actors illegally move large amounts of money or value over national borders via misreporting or misrepresenting the total value of a given commercial transaction exchange. Similarly, tax avoidance and trade misinvoicing both utilize mispricing to

accomplish their illicit ends. Multinational corporations often engage in aggressive schemes of tax avoidance. In and of itself, this
is not misinvoicing even though many multinationals do practice
illegal and incorrect invoicing.[19]

Somewhat similar to trade misinvoicing, transfer pricing[20] is not
used to launder criminal proceeds, but rather to lower taxes and
increase profits. It is not illegal. Transfer pricing is a fact of international commerce and occurs millions of times every day. However,
abusive transfer pricing, or the manipulation of the international
trading system within the same multinational group to take advantage of lower jurisdictional tax rates, represents enormous tax loss
in the producing country. The magnitude of transfer pricing is difficult to determine but is believed to be in the hundreds of billions
of dollars per year. Transfer pricing is found in both the developed
and developing world but most dramatically affects poor countries
robbing them of needed revenue. According to Lee Sheppard of
Tax Analysts, "Transfer pricing is the leading edge of what is wrong
with international tax."[21]

A transfer price, or transfer cost, is the price at which related
parties transact with each other, such as during the trade of supplies or labor between departments. This frequently occurs within
multinational corporations. Approximately 60 percent of international trade happens within multinationals — not between. In other
words, the transfer trade flows across national borders but stays
within the same corporate group.[22] Transfer prices are used when
individual entities of a larger multi-entity and multi-national firm
are treated and measured as separately run entities. It is common
for multi-entity corporations to be consolidated on a financial reporting basis. For tax purposes, they may report each entity separately for tax purposes. In other words, if two companies owned
by a parent multinational group artificially distort the price of the
recorded trade or associated costs to minimize the tax bill, this
becomes an issue of concern — particularly when the tax liability
is shifted to a low-tax or tax-free haven. Much of this is facilitated

by offshores and other non-transparent corporate structures that we will discuss further in Chapter 13.

In our discussion of illicit financial flows, we demonstrated the hemorrhage of much needed tax revenue particularly from the developing world. Transfer pricing is a big component in bleeding the world's poorest economies.

Therefore, from a law enforcement viewpoint, I feel it is a bit hypocritical when multinationals legally use subterfuges such as transfer pricing; when criminals and money launderers use many of the same techniques, however, it is considered criminal. The difference, of course, is the source/origin of the funds. Nevertheless, I'm not sure if there is much of a difference when it comes to ethics.

Case Examples
The following cases show just how varied TBML is:

False Invoicing Using Polypropylene Pellets
A narcotic trafficking and money laundering network inflated the value of high-volume shipments of polypropylene pellets exported from the United States to Mexico. Polypropylene is used to make a variety of plastic articles. Eventually, the operation caught the attention of bank compliance officers, and they discontinued letters of credit used by the suspected launderers. Law enforcement investigated the network. It is believed the operation was hiding approximately $1 million every three weeks. One individual involved said, "You generate all of this paperwork on both sides of the border showing that the product you're importing has this much value on it, when in reality you paid less for it. Now you've got paper earnings of a million dollars. You didn't really earn that, but it gives you a piece of paper to take to [Mexican authorities] to say: 'These million dollars in my bank account — it's legitimate. It came from here, see?'"[23]

TBML and Iranian Sanctions

Before the Iran nuclear agreement or Joint Comprehensive Plan of Action (JCPOA), much of Iran's foreign currency was locked in overseas escrow accounts. The Iranian regime needed access to hard currencies to import needed goods. Front companies in Turkey were conduits for Iranian attempts to access the frozen funds. Turkish front companies issued fraudulent invoices for transactions such as importing food and medicine that were permitted to be shipped to Iran under humanitarian grounds. For example, a Turkish prosecutor's report details a 2013 invoice involving a Turkish luxury yacht company selling nearly 5.2 tons of brown sugar to Iran's Bank Pasargad, with delivery to Dubai. Turkey's state-owned Halkbank facilitated the transaction. The sugar was invoiced at the price of 1,170 Turkish liras per kilo or approximately $240 per pound![24] As part of the overall conspiracy, in early 2018, a Turkish banker was found guilty in a New York courtroom of engaging in a complex TBML scheme where gold and cash was routed from Turkey to Iran through an elaborate network of businesses, banks, and front companies. Various schemes were employed including over-invoicing and circular invoicing (making multiple transactions involving the same funds or goods to hide a money trail or even benefit from arbitrage). It is estimated the money laundering and value transfer could have helped Iran pocket more than $100 billion![25] This could be one of the largest — if not the largest — money laundering case in history.

Inferior Coal

In 2018, the Central Bank of India announced an investigation into malfeasance by three large public sector firms for allegedly causing a loss of Rs 487 crore (approximately $85 million) to the government exchequer by importing inferior coal from Indonesia and passing it off as superior quality. India's Directorate of Revenue Intelligence's investigation into TBML focused on the "artificial inflation" of coal imports of Indonesian origin with lower GCV (gross calorific value) through intermediary firms in Dubai. The imports occurred during a multi-year period. The fraudulent transactions were facilitated "with active participation of public servants."[26]

Used Cars

From approximately 2007 to 2011, there was a widespread multi-hundred million dollar TBML scheme spanning five continents and operating through the Lebanese Canadian Bank (LCB). The scheme involved the sale of Colombian cocaine in Europe; the proceeds from which would be mixed with revenue from sales of used cars in West Africa. The combined funds were then sent through exchange houses to accounts with the LCB. Some of the funds were siphoned off through Hezbollah-controlled money laundering channels including cash smugglers, hawaladars, and currency brokers. The rest were used to purchase used cars from the United States for resale in Africa. Goods were also purchased from China in exchange for Colombian cocaine. In 2013, the LCB settled with the U.S. Department of Justice and agreed to pay a $102 million fine.[27]

Textiles

Another high-profile trade-based money laundering case involved multiple firms located primarily in the Los Angeles Fashion District. The primary scheme used by the launderers was a spin on the Black Market Peso Exchange (BMPE). Though the specifics varied, the overall scheme involved a peso broker who would work with firms in Mexico seeking to purchase goods from firms in the United States. The broker would provide the dollars from U.S. drug sales to firms located in the Fashion District who would then ship garments and textiles to the firms in Mexico. The Mexican firms would then sell the goods in Mexico and provide the revenue in pesos to drug cartels.[28]

One of the companies involved with exporting garments allegedly mixed customs fraud into the BMPE conspiracy. "Made in China" labels were removed from thousands of imported garments.

One of the suspects was paid 50 to 75 cents for each of the altered garments. The fraud saved the co-conspirators from paying taxes on the "Made in China" imports because on paper they appeared to be American-made and exempt from customs duties under the North American Free Trade Act or NAFTA.[29]

Gold

Just about any commodity can be used in TBML. I could launder money with a shipment of apples! However, if a criminal organization wants to launder lots of dirty money or transfer significant value via trade, gold is one of the favored commodities. As discussed in Chapter 10, there are many reasons why gold is the preferred vehicle. Its intrinsic value is high and so is its value to mass. It's both a commodity and a monetary instrument and is a readily acceptable medium of exchange anywhere in the world. There is a tremendous demand for gold in various cultures around the world. Gold offers easy anonymity and, depending on the need, its form can be altered. Also, gold is very susceptible to double invoicing, false shipments, and other fraudulent schemes. Some of the largest money laundering cases in history involved the misuse of the international gold trade.

To help put things into perspective, Colombia exported 64 tons of gold in 2016, much of it to the United States. Yet according to the Colombian Mining Association, that same year, Colombia's large-scale, legal mining operations produced only eight tons. A substantial part of the gap between what Colombia's mines produce and what the country exports is unlicensed gold — sometimes controlled by narco-traffickers and other criminal groups. Because of illegal mining, smuggling, and corruption, it is impossible to know where all the illegal gold is coming from — even though it's clear where most of it ends up. In 2015, Latin America accounted for nearly three-quarters of the gold imported into the United States. That's approximately the total amount of gold mined in the United States annually.[30]

In a 2015 investigation centered in Chicago, 32 people from the United States and Mexico were accused of being involved in a "cash-for-gold" conspiracy that laundered more than $100 million in U.S. drug proceeds for Mexico's Sinoloa drug cartel. Individuals used cash from narcotics sales to purchase gold scrap and gold jewelry in a multi-state area. The gold was later sent to precious metal refineries in Florida and California. The refineries sometimes transferred payments for the gold directly to Mexico.[31]

Oil Smuggling and Terror Finance

Law enforcement and the intelligence communities have long observed that terrorist groups often use the trade in benign commodities such as honey, fish, and antiquities to help finance their operations. For example, terrorists take advantage of peoples' need for oil and its derivative products. Authorities look the other way when citizens naturally shop for discounts and find cheaper-than-market-price fuel. They disregard what seem to be low-scale illicit operations as not meriting the attention of law enforcement. (This phenomenon is also very similar to law enforcement often ignoring the trafficking in popular counterfeit goods.) This salutary neglect of black-market fuel trading burnished by corruption and invoice manipulation is easily influenced by terrorist groups looking for under-the-radar income streams. Proceeds from illicit oil and fuel activities were the Islamic State in Iraq and Syria's (ISIS') most important funding source. In the Philippines, Abu Sayyaf used fuel smuggling to fund itself and to facilitate the movement of weapons and ammunition. In Trinidad and Tobago, ISIS sympathizers have engaged in rampant fuel smuggling and illicit sales. [32]

Countermeasures and a Few Proposals

Around the time of my conversation with the Pakistani businessman noted at the beginning of this chapter, I was very concerned about how the U.S. government was fighting the war against terror

finance. We were spending an incredible amount of resources looking in many of the wrong places for terrorist assets while almost
ignoring indigenous methods terrorists and their facilitators used
to launder money, transfer value, and finance terror. I was convinced there could be a "back door" into some of the underground
financial networks.

In 2004, the United States government adopted a proposal I advanced. Homeland Security Investigations (HSI) created the world's
first trade transparency unit (TTU). [33] The initiative seeks to identify
global TBML trends and conduct ongoing analysis of trade data provided through partnerships with other countries. We have learned
that one of the most effective ways to identify instances and patterns of TBML is through the exchange and subsequent analysis of
trade data. Anomalies can often be spotted only by examining both
sides of a trade transaction, i.e. "trade transparency."

A TTU is formed when HSI and any of the United States trading
partners agree to exchange trade data via a "customs-to-customs"
agreement for the purpose of data identification, comparison and
analysis. The wonderful thing about TTU initiative is that the data
already exists. There is no need for vast new expenditures or to
struggle through labyrinths of bureaucratic hoops and approvals.
Every country in the world already collects import and export data
and associated information. Moreover, there has been an explosion of commercially available trade data over the last few years.
To help analyze the data, HSI has developed specialized software.
Containing both domestic and foreign trade data, the system allows users to see both sides of a trade transaction at a macro level,
making it transparent to both countries. Added value is created by
overlaying financial intelligence, travel data, business registrations,
criminal records, and other data sets. As a result, TTUs can easily
identify trade anomalies that could be indicative of customs fraud,
TBML, contraband smuggling, tax evasion, and even underground
finance. Once the macro anomalies have been identified, customs
and law enforcement can drill down further. Investigations are
still required.

The TTU investigative tool has been proven to be effective. As of 2015, the TTU network had seized well over $1 billion of assets.[34]

Frankly, many countries are not interested in TBML. Nonetheless, they are interested in combating trade fraud because it is a revenue maker. Governments around the world are increasingly cash strapped and looking for new revenue streams. Most people don't realize it, but in the United States before the ratification of the 16th amendment to the constitution in 1913 that established Congress' right to establish a national income tax, the U.S. government depended on customs duties for the majority of our national revenue. The same holds true today in many countries. Their income tax systems are ineffectual, rife with abuse, evasion, and corruption. Hence countries are once again looking at increasing customs duties.

In 2020 there are approximately 20 operational TTUs in the international network. Most are located in the Western hemisphere. In the "next frontier of international money laundering enforcement," I believe a global TTU network will be created that is somewhat analogous to the Egmont Group of Financial Intelligence Units. (There are over 160 FIUs in the Egmont Group network.) I also believe the concept of trade transparency should be built into the U.S. and other countries' trade agendas. I don't have a position on the pros and cons of free trade. But the volume of ever-increasing global merchandise trade will provide additional opportunities for trade-based value transfer and money laundering. I suggest we help protect abuse by insuring that trading partners establish a TTU or the equivalent and share appropriate targeted trade data to spot anomalies that could be indicative of trade fraud at best and TBML at worst.

TBML could be the largest and most pervasive money laundering methodology in the world. However, we do not know for certain because the issue has never been systematically examined. This is even more surprising in the United States because annually we are possibly losing billions of dollars in lost taxes due to trade-mispricing alone. While not necessarily true for all money laundering methodologies, trade generates data. I believe it is possible for economists, statisticians, and analysts to come up with a fairly accurate estimate of the overall magnitude of global TBML and value transfer. Narrowing it down to specific problematic countries is still easier.

The Department of Treasury's Office of Intelligence and Analysis (OIA) or another appropriate government office or agency should examine U.S.-related data and come up with an official estimate for the amount of TBML in all its varied forms that impacts the U.S. A generally accepted estimate of the magnitude of TBML is important for a number of reasons: a.) It will provide clarity; b). It will focus attention on the issue; c.) From an enforcement perspective, the supporting analysis should provide both excellent insight into specific areas where criminals are vulnerable and promising opportunities for targeting; and d.) A systematic crack down on TBML and customs fraud will translate into enormous revenue gain.

The FATF makes AML/CFT happen. The FATF recognizes TBML is a huge concern, and discussed the threats in a special 2006 typology report on TBML. It was followed by an excellent report on TBML by the Asia Pacific Group (a FATF-style regional body) in 2012. However, in 2012 when the current FATF recommendations were reviewed and promulgated, TBML was not specifically addressed. It is past time this is done. So, I think the U.S. Department of Treasury (which heads the U.S. FATF delegation) should introduce a resolution calling for the misuse of trade to launder money and transfer value to be examined as a possible new FATF recommendation.

But a FATF recommendation on TBML by itself is not enough. Historically, the FATF (like FinCEN) is wedded to financial intelligence as the primary AML/CFT countermeasure. The numbers suggest that the filing of financial intelligence on TBML is not the end-all solution. This is because the overwhelming majority of standard commercial trade is accomplished through open-account trade; in open-account trade the financial transaction between the buyer and seller — which underpins the trade transaction — is usually processed through a bank's automatic payment systems. Trade finance is not involved. As such, the financial institution has limited visibility into the underlying reason for the payment. In open-account trade, banks generally do not review documentation such as invoices, bills of lading, or customs declarations as would be the case for transactions that are financed by the bank and where the bank is exposed to greater financial risk.

Financed trade, on the other hand, requires direct involvement from banks and a review of the transaction and parties to the transaction. Still, financed trade represents just 15 percent of the total volume of goods traded.[35] In theory, bank-financed trade should generate SARs which should trigger investigations. But statistics in the United States do not bear this out. FinCEN added a dedicated "TBML box" to its SAR form in 2012. According to data obtained from FinCEN in a 2020 report[36] on TBML by the Government Accountability Office or GAO, there were 7,044 SAR filings for TBML from 2014 to 2018. However, that is a tiny fraction of the 9.6 million SAR filings by financial institutions, money service businesses, and other obligated entities during the same time frame. Additionally, the situation is made even worse because I doubt whether more than a few hundred SARs dedicated to TBML were even comprehensively examined/investigated by law enforcement.

Fortunately, the good news is that there is increasing access to trade data, international pricing norms, shipping records, and other enhanced types of monitoring technology. By using big data analytics, software makes links and connections. The ability to contextualize each transaction means that financial analysts have an increasingly holistic understanding of various trade transactions. So just like some financial institutions have internal financial intelligence units (FIUs), some financial institutions that are heavily involved with trade should consider establishing internal TTUs that focus on trade-related transactions — both open-account and trade financed.

Of course, everything with TBML still comes down to investigations, enforcement, fines, penalties, prosecutions, and convictions. I will address this further in the final chapter.

Together, these commonsense and relatively inexpensive coun-termeasures could help moderate the threat posed by the probable largest money laundering methodology in the world. By cracking down on widespread customs fraud, they would also bring much needed revenue in the form of increased taxes and tariffs to cash starved governments.

NOTES

1 Much of the material in this chapter comes from: John Cassara, Trade-Based Money Laundering: the Next Frontier in International Money Laundering Enforcement; Wiley, Hoboken, New Jersey, 2015. The material in the book was summarized in the author's Written Statement for the Hearing On "Trading with the Enemy: Trade-Based Money Laundering is the Growth Industry in Terror Finance" Before the Task Force to Investigate Terrorism Financing of the House Financial Services Committee, February 3, 2016; https://financialservices.house.gov/uploadedfiles/hhrg-114-ba00-wstate-jcassara-20160203.pdf

2 FATF; Trade Based Money Laundering (Paris: FATF, June 23, 2006), p. 1; http://www.fatf-gafi.org/media/fatf/documents/reports/Trade%20Based%20Money%20Laundering.pdf

3 Ibid

4 World Trade Statistical Review 2016, World Trade Organization; https://www.wto.org/english/res_e/statis_e/wts2016_e/wts2016_e.pdf

5 William M. Sullivan, Jr., Fabio Leonardi, "Bank Secrecy Act Prosecutions: Trade Based Money Laundering," Pillsbury Alert, July 14, 2016; https://www.pillsburylaw.com/en/news-and-insights/new-frontier-for-bank-secrecy-act-prosecutions-trade-based-money.html

6 Analysis given to the author by Dr. John Zdanowicz via June 30, 2015 email.

7 Data given to the author by Dr. Zdanowicz.

8 "The Economist Highlights the Scourge of Trade Misinvoicing," Global Financial Integrity, May 2, 2014; http://www.financialtransparency.org/2014/05/02/the-economist-highlights-the-scourge-of-trade-misinvoicing/

9 "Illicit Financial Flows in Developing Countries Large and Persistent," Global Financial Integrity, May 1, 2017; https://gfintegrity.org/press-release/new-study-illicit-financial-flows-in-developing-countries-large-and-persistent/

10 Brett Wolf, "The Hide and Hair of Terrorist Finance in Pakistan," Complinet, January 17, 2007

11 Raymond W. Baker, Capitalism's Achilles Heel, John Wiley & Sons, Hoboken, New Jersey, p. 134

12 Dr. John Zdanowicz, Trade-Based Money Laundering and Terrorist Financing; https://datapro.fiu.edu/campusedge/files/articles/zdanowiczj3008.pdf

13 "Global Financial Integrity Releases New Study on Trade Misinvoicing in South Africa," Global Financial Integrity, November 13, 2018; https://www.gfintegrity.org/press-release/global-financial-integrity-releases-new-study-on-trade-misinvoicing-in-south-africa/

14 John Cassara, "Service-Based Money Laundering: The Next Illicit Finance Frontier," Foundation for the Defense of Democracies, May 19, 2016; http://www.defenddemocracy.org/media-hit/john-cassara-service-based-money-laundering-the-next-illicit-finance-frontier/

15 International Narcotics Control Strategy Report, Volume II Money Laundering, March 1, 2015, see Montenegro Country Report; https://www.state.gov/documents/organization/239329.pdf

16 David Luna, "Countering Illicit Trade: Why It Matters," David Luna blog, December 12, 2015; https://www.linkedin.com/pulse/countering-illicit-trade-why-matters-luna-%E7%BD%97%E6%96%87%E7%A4%BC-u-s-diplomat?forceNoSplash=true

17 Ibid

18 "Trade Misinvoicing," Global Financial Integrity; https://gfintegrity.org/issue/trade-misinvoicing/

19 Ibid. Also see, "What is Trade Misinvoicing," Herald Financial Dictionary; https://www.financial-dictionary.info/terms/trade-misinvoicing/

20 Cassara, TBML, pages 118-119

21 "Top U.S. tax expert in savage attack on transfer pricing rules," Tax Justice Network, August 23, 2012; http://taxjustice.blogspot.ch/2012/08/top-us-tax-expert-in-savage-attack-on.html

22 "Transfer Pricing," Tax Justice Network; http:///www.taxjustice.net/topics/corporate-tax/transfer-pricing/

23 Tracy Wilkinson and Ken Ellingwood, "Cartels Use Legitimate Trade to Launder Money, U.S., Mexico Say," Los Angeles Times, December 19, 2011; http://articles.latimes.com/2011/dec/19/world/la-fg-mexico-money-laundering-trade-20111219

24 Jonathan Schanzer and Emanuelle Ottolenghi, "Turkey's Teflon Don," Foreign Policy, March 31, 2014; http://www.foreignpolicy.com/articles/2014/03/31/turkey_teflon_don_erdogan_elections_corruption

25 Jonathan Schanzer, "The Biggest Sanctions-Evasion Scheme in Recent History," The Atlantic, January 4, 2018; https://www.theatlantic.com/international/archive/2018/01/iran-turkey-gold-sanctions-nuclear-zarrab-atilla/549665/

26 Ananya Bhardwaj, "Coal import scam: CBI files case against officials of state-run units," The Print, January 24, 2018; https://theprint.in/2018/01/24/coal-import-scam-cbi-files-case-officials-state-run-units/

27 John Cassara, Trade-Based Money Laundering: the Next Frontier in International Money Laundering Enforcement; Wiley, Hoboken, New Jersey, 2015, page 24. Also, see Clay R. Fuller, PhD, "Defeating the Authoritarian-Corruption Nexus Strategic Disentanglement and Realignment," American Enterprise Institute, November 2018, page 11.

28 See Fuller, page 12.

29 Cassara TBML – The Next Frontier page 41.

30 Jay Weaver, Nichols Nehamas and Kyra Gurney, "How drug lords make billions smuggling gold to Miami for your jewelry and phones," Miami Herald, January 16, 2018; http://www.miamiherald. com/news/local/community/miami-dade/article194187699.html

31 "Thirty Two Defendants Facing Federal or State Charges Alleging the Laundering of over $100 Million in Narcotics proceeds Through Cash-For-Gold Scheme," U.S. Attorney's Office Northern District of Illinois Press Release, February 11, 2015; http://www.justice.gov/ usao/iln/pr/chicago/2015/pr0211_02.html

32 Ian Ralby, "The Funding of Terrorism – Hookahs and Honey: Funding of Terrorism Through Benign Activities," Strife, August 3, 2019; http://www.strifeblog.org/2019/08/03/the-funding-of-terrorism-part-i-hookahs-and-honey-funding-terrorism-through-benign-activities/

33 For further information see the TTU website at: https://www.ice. gov/trade-transparency

34 March 26, 2015, email exchange between the author and Hector X. Colon, he unit chief/director of the TTU

35 Alexon Bell, "Why trade-based money laundering is the final frontier of AML," Information Technology, February 1, 2018; http://www.thecsuite.co.uk/cfo/information-technology-cfo/ why-trade-based-money-laundering-is-the-final-frontier-of-aml/

36 "Countering Illicit Finance and Trade," General Accountability Office, December 29, 2019; https://www.gao.gov/products/gao-20-314r

CHAPTER 7
Alternative Remittance Systems

THERE ARE AN ESTIMATED 244 million migrant workers around the world.[1] Globalization, demographic shifts, regional conflicts, income disparities, and the instinctive search for a better life continue to encourage ever more workers to cross borders in search of jobs and security.

Many countries are dependent on remittances as an economic lifeline. Although estimates vary, according to the World Bank, global remittances totaled approximately $625 billion in 2018.[2] Western Union, Money Gram, Ria Money Transfer, Dahabshill are just a few of the well-known companies that provide official remittance services for the world's migrants. Of course, banks and non-bank financial institutions are also used. Some of the top recipients for officially recorded remittances in 2018 were India (an estimated $79 billion), China ($67 billion), the Philippines ($34 billion), Mexico ($36 billion), and Pakistan ($17 billion). Nigeria, Egypt, Bangladesh, Vietnam, and the Ukraine were other large beneficiaries of remittances. As a percentage of GDP, some of the top recipients were Tajikistan (48 percent), the Kyrgyz Republic (31 percent), Lesotho (25 percent), and Moldova (24 percent). For over 31 countries around the world, remittances provide more than 10 percent of the total GDP.[3] In Central America, for example, remittances sent to El Salvador are now equal to 20 percent of its GDP; Guatemala, 11 percent; and Honduras, 18.8 percent.[4]

Remittances from the United States are growing. In 2016, approximately $138,165,000,000 in remittances was sent from the United States to other countries. Top recipients included Mexico ($28,126,000,000), China ($15,418,000,000), India ($10,657,000,000), and the Philippines ($10,536,000,000).[5] In 2017, approximately $150 billion was sent from the United States.[6] The numbers continue to rise.

The above are estimates of what is officially remitted. Unofficially, nobody knows. However, the IMF believes, "Unrecorded flows through informal channels are believed to be at least 50 percent larger than recorded flows."[7] Thus using the above World Bank and IMF estimates, unofficial remittances are enormous!

Informal remittances are sometimes touted as a new phenomenon and a symptom of the emerging borderless world. Policy makers also erroneously promote their increased use and recognition as a "measure of success" in our efforts to combat international money laundering and terrorist finance due to our crack down on illicit money moving through formal banking channels. Yet diasporas and remittances have existed since ancient times. For example, fei-chien alone dates back to the T'ang Dynasty (618 to 907 AD).[8] Also, hawala existed in the Middle East and South Asia for centuries or certainly long before American policy makers discovered the underground system after September 11. Trade-based value transfer which is the backbone of these systems has been used for millennia.

Alternative remittance systems (ARS) are sometimes also called "underground banking," "parallel banking," or "informal value transfer systems." Occasionally everything is erroneously labeled "hawala" (see below). Informal channels operate outside of the ironically labeled "traditional" channels. It's ironic because for most of the migrants involved, the alternatives to Western-style or formal remittances are very traditional for them.

The following is a partial list of worldwide underground remittance systems. The names vary based on a number of factors including geographical locations and ethnic groups:

- Hawala – India, Afghanistan, Africa, the Middle East, Gulf, parts of the Americas

- Hundi – Pakistan, Bangladesh

- Undiyal – Sri Lanka

- Havaleh – Iran

- Door-to-door/padala – the Philippines

- Black market currency exchanges – Nigeria, South America, Iran

- Stash houses/casas de cambio – Latin America

- Phoei kuan – Thailand (Teochew Chinese)

- Hui kuan – China – (Mandarin Chinese)

- Fei-chien – "flying money" China

- Ch'iao hui – overseas remittances – (Mandarin Chinese)

- Chop shop – foreigners sometimes use this term for one of the Chinese systems

- Chiti-banking – refers to the "chit" used for receipt or proof of claim in transactions; introduced by the British in China

The two largest underground remittance systems are hawala (and its various sister systems such as hundi and undiyal) and the Chinese fei-chien (and related schemes). They are both global in scope. While there are no reliable estimates as to the magnitude of these two informal remittance systems, both are probably responsible for hundreds of billions of dollars in unregulated (and non-taxed) money transfers a year.[9]

Although diverse alternative remittance systems are found throughout the world, most share a few common characteristics. The first is that they all transfer money without physically moving it. Another is that these systems all offer the three C's: they are certain, convenient, and cheap. They are all ethnic-based, sophisticated, and efficient. And finally, historically and culturally, most alternative remittance systems use trade as the primary mechanism to settle accounts or balance the books between brokers.

I would like to emphasize that I am not using ethnic in a pejorative sense. My views are far from that. I have the utmost respect for these systems. Many have been around for hundreds and in some cases over a thousand years. They are based on trust, simple, inexpensive and effectual; they serve their clientele well.

The overwhelming percentage of money transfers generated by the use of these informal remittance systems is benign. They are primarily used to remit a portion of migrants' earned wages back to their home countries to support their families. We, of course, do not wish to interfere with this process.

However, there are problems when it comes to AML/CFT. Because these systems are opaque and based on trust, they avoid our primary AML/CFT countermeasures. They operate with almost total impunity. As Osama bin Laden once said, jihadists are aware of the "cracks" in our Western financial system.[10] Informal remittances are not just a crack but a Grand Canyon. Alternative remittance systems represent a classic example of how money and value are being moved right under our noses. But we don't see it.

I first encountered the best known alternative remittance system — hawala — during my travels to the Middle East. In the early 1990's, I saw it in the souks (markets) of Dubai and many other trading centers. However, I didn't know what the system was actually called. When I transferred to FinCEN in 1996, I met Patrick Jost. At the time, Patrick was one of the most brilliant people at FinCEN. He had a background in anthropology and economics, spoke numerous languages, and was very familiar with the culture and ways of doing business in South Asia. When I arrived at FinCEN, prior to September 11, he was desperately trying to bring attention to the ancient underground South Asian system of moving money and transferring value. He even had a personalized license plate on the car he drove that read "HAWALA."[11]

Patrick tutored me in hawala and together we began to explore how alternative remittance systems were abused for criminal purposes. I soon found that hawala overlapped with issues that intrigued me such as the misuse of the international gold trade and trade-based money laundering. After September 11, so called "experts" and talking heads "discovered" hawala and its link to terror finance.

How They Operate[12]

The definition of hawala was concisely expressed during the 1998 U.S. federal trial of Iranian drug trafficker and money launderer, Jafar Pour Jelil Rayhani, and his associates. During the trial, prosecutors called hawala "money transfer without money movement." That is, a broker on one side of the transaction accepts money from a client who wishes to send funds to someone else. The first broker then communicates with the second broker at the desired destination who distributes the funds to the intended recipient (less small commissions at both ends). The money does not physically move from Point A to Point B. The key ingredient is trust. Most brokers are of the same ethnic group and many are members of the same family, tribe, or clan.

To illustrate how the hawala remittance process works, we will use a typical example. Ali is an Afghan national, recent immigrant, and a construction worker in New York City. (Note: While in this example, Ali is Afghan; he could just as easily be Pakistani, Iraqi, Syrian, Somali, North African, Lebanese, Indian, etc.) Ali emigrated to the United States years ago and earns money that helps support his family. He periodically sends a portion of his salary back to his elderly father, Jafar, who lives in a village outside of Kandahar in southern Afghanistan. To make his monthly transfer — usually about $200 — Ali uses hawala. This is very common in Afghanistan. About 30 percent of its population is externally and internally displaced, and about 15 percent of the rural population receives remittances from outside of Afghanistan. Hawala has been described as the de facto national banking system of Afghanistan.

If Ali went to a bank in New York City to send the money home to his father, he would have to open an account. He doesn't want to do that for a number of reasons. First, Ali grew up in an area of the world where banks are not common. He is not used to them and doesn't trust them. Next, Ali has little faith in governments and wants to avoid possible scrutiny. Many immigrants believe the government is monitoring their immigration status and/or will make them pay taxes. He also doesn't want the U.S. government to screen his money transfers to Afghanistan. In addition, although Ali has lived in NYC for a few years, he is still a bit intimidated. His English is marginal. He is only semi-literate (the literacy rate in Afghanistan is quite low) and cannot fill out the necessary forms. Moreover, banks charge their customers assorted transfer fees and offer unfavorable exchange rates. If Ali only earns a little money and is sending $200, bank transfer fees of 10 percent or more are quite substantial.

Generally speaking, the average cost of transferring funds through an alternative remittance system, such as hawala, between major international cities is about 2 to 5 percent of the value transferred. Globally, the cost of sending $200 through formal remittance companies averaged 7.45 percent in 2017 — significantly higher than the Sustainable Development Goal (SDG) target of 3 percent.[13] The price differential is in large part due to the fact that hawaladars (hawala brokers) generally don't have large brick and mortar businesses. Since they operate in the shadows, taxes and regulatory fees are minimal as well as administrative and personnel costs. Of course, prices in both the formal and informal remittance industries are influenced by a variety of factors. Hawala networks are most competitive when they operate in areas where banking systems and overt money remittance chains find it difficult, expensive, or high risk to operate — particularly in areas where our adversaries operate.

Delivery of a bank transfer to Jafar would pose additional problems. The number of licensed banks in Afghanistan is still small. They are used by only about 10 percent of the population.[14] Particularly in a poorly secured area such as Kandahar, Jafar does not want to leave his village home and travel a far distance to a bank.

In light of these problems and concerns, Ali uses a hawaladar in NYC who is a member of his extended clan and family. He feels comfortable dealing with him. The hawaladar also owns and operates an "import/export" company in NYC. The hawaladar completes the transaction for a lower commission than banks or money service businesses charge. In addition, he obtains a much better exchange rate. Delivery direct to Jafar's home in the Kandahar area village is also included in the price. In fact, in certain areas of the world, hawala is advertised as "door-to-door" money remitting.

Ali gives the $200 to the hawaladar in NYC that he wants to transfer. The hawaladar takes his small commission. Ali is not given a receipt because the entire relationship is based on trust. This is a different from financial institutions' "know your customer" (KYC) policies. For purposes of illustration, particularly if this is a first-time transfer, Ali may be given a numerical or other code, which he can then forward to Jafar. The code is used to authenticate the transaction. But in the nature of hawala networks codes are not always necessary. As opposed to the often lengthy formal operating requirements of bank-to-bank transfers, this informal transaction can be completed in the time it takes for the hawaladar in NYC to make a few telephone calls or send a fax or e-mail to the corresponding hawaladar in his network that handles Kandahar.

Hawaladars maintain very few records, offering customers near anonymity. They only keep simple accounting records, and even these are often discarded after they settle-up with one another. This means the paper trail is limited or nonexistent, making transactions very difficult to track for law enforcement. Even when records are kept, they are often in a foreign language or code, making them very challenging for Western authorities to decipher.[15]

Although some transactions are arranged directly between the two hawaladars involved, many are cleared or pass through regional hawala hubs such as Dubai, Mumbai, Karachi, and Kabul. So generally speaking, money can be delivered directly to Jafar's home within 24 hours, and the transaction will not be scrutinized by either U.S. or Afghan authorities.

The above scenario with Ali in NYC could just as easily take place in Minneapolis with its large Somali community, northern Virginia with its large Indian community, Los Angeles with its large Iranian populace, or Detroit with its large Arab community.

Similarly, hawala transfers are very common in London, Frankfurt, Dubai, Damascus, Baghdad, Tehran, Karachi, Zanzibar, Durban, the Colon Free Trade Zone, the Tri-Border region of South America, and many other locations around the world. For example, according to the U.S. State Department 2015 INCSR report in the West African country of Gabon, "There is a large expatriate community engaged in the oil and gas sector, the timber industry, construction, and general trade. Money and value transfer services, such as hawala, and trade-based commodity transfers are often used by these ex-patriates, particularly the large Lebanese community, to avoid strict controls on the repatriation of corporate profits."[16]

Settling Accounts

Hawaladars eventually have to settle their accounts with each other. Frequently, the close relationships between the brokers help facilitate the settlement. Remember, the key ingredient in hawala is trust. Kinship, family, tribal and clannish ties often enable the settlement process. For example, in Afghanistan, intermarriages between the families of hawaladars are common because they help cement confidence between the parties. Brothers, cousins, or other relations often operate in the same hawala network. Lebanese family members that operate in the same hawala networks can be found in Beirut, Dubai, the Colon Free Trade Zone, and various locations in Africa. Yet even though they may have familial or other ties, they are still in business to make money. Somebody is running a surplus and somebody a deficit. Payments go in both directions. For example, remittances may flow into South Asia from the United States and Europe, but money and various goods flow back as well. Periodically, accounts must be settled. Generally, money transfers between hawaladars are not settled on a one-to-one basis but are bundled over a period of time after a series of transactions. A variety of methods are used to make payments and settle the accounts.

Trade: From the earliest times — before modern banking and before modern monetary instruments — trade-based value transfer was used between hawala brokers to settle accounts and balance their books. The use of trade remains widespread. Settling accounts through import/export clearing is somewhat similar to bilateral clearing using bank transfers, but it uses the import/export of trade goods. That is why many import/export concerns are associated directly or indirectly with hawaladars. If a debt needs to be settled, hawaladar A could simply send goods to hawaladar B such as gold, electronics, or a myriad of other trade items. Or at the end of a reporting period, if an outstanding balance exists between hawaladar A in Somalia and hawaladar B in Dubai, B can use a Japanese bank account to purchase cars for export to Somalia. Once the cars arrive, they would be transferred to A to settle the debt and/or sell them for profit. The transaction would clear the debt between the two hawaladars.

Invoice fraud and manipulation is also widespread. As discussed in Chapter 6, to move money/value out of a country, a hawaladar or his agent will import goods at overvalued prices or export goods at undervalued prices. To move money/value in, a hawaladar or his agent will import goods at undervalued prices or export goods at overvalued prices. This type of procedure is called counter-valuation. Most other worldwide alternative remittance systems or informal value transfer networks are similarly based on trade. Historically and culturally, trade is still the preferred method of account settlement. [17] And most of the above bypass our traditional financial transparency reporting requirements.

Banks: Most major hawala networks have access to financial institutions either directly or indirectly. A majority of international hawaladars have at least one or more accounts with formal financial institutions. Bi-lateral wire transfers between brokers to settle accounts are sometimes used. If a direct wire transfer is made between international brokers, hawaladar A would have to wire money directly to hawaladar B's account to clear a debt. This could be problematical because the banks' foreign exchange rate procedures would be triggered. So in this case, hawaladar A might choose to deposit the funds into B's foreign account.

Cash couriers: Direct cash payments are also used to settle debts. This is particularly true in areas of the world that have cash-based economies. Sometimes overlooked is that hawala networks also operate domestically between states and provinces. For example, in Afghanistan, hawala networks are found in each of the 34 provinces. Periodically, the brokers settle accounts and often use cash. Hawala couriers have been identified transporting money within Afghanistan and across the border into Pakistan. Cash couriers representing hawala networks also frequently travel from Karachi to Dubai to settle accounts. Cash is also used frequently to settle accounts between Indian hawaldars and Chinese traders.[18]

Other methods: Over the last few years, there are indications that new payment methods are being added to the mix: cyber currencies and transfers, mobile payments via cell phones, and other forms of person to person (P2P) money transfers.

Although open source reporting is very sparse, there is reason to believe that some underground remittance networks are now using cyber currencies including Bitcoins. For example, Indian police raided a money exchanger/hawaladar that allegedly used Bitcoins.[19] Yet Egyptians, Saudis, Turks and Lebanese are officially discrediting the use of bitcoin feeling that digital money carries great risk of deception, fraud and terrorist finance.[20] I don't think Bitcoins will rival hawala as a remittance service. The danger is that over time the use of cyber currencies could potentially have a great impact on the hawala settlement process. I can envision how an enterprising hawaladar will acquire Bitcoins and use them not only to settle accounts between fellow brokers, but also use them as cash-out service for their clients. Since most hawaladars have side businesses, Bitcoins could also be used to purchase product.

In many areas of the world, mobile payments or M-Payments — particularly via the use of cell phones — are an increasingly popular vehicle for the remittance of wages. It is also quite possible for M-Payments to be used in the settling of accounts between underground money remitters including hawaladars.[21] M-Payments are recognized as a growing money laundering threat — particularly in areas of the world where our terrorist adversaries operate.[22] We will discuss M-Payments further in Chapter 12.

Etisalat Afghanistan, the Afghan telecommunications company, is now offering "M-Hawala." From its website, Etisalat Afghanistan boasts that "M-Hawala is an innovative mobile financial services solution that will enable Etisalat Afghanistan's customers to purchase airtime directly from their handsets, send money from their mobile phones to family and friends, pay their bills via their mobile phones, purchase goods and services from shops and or retail outlets and deposit or withdraw cash from Etisalat authorized M-Hawala distributors or Etisalat partner banks." [23]

Over the last few years P2P money transfers have grown exponentially. There are many domestic and global services (some are interoperable) that make it easy to transfer money from one party to another via a phone number or email. Parties can send cash from an attached digital wallet account, or a linked debit card, bank account, or credit card. It is also easy to receive money; some services offer payments in brick-and-mortar stores as well.

In many respects, the growing use of P2P could mitigate the widespread use of hawala for traditional remittance purposes. I am not aware if P2P transfers are being used in the hawala settlement process. If it is occurring, I suspect it is happening overseas and is linked to other forms of M-Payments that we will discuss in Chapter

12. Once again, most of these developments are not monitored, regulated, or investigated.

Worrisome Links

Unfortunately, hawala is abused by terrorists. Hawala networks are used by ISIS in war-torn Syria, Iraq, and Afghanistan.[24] Hawala is used in Europe to support terror groups. For example, a network of 250 to 300 shops — such as butchers, supermarkets and phone call centers — run by mostly Pakistani brokers across Spain have supported ISIS and the al-Qaeda-affiliated Nusra Front through their hawala operations.[25] There are reports that hawala was used to help finance the 2015 ISIS attacks in Paris.[26]

Hawala is widespread in South Asia and is heavily used by drug warlords and both the Afghan and Pakistani Taliban. Hawala networks exist in other troublesome spots where our adversaries operate such as the Horn of Africa.[27] Hawala is "central" to Libya's underground economy.[28]

Boko Haram's funding is likely to withstand most restrictions on accessing the banking sector, as it uses hawala and cash couriers to move funds, some of which originates from supporters outside Nigeria.[29]

Media reports indicate a surge in hawala funding from charity organizations in the Persian Gulf to madrassas and seminaries in the Kashmir Valley used to indoctrinate local youth.[30]

Iran, a U.S.-designated state sponsor of terror, also uses hawala — locally known as havaleh. The underground money transfer system has also been used to circumvent sanctions.[31] Reportedly some financial exchanges between Iran and Pakistan are routed through hawala instead of the legal channels of the Asian Clearing Union.[32]

Iran's merchant community makes active use of money and value transfer systems, including hawala and moneylenders. Many hawaladars and traditional bazaari are linked directly to the regional hawala hub in Dubai. Over 300,000 Iranians reside in Dubai, with approximately 8,200 Iranian-owned companies based there. The trading companies are instrumental in settling accounts between hawaladars. There are reports that billions of dollars in Iranian capital have been invested in the United Arab Emirates, particularly in Dubai real estate. Iran's real estate market is also used to launder money. [33]

The United States is not immune. Hawala has repeatedly been used to finance terror attacks against the U.S., including the 1998 bombing against our embassy in Nairobi, attacks against our troops in Afghanistan and Iraq, and the 2010 Times Square bombing in New York City. [34] In 2013, a federal judge in San Diego sentenced three Somali immigrants for providing financial support to al-Shabaab — a designated terrorist organization. Evidence presented during trial showed that the defendants conspired to transfer funds to Somalia via hawala to wage jihad. [35]

Hawala is often used in other criminal activity. For example, in 2013 a naturalized U.S. citizen and his wife were indicted for medical billing fraud in Texas, and for sending the illicit proceeds to Iran via hawala. [36] In November 2015, authorities in Los Angeles announced they had broken up an international hawala network with ties between Canada, India, the United States and other locations that moved millions of dollars for the Sinaloa drug cartel and other criminal groups. [37] International criminal organizations from sex traffickers in Nigeria, fraudsters in Eastern Europe, to drug traffickers in Southeast Asia also use hawala. Many of these criminal networks impact the U.S.

In 2018, authorities in the Central District of California announced the conviction of Harinder "Sonu" Singh for laundering drug money through an international hawala network. The indictment alleges that the Singh used hawala to transfer money he received from narcotics traffickers, including some associated with the Sinaloa Cartel based in Mexico's Sinaloa province. Federal agents succeeded in wiretapping calls in the Punjabi language that allowed them to track the transfers. Singh was originally stopped by the California Highway Patrol in October 2012, which led to the discovery of $274,980 in U.S. currency. DEA agents monitoring Singh's southern California apartment complex caught his wife carrying a bag found to contain $388,100 in U.S. currency. The subjects are part of a much larger successful multi-year investigation into the trafficking of cocaine, methamphetamine, "ecstasy," and heroin.[38]

Countermeasures and a Few Proposals

Because hawala and similar alternative remittance systems are based on trust, leave few if any paper trails, are opaque by nature, and are resistant to our traditional AML/CFT countermeasures such as financial intelligence there are few effective countermeasures. Nevertheless, I have a few proposals:

Registration

In the United States, similar to Western Union, Pay-Pal, casa de cambios, and "Mom and Pop" check cashing services, Treasury's FinCEN classifies hawala as a money services business or MSB.

As a result, hawala and other informal money transfer systems are legal as long as the operation is registered with FinCEN and meets individual state licensing requirements. Unfortunately, the regulatory response hasn't worked. According to the 2007 National Money Laundering Strategy, "While the exact number of money service providers in the United States is difficult to determine, es-timates suggest that fewer than 20 percent of MSBs are registered with FinCEN. It is not known what percentage of unregistered MSBs are exempt from registration, due, for example, to their low busi-ness volumes or agent status. Regardless, the result is that the vast majority of MSBs operate without direct Federal regulatory supervision."[39]

Hawaladars are also supposed to file Suspicious Activity Reports (SARs). Very few do. Should we be surprised? Hawala is based on trust. Why would a hawaladar file a suspicious activity report on an extended family, tribe, or clan member?

Requiring the registration of hawaladars was implemented after September 11 when Congress wanted a solution (or the political appearance of a solution) to underground financial systems. While I do not believe registering hawaladars and other alternative remittance system brokers is effective, having a law on the books can be a valuable tool for law enforcement. How? It is a means to ensure cooperation and develop sources. For example, if federal, state, or local law enforcement spots a non-registered hawala-like network or any other informal money transfer system, they can approach the hawaladar/broker operating in the given community and ask for his or her cooperation in shedding light on the operation. They explain the registration and licensing requirements. Simply put, if the hawaladar does not cooperate with the investigation then charges of acting as an unregistered/unlicensed money remitter can be filed.

The IRS/Criminal Investigation Division has the law enforcement mandate to ensure MSB compliance. Unfortunately, due to budget cuts and manpower constraints, the IRS has not been unable to conduct necessary assessments or compel MSBs to register. Mandated "outreach" programs that are designed to advise informal remittance networks of their registration and reporting responsibilities have also fallen short.

In the United States, an enhanced MSB registration must be formulated. Before that is possible, Congress should exercise its oversight authority and ask FinCEN the following questions:

1. Over the last five years, how many hawaladars, fei-chien brokers, and other similar informal remittance operators have actually registered with FinCEN?

2. Of those that have registered, how many SARS have been filed? Per year?

3. A FinCEN request should be made to the Egmont Group of Financial Intelligence Units (FIUs) to poll its international members regarding questions 1 and 2 above.

4. Request that FinCEN estimate the number of informal un-registered money remitting entities currently in operation in all 50 states.

5. For the last five years, have FinCEN and the IRS detail their "outreach" programs to ethnic communities throughout the United States regarding the obligation to register and license money remitters.

6. Ask IRS/CI what it would need in additional budget and personnel to launch an aggressive campaign that targets unregistered and unlicensed money remitters.

Accountability

The U.S. government's 2007 Inter-Departmental National Money Laundering Strategy report's goal #2 is to "Enhance Financial Transparency in Money Service Businesses." The laudable goal contains eight "action items." I urge Congress to exercise its oversight responsibilities and determine whether or not the action items were fulfilled and hold the departments, offices, and bureaus involved responsible if they have not.

Examine the "Back Door" of Trade

Hawaladars are most vulnerable when they settle accounts. As discussed above, historically and culturally, in many parts of the world settling accounts via trade-based value transfer is the preferred technique. One does not understand hawala and other alternative remittance systems unless one understands this concept.

Particularly in areas where our adversaries operate, examining trading records for signs of "counter-valuation" or a method of settling accounts between hawala traders could be the backdoor into their operations. Systematically cracking down on associated trade fraud could also be a boon to revenue strapped governments.

(Sometimes offering the "carrot" of increased revenues to cash-strapped governments is often more effective than the "stick" of heavy-handed enforcement.)

As discussed in Chapter 6, Trade Transparency Units or TTUs are used to spot trade anomalies that could be indicative of customs fraud and forms of TBML. TTUs could be "the back door" into underground financial systems such as hawala.[40] The concept is now part of our national anti-money laundering strategy. The biggest reason why TTUs have not expanded is funding and dedicated personnel. The funding issue is ludicrous because systematically cracking down on trade fraud is a huge revenue booster. Congress should create a specific line item (specific so that Homeland Security Investigations can't use the money for own preferred priorities) that funds the expansion of the U.S. TTU to include additional dedicated personnel and advanced analytics. For example, over the last few years, there has been an explosion in trade and related data. Advanced analytic programs are available. Trade anomalies can be identified. We could specifically risk-score the probability of informal value transfer /counter-valuation. Analytics are available to help over worked analysts and investigators prioritize TBML-related investigations and help with investigative decision making. Funds should also be provided to the U.S. TTU and the State Department's Bureau of International and Narcotics Affairs (INL) that will assist with the creation of additional foreign TTUs. Any funds expended will be more than made up by enhanced revenue collected by cracking down on associated customs fraud.

Examine Fei-Chien

While hawala gets attention because of its links to terror finance, the Chinese equivalent fei-chien or "flying money" is undoubtedly as large and pervasive. As we will see in Chapter 11, fei-chien is ancient; it operates in the same manner as hawala; Chinese flying money is international in scope; it relies on trade to settle accounts between brokers; and while used primarily for remittances, the underground system has also been linked to criminal organizations and capital flight.

I believe flying money is used by wealthy Chinese to help purchase high-end residential real estate, including in the United States.[41] Much of this undoubtedly occurs in violation of China's own capital controls. FinCEN is currently studying the purchase of high-end real estate in money laundering in specific geographic areas.

Unfortunately, our law enforcement, intelligence, and regulatory communities have little knowledge or interest in fei-chien and other forms of underground Chinese remittance systems. Open source information on fei-chien is limited and I fear there is little classified information as well. Treasury's FinCEN should be tasked to develop a strategic study on the prevalence of Chinese flying money and how it impacts the United States. The FATF should also construct a typologies study on the use of Chinese underground financial systems.

Data and Analysis

Since many hawaladars and similar underground financial networks often use financial institutions, advanced analytics should be employed to provide the transparency the hidden systems seek to deny. For example, AML/CFT compliance software could be coded that would provide red flag alerts and/or risk scoring specifically for informal remittance systems such as hawala. Diverse data sets (financial, social media, etc.) could be examined and suspicious activity indicators installed for transfers to/from suspect locations, suspect businesses, individuals on designated lists, etc.

The same type of thing should be done with financial institutions that deal heavily in trade finance. AML/CFT compliance software should be engineered to flag alerts for indications of trade-based money laundering which, per the above, could be the back door into underground remittance networks.

Inclusion

One of the primary reasons immigrants use informal remittances is cost. As a result, the formal financial system — banks and remittance services — should improve their services and reduce charges and fees for remittances. This will attract more customers into the formal and transparent banking and remittance sectors.

Training

In my opinion, a staggering amount of compliance officers and those involved with trade finance do not understand informal remittance systems and how to recognize them. Only with specific insight into hawala and other similar systems will AML/CFT compliance staff responsible for risk monitoring be able to properly react to flagged transactions or adjust risk exposure. Financial institutions and MSBs that are exposed to informal remittance systems and TBML should do more to provide training and assistance to staff. Training in this area should be part of AML/CFT compliance review.

I have firsthand knowledge that law enforcement personnel at the federal, state, and local levels as well as intelligence officers, regulators, analysts, etc., similarly do not understand informal remittance systems and TBML and how to recognize them in their area of operations.

Even though I can demonstrate how informal remittances and TBML affects state and local law enforcement, most often the consensus opinion is, "This is a federal issue and doesn't concern us."

Yet it is precisely because police and local law enforcement officers are on the front lines in their communities and know their operating environment well, they should notice if a local business or commercial activity does not make market or economic sense. For example, a normal business should not remain in operation with only sporadic commercial activity or when it is consistently selling goods far above or below market norms. Numerous businesses in the U.S. and elsewhere are involved at the local level in TBML schemes and deal with goods that are frequently manipulated to transfer value.

Underground remittance networks such as hawala and fei-chien are found in local communities throughout our country and they often depend on trade and local business networks.

Accordingly, I urge my state and local law enforcement colleagues to become more familiar with issues surrounding TBML and informal remittance schemes and how they affect the local community.

NOTES

1 United Nations; http://www.un.org/sustainabledevelopment/
blog/2016/01/244-million-international-migrants-living-
abroad-worldwide-new-un-statistics-reveal/

2 "Five countries that Benefit Most from Remittances,"
CompareRemit, July 3, 2019; https://www.
compareremit.com/money-transfer-guide/
top-five-countries-that-benefit-most-from-remittance/

3 Ibid and United Nations

4 Michelle Malkin, "Illegal Criminal Caravans and Criminal
Catholics," Townhall, January 22, 2020; https://town-
hall.com/columnists/michellemalkin/2020/01/22/
illegal-immigrant-caravans-and-criminal-catholics-n2559915

5 "Remittance Flows Worldwide in 2016," Pew Research Center, January
23, 2018; http://www.pewglobal.org/interactives/remittance-map/

6 "Remittance flows worldwide in 2017," Pew Research
Center; https://www.pewresearch.org/global/interactives/
remittance-flows-by-country/

7 Dilip Ratha, "Remittances, Funds for the Folks Back Home,"
International Monetary Fund; http://www.imf.org/external/pubs/ft/
fandd/basics/remitt.htm

8 Leonides Buencamino and Sergei Gorbunov, "Informal Money
Transfer Systems: Opportunities and Challenges for Development
Finance," November, 2002, United Nations; http://www.un.org/esa/
esa02dp26.pdf

9 Estimates vary as to how much money is pumped annually through
the global hawala network but according to Gretchen Peters research in Seeds of Terror, St. Martins Press, 2009, p. 170, economists put the total figure at about $100 billion per year. Others
estimate hawala transfers approach $400 billion annually; see Jack
Moore, Hawala, The Ancient Banking Practice Used to Finance

Terror Groups, Newsweek, February 24, 2015; http://www.news-week.com/underground-european-hawala-network-financing-mid-dle-eastern-terror-groups-307984. Because the global nature of the Chinese diaspora, I believe "flying money" is at least equal to or surpasses the magnitude of hawala.

10 Chairman Evan Bayh, "Hearing on "Hawala and Underground Terrorist Financing Mechanism," November 14, 2001; https://www.banking.senate.gov/01_11hrg/111401/bayh.htm

11 John A. Cassara, Hide & Seek: Intelligence, Law Enforcement, and the Stalled War on Terror Finance, Potomac Books Inc., Washington, D.C. 1996; pages 143-144.

12 Much of the information in this section is taken from John Cassara, Trade-Based Money Laundering: The Next Frontier in International Money Laundering Enforcement, Wiley, 2015; see chapter on Hawala: An Alternative Remittance System, pages 49 – 69 and original references.

13 The World Bank; http://www.worldbank.org/en/news/press-re-lease/2017/04/21/remittances-to-developing-countries-decline-for-second-consecutive-year

14 International Narcotics Strategy Report Volume II on Money Laundering, State Department, 2015, see Afghanistan country report; https://www.state.gov/j/inl/rls/nrcrpt/2015/supplemen-tal/239124.htm)

15 Financial Crimes Enforcement Network (FinCEN) # 33, March, 2003; https://www.fincen.gov/sites/default/files/advisory/advis33.pdf

16 International Narcotics Control Strategy Report, Volume II, Money Laundering, Department of State, 2015; https://www.state.gov/j/inl/rls/nrcrpt/2015/vol2/index.htm. See Gabon country report.

17 Trade-based money laundering being used as counter valuation for hawala and other informal value transfer systems is described in detail in John Cassara's Trade-Based Money Laundering: The Next Frontier in International Money Laundering Enforcement

18 Sachin Dave and Maulik Vyas, "Importers of Chinese Goods Face Supply Constraints, Unable to Pay Via Hawala Routes," Economic

Times, February 15, 2020; https://economictimes.indiatimes.
com/news/economy/foreign-trade/importers-of-chinese-goods-
face-supply-constraints-unable-to-pay-via-hawala-routes/article-
show/74143982.cms

19 "Bitcoins May be Used by Hawala Traders: Official," The Times of
India, December 29, 2013; http://timesofindia.indiatimes.com/city/
ahmedabad/Bitcoin-may-be-used-by-hawala-traders-Officials/ar-
ticleshow/28067184.cms

20 Rashmee Lall, "Bitcoin is the new hawala — no more, no less,"
Arab Weekly, January 7, 2018; https://thearabweekly.com/
bitcoin-new-hawala-no-more-no-less

21 For an overview of Mobile Payments see John A. Cassara's , Written
Statement for the Hearing On "The Next Terrorist Financiers:
Stopping Them before They Start" Before the Task Force to
Investigate Terrorism Financing Of the House Financial Services
Committee, June 23, 2016; https://financialservices.house.gov/up-
loadedfiles/hhrg-114-ba00-wstate-jcassara-20160623.pdf

22 Ibid

23 See Etisalat press release - http://www.etisalat.af/about-us/press-
releases/183-etisalat-launches-mhawala-mobile-financial-services-
in-afghanistan) and the Mhawala website - http://mhawala.af/

24 See Yaya J. Fanusie and Alex Entz," Islamic State - Financial
Assessment," Foundation for the Defense of Democracies, March
2017; http://www.defenddemocracy.org/content/uploads/docu-
ments/CSIF_ISIS_Finance.pdf

25 Jack Moore, "Hawala, The Ancient Banking Practice Used to Finance
Terror Groups,"Newsweek, February 24, 2015; http://www.news-
week.com/underground-european-hawala-network-financing-mid-
dle-eastern-terror-groups-307984

26 Rukmini Callimachi, Alissa J Rubin, Laure Fouquet," Paris attacks:
terrifyingly fatal layers of resources and tactics," The Irish Times,
March 20, 2016; http://www.irishtimes.com/news/world/europe/
paris-attacks-terrifyingly-fatal-layers-of-resources-and-tac-
tics-1.2580749

27 See Yaya J. Fanusie and Alex Entz," Al-Shabaab - Financial Assessment," Foundation for the Defense of Democracies, May, 2017; http://www.defenddemocracy.org/content/uploads/documents/CSIF_TFBB_Al-Shabaab_v05_web.pdf

28 Yaya Fanusie and Landon Heid, Foreign Affairs, June 17, 2016; https://www.forbes.com/sites/realspin/2016/06/17/what-isis-is-banking-on/#50fe1cc11651

29 See Yaya J. Fanusie and Alex Entz, "Boko Haram Financial Assessment," Foundation for the Defense of Democracies, May, 2017; http://www.defenddemocracy.org/content/uploads/documents/CSIF_Boko_Haram.pdf) and Kathleen Caulderwood, "Fake Charities, Drug Cartels, Ransom and Extortion: Where Islamist Group Boko Haram Gets Its Cash," International Business Times, May 16, 2014. (http://www.ibtimes.com/fake-charities-drug-cartels-ransom-extortionwhere-islamist-group-boko-haram-gets-its-1585743

30 "Gulf funds being used to radicalize Kashmir youth", Daily Excelsior, 24 April 2016; http://www.dailyexcelsior.com/gulf-funds-used-radicalise-kashmir-youth/

31 Rick Gladstone, "Iran Finding Some Ways to Evade Sanctions, Treasury Department Says," New York Times, January 10, 2013; http://www.nytimes.com/2013/01/11/world/middleeast/iran-finding-ways-to-circumvent-sanctions-treasury-department-says.html

32 Reschikov, Oleg, "Iran: Opposition to Western Sanctions in the Banking Sector", New Eastern Outlook, January 30, 201; http://journal-neo.org/2015/01/30/rus-iran-protivodejstvie-zapadny-m-sanktsiyam-v-bankovskoj-sfere/

33 International Narcotics Control Strategy Report, Volume II on Money Laundering, U.S. Department of State, 2015, See Iran country report; https://www.state.gov/j/inl/rls/nrcrpt/2015/supplemental/239219.htm

34 "Manhattan U.S. Attorney Charges Long Island Man with Engaging in Hawala Activity That Funded Attempted Times Square Bombing," FBI Press Release, September 15, 2010; https://archives.fbi.gov/archives/newyork/press-releases/2010/nyfo091510a.htm

35 "Three Somali Immigrants Sentenced for Providing Support to Foreign Terrorists," FBI Press Release, November 18, 2013; https://archives.fbi.gov/archives/sandiego/press-releases/2013/three-somali-immigrants-sentenced-for-providing-support-to-foreign-terrorists

36 "Healthcare Fraudsters Sent $1.1 Million to Iran," Money Jihad, March 26, 2013; https://moneyjihad.wordpress.com/2013/03/26/health-care-fraudsters-sent-1-1-million-to-iran/

37 Joel Rubin, "Drug cartel money laundering indictment is first major effort against hawala tactics," Los Angeles Times, October 2, 2015; http://www.latimes.com/local/crime/la-me-hawala-drug-money-20151003-story.html

38 Howard Fine, "Monrovia Man Convicted in Scheme Using Brokers to Launder Drug Money," Los Angeles Business Journal, January 23, 2018; http://labusinessjournal.com/news/2018/jan/23/monrovia-man-convicted-scheme-using-brokers-launde/)

39 2007 National Money Laundering Strategy Report; https://www.treasury.gov/resource-center/terrorist-illicit-finance/Documents/nmls.pdf)

40 See John Cassara's February 3, 2016 testimony before the Task Force to Investigate Terrorism Financing of the House Financial Services Committee; https://financialservices.house.gov/upload-edfiles/hhrg-114-ba00-wstate-jcassara-20160203.pdf. See also John Cassara, Trade-Based Money Laundering: The Next Frontier in International Money Laundering Enforcement, 2016 John Wiley & Sons, Hoboken, New Jersey - Chapter 9 page 145 on "Monitoring Trade."

41 John Cassara, "Flying money" may land in U.S. - Is Chinese money laundering "flying" into real estate?" February 21, 2016, Banking Exchange; http://www.bankingexchange.com/news-feed/item/6079-flying-money-may-land-in-u-s

CHAPTER 8
Real Estate

IN CHAPTER 2 WE USED a few sobering statistics to show that out of the multi-trillions of dollars of illicit proceeds generated every year, less than one percent is actually seized and forfeited. Here is another amazing statistic: out of the criminal proceeds and assets seized, 30 percent have historically been real estate or tied to real estate.[1]

Over the last thirty years, we have observed how luxury real estate has increasingly become a significant methodology for the laundering of illicit proceeds. Investment in real estate is often preceded by placement into a financial institution. Generally speaking, the layering stage occurs by wiring funds into various accounts. There is sometimes a lack of transparency regarding ownership in these financial transactions. The use of offshore shell companies, which allow the identity of the ultimate owner to be hidden, have more and more become an area of concern. For example, in New York during the past few years, around $8 billion has been invested annually in residential properties worth $5 million or more. Over half of these transactions are made through shell companies.[2] The use of shell companies is synonymous with the layering stage of money laundering. Of course, there are countless variations in the real estate laundering process including cash purchases, money changing hands under the table, the use of hidden intermediaries, co-mingling illicit with licit cash, etc. The purchase of high-end real estate is generally used by criminal money launderers in the final stage of the money laundering cycle — integration.

I have often mentored law enforcement in the developing world. Invariably, foreign police or intelligence services pose the following scenario and question: Ten years ago, Subject X was a low level street thug. Our service knows he was involved with various types of criminal activity, but we couldn't put a case together. Now Subject X owns a shopping center (or high rise residential building) in our capital city. Can you help us? This type of scenario is all too common. Add to the above picture the frequent influx of foreign money that is invested in real estate. The foreign money is often tied to transnational organized crime. For those readers that have seen the nearly empty shopping centers of Dubai or the vacant high rise apartment buildings in Panama City, let alone Miami, you know exactly what I'm talking about. Coupled with the lack of transparency and financial intelligence reporting covering real estate transactions and we see that the use of real estate to launder illicit proceeds has become one of the money laundering methodologies of choice.

This AML vulnerability affects the developing world but also everyday markets where we all live. The most glaring examples of money laundering via real estate include London, New York, San Francisco, Los Angeles, Vancouver, Miami, Toronto, Hong Kong, Singapore, Doha, Sydney, Panama City, Paris, Sydney, and other international real estate hot spots. Some, if not most, of this involves capital flight. We will explore this further in our discussion of Chinese money laundering in Chapter 11.

In some locales unscrupulous real estate brokers accept cash for properties and do not file mandatory financial transparency reports. More commonly there is an official transaction and then cash is exchanged "off the books." The cash makes up the difference between the official and true price.

For example, the manipulation of property values involves criminals buying and selling real estate at a price above or below market value. Buyers, sellers and/or real estate agents conspire to under or overestimate the value of a property. The difference between the actual and stated values is settled with undisclosed cash payments. Note: this is somewhat analogous to over- and under-invoicing schemes employed in Chapter 6's discussion of trade-based money laundering.

In turn, under-valuation involves recording the property value on a sales contract which is less than the purchase price. The difference between the contract price of the property and its true worth is paid under the table by the purchaser to the vendor using illicit funds. The criminal (purchaser) is able to claim that the amount disclosed in the contract as having been paid is consistent with their legitimate financial means. If the property is later sold at true market or higher value, the profits would serve to legitimize the illicit funds. This method is also used to lower tax obligations.

Criminals may also overvalue real estate with the aim of obtaining the largest possible loan from a lender. Illicit funds can then be used to pay off the loan either in a lump sum or installments.[3]

Remember that fraud in various forms is a predicate offense to charge money laundering. In these cases, the purchase of real estate via cash can be considered the placement stage of money laundering. Unfortunately, there are insufficient money laundering investigations in this area.

Money laundering techniques and real estate shenanigans of all sorts raise the price of homeownership for local residents. Hardworking, middleclass citizens that want to move up the real estate ladder and that play by the rules cannot compete when wealthy outsiders throw money at a property. They are increasingly priced out of their local market. Outsiders' influx of money — some of it with dubious origins — fosters resentment. Just as important, investments in high-end real estate serve as one of the major outlets for the annual $1 trillion[4] or so that is stolen by corrupt officials around the world.

There are a number of other reasons why the purchase of real estate is attractive to money launderers:

- Money launderers are businessmen. Property generally offers stability and reliability.

- Real estate presents the chance for asset appreciation and tax write offs.

- Property renovations and improvements may increase the value of their initial investment.

- The property could be used as a second home or to provide rental income.

- Real estate investments by criminals might provide desired lifestyle choices and the chance to reside in desirable locations.

- The purchase of property is cash intensive.

- In many locations around the world, including the United States, real estate agents are exempt from filing Suspicious Activity Reports.

- The purchase of both commercial and residential real estate — compared to some other laundering techniques — is comparatively straight forward and does not necessitate any special expertise.

- Real estate as an asset class is generally available around the world.

- The purchase of property in a desired location may help with obtaining residency or citizenship or provide housing to college-age children attending a nearby university.

- The purchase of real estate facilitates the movement of a lot of money in one transaction.

- Real estate transactions offer the aura of legitimacy.

Reporting by Real Estate Professionals in the United States

The crux of the problem is that, due to the powerful real estate lobby, there really isn't any financial intelligence reporting by real estate agents.

In the 2016 FATF U.S. Mutual Evaluation Report, the United Stated was rated largely compliant with the FATF 40 recommendations. However, there were a few areas of concern. Among the shortcomings identified by the FATF are vulnerabilities in the U.S. real estate sector, particularly in its high-end segment.[5]

For the purposes of FATF mutual evaluations, real estate agents, notaries, independent legal professionals and accountants are classified as designated non-financial businesses and professions (DNFBPs). Unlike in Canada and some other countries, real estate agents and brokers are not required to file suspicious activity reports or maintain AML/CFT compliance programs. Real estate agents are not subject to due diligence and recordkeeping rules for clients. Background checks for real estate licenses vary by state.[6]

To put things in perspective, in 2019 the real estate lobby spent nearly $90 million dollars. There are nearly 600 registered real estate lobbyists.[7] Succumbing to the dollars, power, and influence Congress granted the real estate industry a "temporary" exemption from the 2001 PATRIOT Act. Recognizing that money laundering via real estate is a growing threat, in 2016 the Department of Treasury started putting band-aids on the problem by issuing Geographic Targeting Orders (GTOs) that require title insurance companies in specific, high-value markets to report the ultimate owner of a "legal entity" that purchases a residential home worth more than $300,000. In short, since real estate agents were politically untouchable, the government mandated title companies to report. Title companies must obtain the names of beneficial owners, but only those with 25 percent or greater ownership interest. In theory, GTOs are temporary and targeted. Nevertheless the FinCEN action has been renewed and expanded a number of times.

According to the FinCEN renewal of May 2019, "GTOs continue to provide valuable data on the purchase of residential real estate by persons possibly involved in various illicit enterprises. Reissuing the GTOs will further assist in tracking illicit funds and other criminal or illicit activity, as well as inform FinCEN's future regulatory efforts in this sector. . . GTOs cover certain counties within the following major U.S. metropolitan areas: Boston, Chicago, Dallas-Fort Worth, Honolulu, Las Vegas, Los Angeles, Miami, New York City, San Antonio, San Diego, San Francisco, and Seattle."[8]

Per the above, FinCEN believes that the financial intelligence generated from the GTOs has proved valuable. FinCEN also estimates that requiring the mortgage lending industry to file SARs puts 78 percent of residential purchases in the U.S. subject to BSA/AML compliance.[9]

The problem with this line of reasoning is that real estate agents are in the best position to know their customer/KYC. Many spend long periods of time with the prospective buyer(s). Like any sales professional, real estate agents assess their buyers. They pick up on a wide variety of verbal and non-verbal clues from perspective clients that help them formulate sales. They have access to documentation provided by their clients. They are in a perfect position to discern suspicious behavior, motives, or a sale that could be tainted. Yet similar to the objections that bankers raised thirty years ago, real estate agents, like other DNFBPs, do not want to be "police" or "informers." They have no desire for the administrative headaches of filing SARs. The regulatory burden would be expensive. Most importantly, the real estate industry must surmise that filing SARs could possibly jeopardize their high commissions.

There are other practical loopholes covered by the GTO band-aid. For example, criminals can simply bypass the GTO half-measure by purchasing property outside the designated GTO areas. They could also simply take out a loan under the reporting threshold or avail themselves of the fictitious valuing ruses discussed above. A 2015 report by the U.S. National Association of Realtors found that almost 60 percent of purchases by international clients are made in cash.[10]

Hence, while GTOs are a step in the right direction, it isn't solving the problem of money laundering via real estate in the United States. Besides, even though GTOs provide "valuable information" to FinCEN, there is still a dearth of actual ground level investigations using the GTO generated data.

Shell Companies and LLCs

In 2018/2019 the case against Paul Manafort made international headlines. He was charged with money laundering and tax evasion. One of his techniques used real estate transactions and offshores. Manafort was accused of opening bank accounts in Europe with tainted funds. Money was then wired from the European bank directly into a U.S. escrow account to close all cash purchases of property. Subsequently, a loan was placed on the property to obtain cash on a tax-free basis.[11] Testimony in his trial also outlined an elaborate operation where Cyprus shell companies were used to secretly accept millions of dollars of work done in Ukraine. Much of the money was later routed to the U.S.[12]

Coached by networks of complicit investment advisors, international bad actors have used similar approaches for the purchases of both commercial and residential properties. Many suspect real estate purchases are made through LLCs formed specifically to purchase and own the individual property. These LLCs can be formed by anyone. The actual or "beneficial owner" may not be fully disclosed in the operating agreements. The agent or broker forming the LLCs may be cut-outs for the real owners. These "fronts" or "straw men" are active for shadow parties in a wide variety of legal and illegal activity. As noted above, property purchases are ideal for money launderers because the size of these transactions can move a significant amount of money at one time.[13] In Chapter 13, we will discuss offshores and lack of beneficial ownership information in more detail.

The United States is one of the easiest places in the world to establish an anonymous company. Law enforcement has observed that these companies are used time and time again in suspect purchases of properties. While national legislation is pending that would provide registration transparency, currently no U.S. state collects information about beneficial owners of shell companies.

Over the past few years, several troublesome cases involving shell companies have come to light including the trial of Teodoro Obiang, son of the president of Equatorial Guinea; Malaysia's 1MDB scandal; the Brazilian Car Wash Operation; and the Panama Papers' revelations. According to Transparency International, these cases ". . . offer examples of how property in key markets may have been used to launder money. In many such cases, property is purchased through anonymous shell companies or trusts without undergoing proper due diligence by the professionals involved in the deal." [14] In Chapter 11, we will discuss offshores and shell companies focusing on Chinese investment in international real estate including investment of illicit proceeds from drug trafficking. The following are a few other examples and illustrative investigations.

Canada

In 2018 a media exposé in Canada followed by a Royal Canadian Mounted Police investigation revealed that drug traffickers dealing in fentanyl had invested CAD $47 million in the Vancouver property market through unofficial cash loans and other techniques. The organized crime syndicates also earned significant interest on their investments in addition to laundering their funds. [15]

The Vancouver residential real estate market is exploding. According to 2017 statistics, with a median home sale price of $1,108,345 and a median family income of $63,944, Vancouver is the most unaffordable market in North America. This includes other more expensive housing markets such as Manhattan and San Francisco. [16] Moreover, law enforcement, outside observes, and increasingly politicians concur the culprit in the escalation of housing prices has been money laundering — by criminals, kleptocrats, tax evaders, and foreign nationals.

In 2018, foreign influence in the hot real estate market was demonstrated by both Ontario and British Colombia when the two provinces imposed a new 15 percent tax on non-resident buyers. This resulted in home sales falling around 40 percent in Vancouver in January compared to the same period the year before.[17] Of course, foreigners can still get around the tax by using straw buyers or friends and family members that are citizens. Once again, the problem is lack of "beneficial ownership" information.

United Kingdom

In 2019, analysis by Global Witness showed that over 87,000 properties in England and Wales are owned by anonymous companies registered in worldwide tax havens. The value of these properties is at least £56 billion and likely to be in excess of £100 billion when accounting for inflation and missing price data.[18]

The estimates buttressed earlier Transparency International reporting on the London property market. Moreover, Transparency International's research also shows that 75 percent of UK properties under investigation for corruption between 2004 and 2015 were registered with offshore companies incorporated in secrecy jurisdictions, such as the British Virgin Islands.[19] Illicit funds help sustain Britain's inflated property market.

There have been legislative proposals in the UK to create an online register which would require the owners of overseas companies that own UK properties to be named. It is believed this kind of transparency would stop people from hiding their identity when buying a property by allowing checks to be carried out on the source and legitimacy of the subject funds.

Spain's Costa del Sol

For the last 25 years, tainted money has flooded into Spain's Costa del Sol real estate market. Much of the suspect money appears to originate from Russian organized crime. Using some of the techniques outlined above including all cash purchases, the use of anonymous shell companies, and under-the-table dealings between buyer, seller, and broker, multi-hundreds of millions if not billions of dollars equivalent was placed, layered, and integrated into Costa del Sol property.

For example, in 2015 Spanish Guardia Civil and National Police investigation concluded that the money laundering network of the Kremliovskaya, a Russian mafia organization, moved more than 200 million euros in cash into the Costa del Sol market.[20] The launderers used more than two dozen companies in different sectors, including property, sports, private security, the media and approximately 100 bank accounts to layer the illicit proceeds. By following the money trail, Spanish investigators found financial tentacles reaching to Belgium, Holland, Germany, Denmark, Italy, the UK, Poland, Switzerland, France and the United States. The investigation was initiated due to filing irregularities at the town hall in the village of Casares, where a huge residential complex called Residencial Majestic was allowed to be built despite it exceeding town planning regulations. [21]

Dubai

In 2005, I wrote my first book Hide & Seek: Intelligence, Law Enforcement and the Stalled War on Terror Finance. In the book I chronicled my early involvement in investigating international money laundering. Assigned to the Office of the Customs Attaché in Rome, Italy, I had a unique vantage point. We were also a regional office. I was on the road a lot following illicit money trails that led to Africa, Europe, South Asia, and the Middle East. Early on I became concerned about money laundering and other financial crimes in Dubai and devoted a chapter in my book to the subject. As I wrote in Hide & Seek, "In ancient times it was said all roads lead to Rome. In modern times coming from Rome, the trails of transnational crime that I followed eventually led to Dubai."[22]

Over the last 30 years, the growth of Dubai in the United Arab Emirates has been simply incredible. Not many years ago it was nothing more than a small Arabian Gulf Coast fishing and pearling settlement. Today, modern Dubai rises where the desert meets the sea like an Emirati Emerald City in an Arabian Oz. In real estate, the experts say the most important thing is "location, location, location." The same holds true for transnational crime. Because of Dubai's magnificent position on the crosswinds and crossroads of the Arabian Peninsula, it has become an attractive location for shopping, trading, finance, communications, and investment. Its remarkable growth has been fueled in part by an influx of foreign capital of suspect origin. The welcoming environment is coupled with the laissez-fair attitudes of the ruling Maktum family. There is also a startling lack of initiative dealing with AML/CFT enforcement. It is a potent mix that unfortunately has been abused.

A 2018 investigative report[23] by the Organized Crime and Corruption Reporting Project (OCCRP) and the Centre for Advanced Defense Studies (C4ADS) showcased how the UAE's secretive and weakly regulated financial sector and unaccountable high-end real estate market combine to offer the world's criminals a range of services. The lack of enforcement and oversight I observed years ago has continued unabated in Dubai's property sector. Dubai's shimmering cityscape is losing its luster with vast amounts of dirty money.

The report also shows that individuals under international sanctions are finding safe haven in Dubai. Leaked private real estate data cited in the report reveals that organized crime figures and politicians are flocking to Dubai to purchase property. Despite international and domestic prohibitions, sanctioned individuals and their associates — terrorists, narco-traffickers, proliferators, and kleptocrats — continue to invest millions of dollars into private luxury real estate.[24]

Similar to other countries and jurisdictions, Dubai has made promises to clean up its act, strengthen its AML/CFT rules, and conduct investigations. For example, real estate agents, developers, trust and corporate services providers and lawyers involved in real estate transactions who are registered in the Dubai International Financial Centre (DIFC) are now required to conduct customer due diligence on customers and register, identify the beneficial owner of customers, and apply extra scrutiny to foreign politically exposed persons. In spite of these improvements, little to no enforcement action appears to have been taken in the real estate sector.

Moscow

While there has been a flood of Russian capital flight and tainted money leaving Russia, there has also been an underreported influx of suspect funds into Moscow real estate. In one example, Global Witness estimates that prominent members of Syria's powerful Makhlouf family, cousins of dictator Bashar al-Assad, own at least $40 million worth of property invested in two Moscow skyscrapers. Makhlouf family members have helped maintain al-Assad's hold on power. However, the specific source of the funds invested in the properties is not known. Global Witness' investigation does show that when buying the Moscow office space in 2016, Makhlouf Russian-registered property companies took out loans using 11 of the properties as collateral. The complex structure of these loans disguises connections to the funds. As Global Witness notes, this is characteristic of money laundering. The loans could have been designed to establish money flows between Russia and Syria, raising the possibility that the ultimate aim is to move the money out of Russia.[25]

Countermeasures and a Few Proposals

In large part countermeasures in the real estate sector are dependent on the country and jurisdiction of concern. Some do a much better job than others in policing suspicious purchases of real estate. Here are a few proposals that for the most part concentrate on the United States.

Real Estate Agents Should File SARS

In the United States, Congress should repeal the exemption in the USA PATRIOT ACT that grants real estate agents an exemption to report SARs. Real estate agents and other DNFBPs including attorneys and accountants should report suspicious activity to FinCEN. This action will make the United States compliant with FATF guidelines. In fact, all governments should require real estate agents and others engaged in real estate closings to identify and report suspicious transactions to the financial intelligence unit. Real estate professional associations or supervisory bodies should provide money laundering guidance, red flag indicators, and training on how to report quality SARS. Real estate agents should take a "fit and proper" or background test in order to operate in the real estate sector.

Require Beneficial Ownership Information

In the United States, FinCEN's "temporary" GTOs governing real estate should end. Per the above, real estate agents should file SARs. They are in the best position to KYC and identify beneficial owners of customers. Transparency should be mandated before proceeding with the sale or purchase of the property. Beneficial ownership information for real estate should be in the public domain.

Tax Foreign Purchases of Real Estate

Canada, for example, currently taxes purchases of property by foreign buyers. States should also consider implementing similar taxes in the U.S. Of course, the tax will easily be circumvented by straw buyers, a proxy person or company. As noted above, typically funds come from a trust; this trust is managed by a shell company owned by another trust with an account in the British Virgin Islands or Cayman Islands run by a Luxembourg banker who doesn't know the owner. Such arrangements should be prohibited. Consequently, the tax can only be implemented in conjunction with meaningful beneficial ownership information. A tax could also be considered on residential properties that stand vacant. Taxes of this type will decrease demand in hot upscale markets. The tax will guard against outside domination and influence and go a long way to ensure people actually live in the purchased property. Demand for the properties by foreign buyers should fall giving locals a better chance at purchasing property in their own neighborhoods.

Unexplained Wealth and Source and Application of Funds

In 2018, law enforcement officers in the UK used a new power — the Unexplained Wealth Order — to investigate how Zamira Hajiyeva, wife of an Azerbaijani banker, managed to acquire an £11.5 million house in Knightsbridge. The banker's salary was far from sufficient for such a purchase, they argued. The Unexplained Wealth Order gives British authorities the power to seize assets over £50,000 owned by a person "who is reasonably suspected of involvement in, or of being connected to a person involved in, serious crime." [26]

The Unexplained Wealth Order uses an IRS "Source and Application of Funds" accounting technique. According to an IRS accounting manual, this method "uses changes in assets and liabilities, along with expenditures for nontaxable income and nondeductible receipts. The applications (increases in assets and decreases in liabilities and nondeductible expenses) are compared against the sources (decreased in assets, increases in liabilities or nontaxable receipts). Any excess of applications over the sources is considered an understatement of adjusted gross income"[27] or "unexplained wealth." However, the U.S. does not have statutory authority to seize unexplained wealth. I urge U.S. lawmakers to consider passing unexplained wealth legislation that includes proper safeguards to guard against civil forfeiture abuse.

NOTES

1 "Sandcastles. Tracing Sanctions Evasion through Dubai's Luxury Real Estate Market," C4ADS, 2018; https://www.c4reports.org/sandcastles/

2 Jay Ryan, "Real Estate Spotlight Series: How US cities are fighting money launderers," Accuity, May 2, 2018; https://accuity.com/accuity-insights-blog/real-estate-spotlight-series-how-us-cities-are-fighting-money-launderers/

3 "Strategic analysis brief Money laundering through real estate," AUSTRAC, 2015, page 8; https://www.austrac.gov.au/sites/default/files/2019-07/sa-brief-real-estate_0.pdf

4 Amanda Abrams, "How Russians Launder Stolen Money Via Real Estate," Newsweek, December 21, 2015; https://www.newsweek.com/how-russians-launder-stolen-money-real-estate-407810

5 The Financial Action Task Force, (2016), Mutual Evaluation Report: United States; http://www.fatf-gafi.org/publications/mutualevaluations/documents/mer-united-states-2016.html

6 "Money Laundering in Real Estate," Conference Report Convened by the Terrorism, Transnational Crime and Corruption Center at the Schar School of Policy and Government, March 25, page 2

7 "Real Estate Lobbying, 2019," Open Secrets; https://www.opensecrets.org/industries/lobbying.php?ind=F10++

8 "FinCEN Reissues Real Estate Geographic Targeting Orders for 12 Metropolitan Areas," FinCEN, May, 15, 2019; https://www.fincen.gov/news/news-releases/fincen-reissues-real-estate-geographic-targeting-orders-12-metropolitan-areas

9 "U.S. regulators tackle money laundering in the luxury home market," Thomson Reuters; https://legal.thomsonreuters.com/en/insights/articles/u-s-regulators-tackle-money-laundering-luxury-home-market

10 "Doors Wide Open," Transparency International, 2017, page 9; https://www.transparency.org/whatwedo/publication/doors_wide_open_corruption_and_real_estate_in_four_key_markets

11 Randy Pereira, "Money Laundering Through Commercial Real Estate and Our "Know Your Client" Obligations," Colliers International, February 28, 2018; https://knowledge-leader.colliers.com/randy-pereira/money-laundering-commercial-real-estate-know-client-obligations/

12 Kevin Johnson, "Paul Manafort trial: Rick Gates admits padding expenses to pay for mistress, may have bilked inaugural committee," USA Today, August 7, 2018; https://www.usatoday.com/story/news/politics/2018/08/07/paul-manafort-trial-rick-gates-reveals-web-secret-bank-accounts/923239002/

13 Ibid

14 "Doors Wide Open," page 5

15 "Sandcastles, page 7;

16 Juliana Mindru, "Housing Affordability: How Fast Could You Pay off Your Home in the 50 Most Populous Cities in North America?" Point2Homes, December 18, 2017; https://www.point2homes.com/news/canada-real-estate/housing-affordability-north-america.html

17 Diane Francis, "Money laundering by foreigners is what's really destroying housing affordability in Canada," Financial Post, February 19, 2019; https://business.financialpost.com/diane-francis/money-laundering-by-foreigners-is-whats-really-destroying-housing-affordability-in-canada

18 "£100BN OF PROPERTY IN ENGLAND AND WALES IS SECRETLY OWNED, ESTIMATES SHOW," Global Witness Press Release, March 17, 2019; https://www.globalwitness.org/en/press-releases/100bn-of-property-in-england-and-wales-is-secretly-owned-estimates-show/

19 Ibid, page 14.

20 Juan Cano, "Russian mafia laundered over 200 million euros in cash on the Costa," SURinEnglish.com, March 15, 2015; http://www.surinenglish.com/20150313/news/costasol-malaga/russian-mafia-laundered-over-201503131140.html

21 Ibid

22 John Cassara, Hide & Seek: Intelligence, Law Enforcement, and the Stalled War on Terror Finance, Potomac Books, Dulles Virginia, 2006, page 108.

23 "Sandcastles." This is an excellent investigative report that goes into detail on how Dubai's real estate market is abused by criminals.

24 Transparency International, "Dirty Money-Hub Dubai Must Clean Up its Real Estate Sector," June 12, 2018; https://www.transparency.org/news/pressrelease/dirty_money_hub_dubai_must_clean_up_its_real_estate_sector

25 "Assad's Henchmen's Russian Refugee," Global Witness; https://www.globalwitness.org/en/campaigns/corruption-and-money-laundering/assad-henchmens-russian-refuge/

26 Ollie Williams, "British Real Estate Agents Hit by Money Laundering Crackdown," Forbes, March 11, 2019; https://www.forbes.com/sites/oliverwilliams1/2019/03/11/british-real-estate-agents-hit-by-money-laundering-crackdown/#634a13d83c88

27 "Cash Intensive Businesses Audit Techniques Guide - Chapter 5 – Examination Techniques," The IRS; https://www.irs.gov/pub/irs-utl/cashchapter5_210639.pdf

CHAPTER 9

The Illicit Tobacco Trade

IN 1990 I WAS ASSIGNED to the American embassy in Rome and headed the first international anti-money laundering task force. We targeted Italian American organized crime — the mafia. Partnering with the Italian Guardia di Finanza (GdF) or the fiscal police, we tried to follow the dirty money trails.

Some of those trails involved illicit tobacco — a big concern of the GdF. The GdF investigators demonstrated the link between contraband tobacco and organized crime; they taught me how tobacco products are traded for guns, drugs and other smuggled goods. They also showed me how contraband smuggling routes and networks overlap. The GdF was very concerned about the enormous proceeds the trade in illicit tobacco generates and the simultaneous loss in revenue for the Italian government. The investigators also lamented that their work received little recognition or respect. Social and political commentators felt that the trade in illicit cigarettes was a "victimless crime." Too many policy makers and those involved with law enforcement opined that the issue had no relevance for them.

The same challenges exist today. However, a convincing argument can be made that the current situation is even worse. According to the World Customs Organization, there has been "an unparalleled growth in the illicit trade of tobacco products over recent years." The WCO continues "that where goods are highly taxed, easily portable and penalties remain relatively light for smuggling, transnational criminal organizations will take advantage of any weaknesses in customs, revenue or other border controls to amass profits."[1]

Today we also see how organized criminal groups involved with the illicit tobacco trade are increasingly linked to other criminal activity, including counterfeit pharmaceuticals, counterfeit currency, counterfeit household goods, narcotics smuggling, and trafficking in weapons and wildlife. For example, in 2018, the same GdF I worked with 30 years ago dismantled a human trafficking organization involved with smuggling people from Tunisia to Italy.[2] On board some of the smuggling vessels were bulk quantities of contraband cigarettes. This kind of thing happens around the world. Transnational organized crime, corruption, smuggling and cigarette trafficking have become deeply intertwined. Unfortunately, ugly violence is sometimes part of the trade. Illicit tobacco also helps fund terror. The laundering of massive amounts of criminal proceeds generated via the illicit tobacco trade continues unabated.

Tobacco trafficking — in varied forms — has been with us for centuries. Today it spans the globe. It occurs in literally every country. As a result, illicit tobacco could be the best understood and most documented sector of the word's dark economy. Thus, this long-standing, robust, and widespread illegal activity is an excellent typology to study the effectiveness of our AML/CFT countermeasures. In order to do so we first have to learn a little bit about how the trade in illicit tobacco works.

The Magnitude of the Problem and the Tobacco Chain

Generally speaking, a "tobacco product" is any item for human consumption that is made from tobacco. The illicit trade in tobacco products is a chain of sometimes interconnected illegal activities that may include uncertain sourcing, unlicensed production, smuggling, fraudulent marketing and tax evasion. Facilitators include corruption and various frauds and related crimes that move the illicit product and money through various transit and financial systems.

The illicit trade in tobacco requires money laundering to disguise the enormous proceeds that are generated.

Each link in this chain of criminality causes direct or indirect harm: it denies legitimate manufacturers, suppliers, and distributors of revenue and sometimes both their physical and intellectual property; the sale of illicit tobacco products deprives governments at various levels revenue in the form of sales and/or value added taxes; the illicit trade in tobacco is a catalyst for corruption; it undermines legitimate employment; illicit tobacco fosters criminality and in certain areas of the world its revenue furthers organized crime and terrorist organizations. Legitimate retailers — very often small family businesses — are damaged as criminal organizations usurp their livelihood. Rules that prevent sales of tobacco products to children are often undermined because the illicit product is purchased away from the eyes of the authorities. Moreover, illicit tobacco is often manufactured at sites without public health protocols. For example, Steve Wilkins, Japan Tobacco International's Anti-Illegal Trade Operations Director, commented on an undercover buy of cigarettes, "Smokers buying cheap fake cigarettes and tobacco on the streets of the UK may be getting more than they bargain for as these fake imitations have been found to contain asbestos, mold, dust, dead flies, rat droppings and even human excrement."[3]

In comparison, licit tobacco is cultivated, processed, manufactured, and distributed through regulated and legal channels. The product is taxed. The companies involved with legitimate tobacco sales practice customer due diligence and know their producers and suppliers (including filters, papers, and packaging), and distributors. The cigarettes and other tobacco products are disseminated through systems of transit companies, wholesalers and retailers. Just over half of legal tobacco products are sold to the consumer through independent retailers, grocery stores/supermarkets, convenience stores and gas/petrol stations, with the rest sold through other legal outlets.[4]

The legal supply chain is controlled to a great extent by the industry. It begins with the growers. Other elements of tobacco production include suppliers of key components such as cigarette paper, filters, acetate tow (a natural product deriving from wood that is produced to maintain cigarette quality and aroma), packaging, and chemicals. Tobacco manufacturers are involved with research and development, production, packaging, shipping to wholesalers and marketing. The manufacturers then distribute to wholesalers or intermediaries. Finally, the consumer purchases product via retailers, duty free sales, or cross-border shopping.

In 2018, the retail value of cigarette sales worldwide was approximately $714 billion.[5] Approximately 5.3 trillion cigarettes were sold to more than one billion smokers worldwide.[6] Concurrently, there is an illicit volume of approximately 600 billion sticks per year.[7] Cigarettes account for about 90 percent of all tobacco products sold worldwide.

The occasional illicit transaction (an estimated 10 percent of the worldwide trade) often gets lost in the majority of licit tobacco trade. This "mixing" or "co-mingling" of illicit with licit or criminally "hiding-in-plain-sight" along with the overwhelming percentage of legitimate activity is often used in criminal schemes. Similar to our discussion of TBML in Chapter 6, it is the very volume of the trade that makes it so difficult to detect.

Another way of looking at the illicit trade is by examining 2017 data that shows around one in 10 cigarettes lit globally, excluding China, was illicit, compared to one in 11 in 2012. Valued collectively at more than $60 billion,[8] that is greater than the value of illicit trade in oil, wildlife, timber, arts and cultural property, and diamonds combined. Some estimates suggest that the worldwide retail value of illicit tobacco products may be comparable to the size of the international cocaine market.[9] Organized crime is increasingly dominant in the illicit trade of tobacco because the rewards can be high and the penalties slight. Just one shipping container full of trafficked cigarettes could earn a criminal group more than $1 million in profit.[10]

The Market

The illicit trade in tobacco products includes various types of tobacco products. Both industry and law enforcement describe the illicit tobacco market as falling into broad categories: 1) contraband, 2) counterfeit, 3) "cheap whites" or "illicit whites," and 4) loose and/or raw tobacco.[11] Mirroring the legal market, a significant percentage of illicit tobacco is in the form of cigarettes.

Contraband tobacco products are legally produced and manufactured but diverted into an illegal market. No taxes, duties, or fees are paid on the contraband product. The diversion from manufacturer to retailer occurs in a variety of ways including theft, smuggling, and bootlegging.

Counterfeit tobacco products are illegally produced. They have fictitious labeling, trademarks, and/or trade names. The sophistication of the counterfeit operations varies greatly. Generally speaking, the quality of the illicit tobacco product as well as the packaging and fictitious authentication have increased over the years due to the sophistication of various technologies. Counterfeit tobacco products deny intellectual property rights; they often do not meet health regulations, and they generally avoid taxes. Illegal factories located in China tend to be the largest supplier of counterfeit cigarettes. Other prominent source countries include Vietnam, North Korea, Iran, Iraq, United Arab Emirates, Paraguay, Uruguay, Belarus, Poland, Romania, Russia, the Czech Republic and Spain.[12]

"Cheap whites" or "illicit whites" or "off-brand" or "new brands" are cigarettes legally manufactured and produced in one country or jurisdiction such as a Free Trade Zone (FTZ) for the sole purpose exporting the product for resale in another country. In the country or jurisdiction of origin, the production is monitored and taxes are paid. The production of cheap whites generally fulfills the specifications of the foreign buyer and market. Since the product is intended solely for export and not offered for sale in the production country, authorities in the manufacturing country tend to ignore applicable regulations and enforcement. They turn a blind eye because the manufacturing and shipping process provide employment, revenue, and enhances exports. However, the cigarettes may not meet the health and other regulations in the destination country and taxes and duties are circumvented. According to INTERPOL, in 2014 the primary sources of illicit white production are located in Belarus, Vietnam, Indonesia, Philippines, India, Cambodia, Paraguay, Ukraine, Russia, the Tri-Border Area, Singapore, Belize, Montenegro, United Arab Emirates (UAE), Kenya and various FTZs.[13]

Loose tobacco refers to tobacco that is often used to manufacture or produce custom or "roll-your-own" cigarettes without payment of tax. It is sometimes misbranded and/or does not meet host country regulatory standards.

Smuggling

According to INTERPOL, "both genuine and counterfeit [tobacco] products rely on large-scale smuggling to achieve distribution via illicit trade. The sophistication and complexity of this activity will depend on the size and ambition of the smuggling/illicit trade and the organized groups."[14]

Over the last twenty years, law enforcement has observed a change in cigarette smuggling practices. Previously, there was large-scale smuggling of genuine cigarettes of well-known brands such as Marlboro. In 1995 two scholars in Europe discovered that almost one-third of the world's cigarette exports had disappeared. Billions of cigarettes, once exported, had mysteriously gotten lost in transit. The mystery was soon solved. A few years later a team of investigative reporters examined thousands of internal industry documents and uncovered how leading tobacco companies were colluding with criminal networks to divert cigarettes to the world's black markets. Big Tobacco was smuggling for profit. The goal was to boost sales and gain market share, all the while avoiding billions of dollars in taxes and simultaneously recruiting growing numbers of smokers around the world. The original investigative findings, and others that followed, lead to government inquiries, lawsuits, and promises of global cooperation to crack down on the smuggling of cigarettes. Manufacturers such as Philip Morris, JTI-Gallaher, and Britain's Imperial Tobacco Group came under intense international, public, and political pressure. Some of the largest manufacturers committed publicly to help fight trafficking in tobacco and clean up their act.[15] They have. There have been significant decreases in seizures of legal but untaxed tobacco products exported from Western producers.

The current trend is the increased production, smuggling, and sale of illicit whites and counterfeit cigarettes. The net result is widening the scope of illicit trade from source to destination countries — often through transit countries which the goods pass through on the way to their intended destination. The underground industry is wide and diverse. There is a wide range of examples: Chinese production of illicit whites; counterfeiters that mimic holograms and packaging to perfection; Russian-owned manufacturing centers that mass produce brands made exclusively to be smuggled into Western Europe; Canadian criminal gangs and Native American tribes' involvement in cigarette trafficking; the cigarette manufacturing and smuggling centers in the Tri-Border Area between Argentina, Brazil, and Paraguay; Mexican cartels exchanging narcotics proceeds for U.S. contraband cigarettes imported into Mexico.

The distribution systems from these and many other problematic locations are complex. The smuggling routes are twisting, circuitous and hard to track. Smugglers often take advantage of a customs "in transit" system used in FTZs and other shipping centers which allows for little or no customs inspections as well as temporary tax suspension while the tobacco product is en route to a third country.

Before modern containerization revolutionized shipping and after coveted goods would arrive at a seaport, organized crime would perfect the routine of having goods accidentally "fall off the truck." The modern version of this ruse is that due to lax oversight and meaningful customs controls, cigarettes get "lost" along the way. Once again, organized crime is involved. Huge numbers of cigarettes fail to arrive at their intended destination. Illicit tobacco may sit for lengthy periods of time in FTZs in Panama or Dubai until they are sold. Then they quickly pass through multiple buyers in a short period of time. The system is comparable to the "layering stage" of money laundering where there is added complexity to transactions in an effort to make it difficult for customs and law enforcement to follow the trails due to issues such as venue and jurisdiction. Cigarettes are even illegally sold or traded at sea, where vessels offload them to smaller boats that take them to shore. In the Balkans, they are sold by the trunk load to smugglers.[16]

Similar to bulk cash smuggling techniques described in Chapter 5, various methods are used in to smuggle illicit tobacco products via land, sea, and air.[17] These include:

- The use of trucks with or without false compartments

- Commercial and passenger vehicles

- Planes, cargo vessels, and trains

- Human couriers (mules)

- The abuse of cross border shopping limits

- Postal services

- Shipping using false declarations

Pricing and Laundering

Pricing (which includes taxes or the lack thereof) drives the trade in illicit tobacco. As mentioned above, a variety of jurisdictions, produce cheap whites. Malaysia, South Africa and Eastern Europe are significant manufacturing centers. There are large concentrations of manufacturers in many United Arab Emirates' FTZs. For example, manufacturers in the UAE will sell a master case of cheap white cigarettes (10,000 cigarettes) for as little as $35.[18] Yet the average legitimate manufacturing cost for a master case is approximately $100. That same master case in the developing world will sell for $400, and in OECD developed countries it will sell for nearly $2000. The potential for profits is both obvious and enormous!

Multiply those profits by container shipping. Standard 40 foot shipping containers are generally used from the point of production to a point of consolidation or distribution via other ports to disguise origin and/or secondary distribution. A single container can hold up to 10 million cigarettes. Thus, the cost of manufacturing a container load of cigarettes is approximately $100,000. The re-sale value escalates to $400,000 in the developing world and $2 million in the developed world. That is a great investment!

For example, in China, counterfeiters produce approximately 190 billion counterfeit cigarettes annually. Just one 40-foot container of counterfeit cigarettes produced in China could procure approximately $2 million in profit when sold in Europe. If all 190 billion Chinese counterfeit cigarettes were exported and sold in Europe, this criminal trade could be worth up to $40 billion a year.[19] Once again, the trade in counterfeit goods including cigarettes is a predicate offense to charge money laundering. It seldom happens.

The point of these statistics is to show that the business of illicit tobacco is almost as large as the drug trade but is accomplished at a fraction of the risk. We hear a lot about narco-trafficking. In fact, our efforts to combat money laundering began in 1970 when Richard Nixon declared "the war on drugs." Yet the trade in illicit tobacco does not receive a fraction of the attention, even though it is perhaps even more effective filling the coffers of criminal organizations.

According to the FATF, the laundering of illicit tobacco proceeds varies little from the laundering of other sources of criminal activity. Common techniques to launder proceeds from illicit tobacco include the use of offshore accounts, the use of front companies, the use of money remitting services and currency exchange houses, the use of hawaladars, cash couriers, bulk cash smuggling techniques, money service businesses, international banking, trade-based money laundering techniques, co-mingling, smurfing, structuring, the use of nominees, the use of professionals such as lawyers and accountants, the purchase of real estate, and the use of casinos.[20]All of the above methodologies are problematic for law enforcement. We have struggled with these techniques and methodologies for the last half century. The futility helps demonstrate why our efforts to combat money laundering via illicit tobacco are also a "decimal point away" from failure.

Situation in the United States

The Surgeon General WARNING on one side of a packet of cigarettes reads, "Smoking causes lung cancer, heart disease, emphysema, and may complicate pregnancy." Perhaps there should be another WARNING by the Attorney General on the other side of the packet, "The illicit cigarette trade facilitates fraud, tax evasion, money laundering, and terrorist financing."

Illicit tobacco in its many forms continues to be a major challenge for U.S. law enforcement. There has been a lack of concerted and coordinated effort to combat it.

According to a 2012 FATF report, the primary international source of counterfeit tobacco products in the United States is China. As we will discuss in Chapter 11, that is changing but other threats are developing. Domestically, Native American reservations, importers, and duty free stores have been a source of untaxed tobacco products. U.S. law enforcement also reports the expanded use of the Internet to sell and purchase tobacco products. In addition, mail and express consignment facilities are also increasingly being used in transport. Shipping illicit tobacco products in small quantities often fall under prosecutorial thresholds in many jurisdictions.[21]

The size of the illicit cigarette market in the U.S. is difficult to gauge, but it is estimated at 8.5 to 21 percent of the total market sold every year. To put things in perspective, Altria, the nation's largest tobacco manufacturer, commissioned a study that collected and analyzed 5,000 empty cigarette packs that smokers discarded in New York City. The findings confirmed research by other organizations and indicates that 50 to 60 percent of cigarettes sold in the city are contraband.[22]

Similar to international markets, domestic taxes drive the trade in U.S. illicit tobacco. State and local taxes vary widely. For example, in New York City, smokers pay a state excise tax of $4.35, a city levy of $1.50, and a federal tax of $1.01. Retail prices often exceed $13 a pack or $130 a carton. By contrast, the state tax in Virginia is 30 cents a pack. A van load of about 600 cartons bought in Virginia and sold without paying New York taxes can produce a profit of $20,000.[23] In the United States criminals may be depriving local governments as much as $10 billion in annual tax revenues. This is money cash-strapped local governments desperately need.

Officials say pricing disparities also foster smuggling of cigarettes purchased in native- American smoke shops. Both Canadian and U.S. laws give native American tribes sovereign status and some tribes assert that cigarettes manufactured on tribal lands aren't subject to normal taxes. This gives the native American enterprises a huge competitive advantage over regulated mainstream brands. For example, the Six Nations of the Grand River Reserve in Ontario manufactures Seneca and other brands of cigarettes at a large sprawling plant on the reserve in Ohsweken, directly across Lake Erie and Lake Ontario from the state of New York. The tobacco products are sold at smoke shops there and also through distributors who market them across Canada, the U.S., Central America, and even Germany where that nation's armed forces have bought them for their personnel.[24]

There is a financial incentive to source a product in lower-priced markets and transport, distribute and sell it in higher-priced markets. The appeal is undeniable. According to Alvise Giustiniani, vice president for illicit-trade strategy and prevention at Philip Morris International Inc., "The economics are tremendous. It's big money that's attracting organized crime and, in some places, terrorism." There's also far less risk of a lengthy prison term than with narcotics trafficking.[25]

According to the Center for the Analysis of Terrorism, nearly 15 worldwide terrorist organizations, including Hezbollah, regularly use smuggling and counterfeiting cigarettes as a funding mechanism.[26]

Criminals are also attracted to the illicit tobacco trade because the very volume masks individual criminal activity. As the premise of this book makes clear, the chances of a criminal being investigated, prosecuted and convicted are remote. Penalties are light. The enormous profits are easily laundered. From the criminal's perspective, involvement in the illicit cigarette trade is low risk and high reward.

Yet despite the threat to our country, the Bureau of Alcohol, Tobacco and Firearms' (ATF) own studies show that from 2010 to 2017, the number of its tobacco investigations has dropped from around 100 investigations to roughly 10 investigations a year![27]

Financial seizures relating to tobacco trafficking have likewise plummeted from around $50 million a year to less than $5 million. Not surprisingly, during this same time, the illegal smuggling of cigarettes has increased.

Case Examples
The following are a few case examples that demonstrate the wide variety of abuse in international illicit tobacco:

Pakistan's Federally Administered Tribal Areas
Much of the trafficking in illicit tobacco occurs in areas of the world where terrorist groups operate. South Asia, the Middle East, and parts of Africa and Latin America all have demonstrated links between the proceeds of illicit tobacco and terrorist groups. Terrorist organizations such as the Pakistani Taliban, Lashkar-E-Taiba, Al-Qaida au Maghreb Islamique, Hezbollah, Hamas, the Revolutionary

Armed Forces of Colombia, the Kurdistan Workers' Party, Euskadi Ta Askatasuna, and the Irish Republican Army have all been reported to be involved with the smuggling and sale of contraband tobacco.

For example, in Pakistan most contraband cigarettes are produced in factories side-by-side with registered production facilities, or by small sites entirely dedicated to the black market. These small production facilities are generally family workshops. The production and trade of contraband cigarettes has developed into a large somewhat clandestine parallel economic system that nurtures armed criminal groups, terrorist organizations, and systemic large-scale corruption. A kind of "nicotine-state" has developed within the state. In Pakistan's Federally Administered Tribal Aras (FATA), one of the world's most entrenched breeding grounds for terrorists and organized criminal groups, it is estimated that nearly 20 percent of the revenue for terrorist groups comes from cigarette smuggling.[28]

Syria

The trafficking in tobacco is a source of revenue for various factions involved in the long running Syrian Civil War — including remnants of the Islamic State. Smuggling groups that used to traffic in weapons and oil increasingly turn to tobacco products. Unlike al-Qaeda, which relied heavily on outside donors for revenue, the Islamic State generated much of its income locally through taxes, extortion, tolls, fees, and ongoing criminal enterprises. The tobacco trade is part of the revenue stream.

Cigarettes offer a business opportunity for those ready to take the risk; desperate refugees try to fund their escape from war-torn cities via the trade in tobacco and so do large smuggling rings that seek high returns on investments or as to use as a commodity in barter transactions. Local brands of cigarettes that once sold for the equivalent of 50 cents a pack now sell for the equivalent of about $2.00 or about what most Syrians live on per day. Loose and flavored tobacco for water pipes — very popular in Syria and the Middle East — is even more in demand and more profitable.[29]

Hezbollah in Latin America

Hezbollah is a U.S.-designated terrorist organization. Hezbollah and its supporters have a growing presence in Latin America. The organization exerts influence and exploits structural weaknesses, corruption, and weak law enforcement in Latin America in places such as Argentina, Brazil, Venezuela, and the Tri-Border Area (TBA) of Argentina, Brazil, and Paraguay. Hezbollah is especially attracted to areas where there are sizable Shi'a Lebanese expatriate communities.

The growing Hezbollah influence in these areas overlaps with the presence of Hezbollah-affiliated companies in the tobacco retail business and the illegal production, sale, smuggling, and laundering the proceeds of illicit tobacco products. Hezbollah partners with local criminal syndicates. For example, drug smuggling and cigarette smuggling routes overlap along the Paraguay-Brazil border. The smuggling businesses are indistinguishable and attract many of the same criminal actors.

Paraguay is considered the principal source of illicit cigarette trade in the Western Hemisphere. With only seven million inhabitants, Paraguay produces over 60 billion cigarettes every year, 90 percent of which are sold on the black market and result in untaxed revenues of $1 billion.[30] Most of its annual production is illegally exported, with only 3 percent being consumed domestically. There are some estimates that Paraguay accounts for approximately 10 percent of the world's illegal cigarette trade. Israel's Ministry of Health reported in 2016 that "illicit trade of tobacco constitutes an important source of funding for Hezbollah."[31]

Operation Black Poseidon

Operation Black Poseidon was a 2013 pan-European enforcement action organized by Interpol with the cooperation of 11 national police forces. The operation targeted counterfeiting, smuggling and the illicit tobacco trade in Eastern Europe. The operation led to the discovery of a complete covert cigarette production factory in Ukraine. The facility was hidden in an underground complex. The manufacturing capacity of the production line is estimated to be between 100,000 to 125,000 individual packs of cigarettes per day. Seizures included machinery used for manufacturing, 30 tons of cut tobacco, 350,000 of ready-to-sell individual cigarettes packs, 1.5 million counterfeit excise stamps, and vehicles.[32]

In addition to illicit tobacco, Operation Black Poseidon was responsible for the seizure of alcohol, electronics, perfumes, cosmetics, and other counterfeit goods. The operation demonstrates the overlap between illicit tobacco and organized criminal smuggling networks. The operation focused on eastern and central Europe. In addition to internal consumption, the area is a major transit zone for counterfeit goods, with illegal products usually making their way to more expensive markets such as the UK, France and Germany.

Jing Ling

Over the last dozen years or more, a network of factories and smuggling routes has been put together across Europe to facilitate the trade of the Jing Ling brand of cigarettes — an illicit white primarily manufactured by the Baltic Tobacco Factory in Kaliningrad, Russia. There are also Jing Ling factories in Ukraine and Moldova. Kaliningrad, a city in the administrative center of a Russian exclave between Poland and Lithuania on the Baltic Sea, went into rapid decline after the fall of the Soviet Union, but has since profited enormously from its close proximity and excellent transport to the European Union. Kaliningrad also has a reputation as a haven for organized crime, corruption, smugglers, money launderers, and for a police force that accommodates smugglers' interests. European law enforcement officials say that Jing Ling is now the top smuggled brand of cigarettes seized in the European Union.

In 2008, the Jing Ling factory manager in Kaliningrad boasted that they could make an entire container of 10 million cigarettes or "sticks" in 8 hours, and that their production lines operated 24 hours a day, 7 days a week. Transport and distribution could also be arranged.[33] For example, at border crossings between Russia and the EU nations of Poland, Latvia, and Lithuania, cigarettes are commonly not only smuggled through in full container loads, they are also broken down by their smuggling bosses into small quantities of personal smugglers.

The profits are enormous. Each box that costs a bit more than $100 at the Kaliningrad factory is worth at least 10 times more if smuggled successfully to Western black markets. The Russian-run factory network claims to be able to produce more than 24 billion cigarettes annually which is the equivalent to 7 percent of legal EU cigarette imports.

Originally an obscure brand exported from China to Russia, Jing Ling features a packet design that closely resembles the legal Camel brand in color, typestyle, and layout. However, instead of a camel, the packs are illustrated by a mountain goat.

Jing Ling cigarettes have no legal market in any European country. The brand is not advertised. The unlicensed cigarettes are bought and sold on the untaxed black market. For example, the cheap whites can be found under-the-counter in small private retail shops, in road side stalls, and sold by street vendors commonly hawking their wares near underground stations. [34]

Tests conducted by the Center for Public Integrity on tobacco leaf used in production of Jing Ling cigarettes by the Baltic Tobacco Factory in Kaliningrad found "[heavy] metals such as cadmium, pesticides, arsenic, rat poison and human feces."[35]

Smuggling Cigarettes via Miami

An Immigration and Customs Enforcement (ICE) investigation uncovered an international criminal organization smuggling cigarettes out of the Port of Miami. The organization operated out of Spain, the United Kingdom, Ireland and Florida. The primary suspect in Miami operated the Miami portion of the operation and arranged for the purchase of hundreds of cases of cigarettes from Panama and the transportation of those cigarettes into the Port of Miami. The criminal group then arranged for the purchase of other cargo, such as wood flooring and building insulation material for use as cover loads to conceal and smuggle the cigarettes. False bills of lading were prepared that only declared the cover load material and were subsequently presented to the shipping companies and overseas customs services. No duties or taxes were paid on the cigarettes. Follow-up investigations linked the organization to multi-shipments of millions of cigarettes shipped to Europe.[36]

Countermeasures

In 1972, the Treasury Department established Alcohol, Tobacco and Firearms (ATF) as a separate bureau. In addition to expertise in specialized investigations, it offered an effective revenue arm for the government giving a 35-to-1 return on every dollar it spent.[37] In 2003, the Homeland Security bill transferred ATF to the Department of Justice (DOJ), and changed the name of the agency to the Bureau of Alcohol, Tobacco, Firearms and Explosives.

The name change reflects new and skewed priorities from its legacy missions. For example, tobacco is included in the very name of ATF, but in its last published Strategic Plan, tobacco is not even included in the table of contents. Perhaps this explains why there are only four ATF Special Agents out of a total workforce of 2,600 devoted to the illicit tobacco product mission — and this at a time when other government agencies are warning of the increased global threat. [38]

As a former Treasury agent, I witnessed how legacy ATF suffered when the Bureau's mission was passed around until reluctantly placed under the DOJ. The FBI pushed back. They wanted ATF's jurisdiction but frankly did not want the ATF agents. Troublesome issues were compounded by lack of funding and questionable management. For example, ATF's "Fast and Furious" gun running scandal and subsequent stonewalling within DOJ are symptomatic of larger concerns that are only now coming to light.

I believe Congress should devote dedicated resources to help the ATF once again focus on one of its core missions — illicit tobacco products and its links to fraud, tax evasion, money laundering and terror financing. While Congress is at it, perhaps they should give thought to returning ATF to Treasury where its crime-fighting expertise and production of revenue will be appreciated.

Internationally the proliferation of illicit tobacco has many causes. Countermeasures vary greatly. One primary shortcoming was identified in a 2012 FATF study on the illicit tobacco trade. Participating member countries were polled regarding the number of tobacco- related crimes. According to the study, it is "clear that authorities are convicting perpetrators of ITT [illicit trade in tobacco] on varying offences but that money laundering is seldom included in the charge sheet."[39] Once again, we see that one of the world's most widespread criminal activities is not effectively tied to money laundering even though, as we highlighted in Chapters 1 and 2, money is the motivation behind the criminality.

Another widespread failure overseas in successfully combatting illicit tobacco and following the dirty money trail is the almost uniform lack of customs investigative authority. I have personally observed this shortcoming numerous times in my overseas investigations, training, and mentoring.

In the U.S., a Customs (now ICE) criminal investigator or Special Agent carries a badge, gun, and has investigative and arrest authority. This rarely happens overseas. Most foreign customs authorities have the mission of inspection, control, and assessing taxes, duties, fees and tariffs. They do not have training, expertise, and the authority to conduct investigations — for example, following the dirty money trails resulting from the seizure of illicit tobacco seized at the border. Although procedures vary from country to country, generally speaking if a customs service feels a particular situation merits investigation, they turn the matter over to the national police force. However, the police force often does not have any familiarization with cross-border issues or for that matter expertise in financial crimes enforcement. They are not trained to ask what I consider the most important question in these types of investigations, "What about the money?" As a result, a courier might be detained and perhaps arrested for smuggling tobacco at the border. Customs and the police both get credit and "stats." But that is generally the end of the matter. The criminal organization remains intact and the financial trails that might lead to the hierarchy and assets of the organization are not followed. I believe countries should provide adequate resources and staff for customs, law enforcement, and magistrate/prosecutorial teams that have a clear mission to investigate illicit tobacco networks including following the money trails. The teams should have the mandate of filing money laundering charges and the seizure and forfeiture of criminal assets.

There are other countermeasures involved with combatting illicit tobacco which are well beyond the scope of this chapter. Some of the issues will be addressed later in the book. Here is a partial list:

- Capacity building, particularly for law enforcement, prosecutors, and customs officers

- Public awareness and educational campaigns regarding the detrimental impact of illicit tobacco on multi-levels of society

- Improving the quality of data concerning illicit tobacco and investing in robust analytic tools

- Improving best practices, supply chain management, and tracking and tracing for licit tobacco products

- Examining punishments associated with the illicit tobacco trade

- Cooperation and intelligence sharing between the tobacco industry and law enforcement that results in enforcement action

- Regulation of tobacco operations in Free Trade Zones (FTZs)

For far too long, organized criminal groups and terrorists have benefited from the enormous proceeds generated from the global and deadly trade in illicit tobacco. Policy makers must prioritize illicit tobacco and give law enforcement and customs services the tools, resources, and mandate to crack down.

NOTES

1 "Illicit Tobacco Trade," The FATF, June, 2012, page 8; http://www. fatf-gafi.org/media/fatf/documents/reports/Illicit%20Tobacco%20 Trade.pdf

2 "Guardia di Finanza: Operazione Scorpion Fish 2," SiciliaOggi, April 10, 2018; http://www.siciliaoggi.com/2018/04/10/guardia-di-finanza-operazione-scorpion-fish-2-smantellata-organizzazione-criminale-italo-tunisina-dedita-al-favoreggiamento-dellimmigrazione-clan-destina/

3 Brittany Vonow, "Up In Smoke," The Sun, May 16, 2017; https://www. thesun.co.uk/news/3572102/illegal-cigarettes-sold-london/

4 "Illicit Trade: Converging Criminal Networks," The OECD, 2016. See Chapter 5: "A brief overview of illicit trade in to-bacco products," pages 123-171; https://www.keepeek.com/ Digital-Asset-Management/oecd/governance/charting-illicit-trade_9789264251847-en#.Wq-e22rwaM8#page12

5 "The Global Cigarette Industry," Tobacco Free Kids," https://www. tobaccofreekids.org/assets/global/pdfs/en/Global_Cigarette_ Industry_pdf.pdf

6 Ibid

7 Testimony of Marc Firestone, Senior Vice President and General Counsel, Philip Morris International, United States Commission on Security and Cooperation in Europe, July 19, 2017; https:// www.csce.gov/sites/helsinkicommission.house.gov/files/ Firestone%27s%20Testimony.pdf

8 "Illicit Trade in Tobacco Products," Euromonitor International, 2018; https://www.euromonitor.com/illicit-trade-in-tobacco-products/ report

9 Professor Ernesto Savona, "Crime Proofing the Policy Options for the Revisions of the Tobacco Products Directive," 2012

10 "The Illegal Tobacco Trade," British American Tobacco; http://www.
   bat.com/theman

11 See The OECD, page 126 - 127

12 "Countering Illicit Trade in Tobacco Products," Interpol, 2014, page
   17

13 Ibid

14 Ibid

15 "Tobacco Underground: The Booming Global Trade in Smuggled
   Cigarettes," Organized Crime and Corruption Reporting
   Project; https://www.reportingproject.net/underground/
   index.php?option=com_content&view=article&id=5:cigaret
   te-smuggling-still-booming-&catid=3:stories&Itemid=1

16 Ibid

17 The FATF, page 29

18 The FATF, page 11

19 Firestone testimony

20 The FATF, page 35-37

21 The FATF, page 26

22 John Reid Blackwell, "Altria fights cigarette trafficking from Virginia
   to New York," Roanoke Times, March 22, 2015; http://www.roanoke.
   com/news/virginia/altria-fights-cigarette-trafficking-from-virginia-
   to-new-york/article_90366994-f636-5cd9-b981-bc7d4eb48c41.html

23 Ibid

24 David Voreacos and Andrew Martin, "Who Gets to Sell Cigarettes
   Without Taxes?" Bloomberg Businessweek, July 27, 2017;
   https://www.bloomberg.com/news/articles/2017-07-27/
   who-gets-to-sell-cigarettes-without-taxes

25 Ibid

26 Douglas Clark, "Legislation targets terrorist organization use of illegal tobacco trade," Homeland Preparedness News, November 8, 2019; https://homelandprepnews.com/stories/39517-legislation-targets-terrorist-organization-use-of-illegal-tobacco-trade/

27 Information provided to the author. See also, John Cassara, "It's Time for the ATF to Refocus its Mission," Federal News Network, October 26, 2017; https://federalnewsnetwork.com/commentary/2017/10/its-time-for-the-atf-to-refocus-its-mission/

28 Thomas Guénolé, "The U.S. Anti-Terrorism Strategy In Pakistan Needs To Change," The World Post, March 20, 2017; https://www.huffingtonpost.com/entry/us-anti-terrorist-strategy-in-pakistan-should-focus_us_58c054bee4b070e55af9eaa6?

29 Erika Solomon, "Syrian smugglers shun weapons and turn to cigarettes for profits," Financial Times, May 1, 2015; https://www.ft.com/content/081071ee-f975-11e4-ae65-00144feab7de

30 Isabela Fernandez, "Big Tobacco Feeds Latin American Corruption," International Policy Digest, November 12, 2017; https://intpolicydigest.org/2017/11/12/big-tobacco-feeds-latin-american-corruption/

31 Dr. Emanuele Ottolenghi, "Emerging External Influences in The Western Hemisphere," Testimony before the Senate Foreign Relations Committee, May 10, 2017; https://www.defenddemocracy.org/content/uploads/documents/51017_EO_Testimony.pdf

32 "The Global Illicit Trade in Tobacco: A Threat to National Security," U.S. State Department, 2015, page 4; https://2009-2017.state.gov/documents/organization/250513.pdf

33 "Going Undercover," International Consortium of Investigative Journalists, May 16, 2012; https://www.icij.org/investigations/tobacco-underground/going-undercover/

34 "Tobacco Underground: The Booming Trade in Smuggled Cigarettes," Organized Crime and Corruption Reporting Project; https://www.reportingproject.net/underground/index.php?option=com_content&view=article&id=3:made-to-be-smuggled&catid=3:stories&Itemid=17

35 Nick Johnston, Walter Kegö and Christina Wenngren, "Cigarette Smuggling: Poland to Sweden," Institute for Security and Development Policy, 2016; http://isdp.eu/content/uploads/2016/10/Cigarette-Smuggling-Report-2016.pdf

36 The FATF, page 42

37 "History of the ATF," Arrowsmith Web, September 14, 2014; http://www.arrowsmithweb.com/2014/09/history-of-the-atf/

38 ATF document provided to the author

39 The FATF, page 21

CHAPTER 10

The Misuse of the International Gold Trade

IN 1990, WHEN I WAS assigned to the American Embassy in Rome to head Operation Primo Passo, I worked with the Italian Guardia di Finanza to combat Italian/American Organized Crime — the mafia — by looking at the flow of suspect money going to/from the United States and Italy.

It turned out that the most complex and far-reaching case we investigated had little to do with the mafia. It began as a spin-off of the then largest money laundering investigation in history, Operation Polar Cap.[1] Operation Polar Cap came to fruition in 1989. Involving the misuse of the international gold trade, to this day it remains one of the largest international money laundering investigations in history. Over thirty years later, Polar Cap is still used as a benchmark to measure and contrast many different money laundering schemes and the success and failure of our resultant countermeasures. The lessons learned (and not learned) in Operation Polar Cap and follow-up investigations surface repeatedly. Unfortunately, many of the techniques used by the Polar Cap conspirators are still in use today.

The drug money belonged to the Medellin cartel. Called "La Amina," the laundering scheme processed nearly $1.2 billion in drug money. Operation Polar Cap — conducted jointly by the DEA, FBI, IRS, Customs, and state and local law enforcement — led to the first conviction of a foreign financial institution, Banco de Occidente/

Panama, for violating U.S. money laundering laws. Law enforcement made more than 100 arrests, and seized some $105 million in assets, including currency, bank accounts, real estate, jewelry, gold, and vehicles.

La Mina involved the buying and selling of gold, both real and fictitious. The multi-agency investigation uncovered multiple laundering schemes. The earliest phase of the criminal operation involved the delivery of bulk drug money to collaborating gold dealers in Los Angeles, Houston, and New York. The principal suspect jewelry retailer in Los Angeles was called Ropex.

A network of primarily immigrant Armenians in the Los Angeles jewelry district manufactured gold chains and jewelry for wholesale distribution and retail sale. Gold is a high value item, so it was the perfect cover to mask deposits of large sums of money (placement) and to wire large sums out of the country (layering) for gold purchases (integration). The money behind the transactions was actually the bulk cash proceeds of the sales of narcotics controlled by the narcotic cartels. Gold purchasing schemes to launder the money became increasingly sophisticated. A variety of schemes were introduced, including paper purchases and sales via fictitious invoicing which replaced the purchase and sale of real physical gold. Later, I was able to track down much of the fictitious invoicing to its alleged origins in Europe and the Middle East. It was my first introduction to what I began to call "trade-based money laundering."

Drug cash was literally carried into the back door of Ropex. Even though it is highly unusual for legitimate jewelry transactions in the United States to deal in the large volume of cash like those generated by Ropex gold "sales," no bank in the Los Angeles jewelry district, save Wells Fargo, was concerned about the origin of the funds. In the still early days of the BSA and KYC, the lack of reporting was tantamount to a form of "willful blindness" by the financial institutions involved. Hundreds of millions of dollars were going through Ropex-controlled bank accounts, and the banks involved with the transactions were making enormous profits. Unfortunately, the same profit-driven scenario has repeatedly played out over the last 30 years. Although the banks did fill out the mandated BSA CTRs, they never reported the transactions as suspicious and the golden money laundering schemes went undetected for years. As a postscript, it was this very failure of banks to report suspicious transactions that led the Department of the Treasury to propose that financial institutions begin filling suspicious activity reports (SARs). SARS reporting was finally implemented in 1996. In addition, the inability to recognize anomalies in the CTR data generated by the gold sales caused Customs and IRS to explore early forms of data mining financial intelligence. They jointly developed "artificial intelligence" features to proactively identify suspect financial patterns and trends. This type of BSA analysis contributed to their joint proposal in 1989 to create Treasury's FinCEN — the world's first financial intelligence unit. I was at Customs Headquarters Anti-Money Laundering Section when the negotiations within the executive branch and Congress for the creation of FinCEN occurred. I also witnessed the earliest forms of BSA data mining via artificial intelligence taking place at Customs headquarters.

As part of the multiagency Organized Crime Drug Enforcement Task Force (OCDETF) investigative efforts in Operation Polar Cap, electronic interceptions of conversations at Ropex were authorized by the courts. The intercepted conversations and hidden cameras established very clearly that the gold transactions covered the laundering of cocaine profits from the United States to accounts controlled by the cocaine cartel in Uruguay, Panama, and Europe. In reviewing the photographs and transcripts of the suspects' conversations in Ropex, a mysterious individual was observed on multiple occasions discussing gold shipments with individuals who appeared to be close friends and business associates. Some of the recorded conversations were in Armenian and others in Arabic. The OCDETF agents could not fully identify this suspect but from taped conversations it seemed he was of Armenian origin. He was called "John" and was from the Milan area of Italy. He was treated by the other conspirators as somebody of prominence. At the conclusion of the investigation, OCDETF agents served a search on Ropex and the subsequent searches uncovered many invoices detailing gold sales between Ropex and John. These investigative leads were sent to the Customs Attaché Rome. Customs agents in Los Angeles asked the Primo Passo task force to fully identify John and determine if he played any role in the laundering of narcotics proceeds via the misuse of the international gold trade.[2]

I devoted a large part of the next two years of my professional life to unravel the mysteries surrounding John of Milan and his gold business. The money and value trails took me to the gold-manufacturing centers of Italy, multiple countries in the Middle East, and back to the United States. I met numerous people in the gold industry and recruited informants in four countries. At the end of the investigation, I was able to present a fairly comprehensive criminal syllabus and affidavit in support of seizure warrants for John's substantial U.S. financial and property holdings. The Italian Guardia di Finanza likewise identified John's Italian properties and assets. Although the Department of Justice officials were supportive of the case, and despite a wealth of excellent information put together by the Primo Passo team, at the end of the day the decision was made not to prosecute John (not his true name) or try to seek the seizure and forfeiture of John's assets. We could not conclusively prove that the assets were a direct result of the proceeds of narcotics sales.

Although the John of Milan investigation did not result in the arrest and seizure statistics that drive law enforcement management, in hindsight it was the single most worthwhile investigation that I ever conducted. We obtained much new information about how the misuse of the international gold trade can launder money or transfer staggering amounts of value around the world. I realized that gold has unique properties that make it a very attractive money laundering methodology. As I have said many times over the years, "there is nothing else like gold out there." The following are some of the primary reasons why.[3]

Gold Has Represented Wealth Since Antiquity

Since the dawn of recorded history, in diverse locales and cultures, gold has symbolized wealth and guaranteed power. Its possession has obsessed men and nations. The quest for gold has destroyed some cultures while helping others expand their influence.

Throughout history, gold has been cherished for its beauty and radiance. The oldest gold objects discovered thus far were the products of the ancient Thracian civilization, dating from 4000 BC. They were found at a burial site in Varna, Bulgaria.[4] Archaeological digs suggest that the use of gold as a measure of wealth was initiated in the Middle East, where the first-known civilizations began. Egyptian tombs from the third millennium BC have been discovered with gold jewelry. The Egyptians obtained gold via trade with the Kingdom of Kush or the Nubians of Sudan and Ethiopia, as well as from their own mines. In West Africa, people traded gold for salt from the Sahara Desert in the north. The Persian Empire, in what is now Iran, made frequent use of gold in artwork as part of the Zoroastrian religion while the Roman Empire used gold coins as currency. In fact, the acquisition of gold was the main focus of some of the Roman conquests, such as Rumania. Gold has also been important in the cultures of South Asia, China, and Central and South America. Finally, gold was one of the main reasons behind the early European exploration of the Americas. In the Inca civilization, gold was considered the blood of the sun. Gold exploration and mining were also keys to the development and settlement of the American West.

Gold is a Readily Acceptable Medium of Exchange

Early in my career, while working for the U.S. intelligence community, I began training for a covert overseas assignment. I was to be clandestinely inserted into one of the most remote areas of Africa to link up with a liberation group fighting a Soviet proxy government. In case I ran into trouble and would have to make my way to a non-hostile area, I was outfitted with boots that had gold coins secreted in the insoles. The assignment never materialized, but the reason for this anecdote is that it is an excellent illustration that gold is recognized as a de factor bearer instrument anywhere in the world. In that sense, it is better than the paper dollar. Gold is an internationally recognized form of currency — even in far-flung and isolated lands.

Gold Offers Stability in Times of Uncertainty

I traveled to Kuwait shortly after Saddam Hussein's Iraqi army was forcibly expelled by coalition forces. At the time, there were many stories of Kuwaiti citizens that had fled their country during the invasion and occupation. Prior to leaving, they had desperately tried to exchange their dinars and dollars for gold. These actions had many historical precedents. In times of economic or political un-certainty, gold generally increases in value as people seek out the comparative stability it offers. Today, in certain parts of the world, individuals continue to stockpile gold holdings in case they find it necessary to flee. Indeed, gold is a much better insurance policy, bribe factor, and source of transportable wealth than currency. In many areas of the world, gold is a hedge against unexpected cur-rency depreciation. Fleeing wars, natural disasters or civil unrest, people can carry much more value on their person than they could even via large-denomination currency. Gold is accepted at almost any destination — the same might not be true of some national cur-rencies. Credit cards don't work when banks fail. Gold always main-tains value. When economic news is bad and/or the stock market tumbles, gold sales generally spike. The price of gold reached highs during the Chinese Coronavirus pandemic. It is not a coincidence.

Weight and Quality Can be Assured

Gold is mined in every continent but Antarctica. China, Russia, South Africa, the United States, Canada, Australia, Ghana and Peru are some of the top-producing countries. China is the top producer with more than 355 metric tons of gold per year.[5] Gold is generally manufactured into bars and other desired forms in gold centers, including Switzerland, London, and Dubai. There are strict international standards and safeguards regarding the purity, sizing, and quality of this manufactured gold.

Solid gold bars must be 99.99 percent pure. These bars are sometimes referred to as "four-nine" gold. Depending on the market, the so-called "good delivery bars" are formed into 35.27-ounce kilo bars, about the size of a small brick; the bars are particularly popular in Western countries and the Middle East. In South Asia, 10-tola bars (an Indian unit of weight) are popular; these 3.75-ounce pieces are approximately the size of a candy bar. Wafer-thin "tael bars" are primarily found in the Far East and are manufactured in various shapes and sizes (the tael is an ancient Chinese weight approximately equal to 1.2 ounces).

Gold Offers Certainty

The price of gold is set in international trading markets, and as with most commodities, it fluctuates daily. Yet if gold is selling for $1,880 per ounce in New York, it will sell for the same price in London, Zurich, Tokyo, Dubai, or Johannesburg. The daily price can easily be determined, whether one is consulting financial markets, the Internet, a major newspaper, or visiting an Arabian gold souk (market).

Although the price of gold varies over time, its value remains relatively constant. This is due to the fact that its supply is limited and generally fluctuates no more than a few percentage points annually; the gold in circulation continues to be recycled. Gold is a highly liquid but scarce asset. All of the gold ever mined would fit into a crate of 21 meters cubed.[6] Thus, it is the value of the dollar that changes which in turn affects the price of gold. Money launderers — like businessmen and investors — are attracted to the relative constancy that gold offers.

Gold Offers Easy Anonymity

When investigating traditional money laundering, authorities try to "follow the money" via a paper trail. There are various tell-tale signs. For example, financial intelligence can be generated from bank records; identifiers like serial numbers and the issuing bank are found on currency; and electronic codes and "travel rules" are associated with wire transfers. Cyber currencies can be traced via blockchain technology.

Gold, the commodity, lacks such identifying records. Gold coins, and even gold bars, may have serial or manufacturing numbers or other telltale signs which are easily removed. Chemical analysis is generally unable to conclusively trace its origin. Although trade data is generally available (see Chapter 6), matters are complicated because gold's form is readily altered. In other words, there are very few effective ways to follow a disguised or laundered "golden trail."

Gold Is Generally Immune to Asset Freezes

Given the proliferation of asset freezing and seizing efforts, criminal and terrorist organizations are often reluctant to deposit liquid assets in financial institutions. Many have realized that it is much more secure to simply hoard assets such as gold outside the formal financial system. For example, in 2007, as part of one of the largest money laundering seizures in history, the Colombian National Police and DEA discovered more than $80 million worth of cash and gold in private residences and businesses, buried in the ground, stashed in private safes, or hidden elsewhere.[7] In 2008, when the European Union threatened new sanctions against Iran, $75 billion worth of Iranian assets were moved from European banks, and some of these funds were reportedly converted to gold.[8] And in a 2009 law enforcement operation targeting a marijuana distribution ring that brought large quantities of the drug from Canada to Saratoga County, New York, authorities found 172 gold bars, 161 gold coins, and a 100-ounce silver bar in one of the conspirator's homes. The items were purchased with money from the drug trade.[9] Sanctions drive both the Iranian and Venezuelan governments' activity in the licit and illicit gold trades.

Worldwide Cultural Demand

Gold has an important cultural role to play in much of the world. For example, throughout their histories, India, China, the Middle East, and Latin America have all treasured gold. It continues to be in high demand whether as jewelry, savings, a type of bearer instrument, a hedge against unexpected currency devaluations, an escape from the tax collector, a means of transporting wealth, or as part of religious/cultural ceremonies such as weddings.

China has surpassed India as the largest consumer of gold. China consumes roughly 984 metric tons of gold per year and India 849 metric tons. The United States uses around 193 metric tons of gold per year. The demand is a mix of industrial, investment, and jewelry use.[10] Historically, Saudis are one of the world's largest spenders on gold per capita. For example, it is not unusual at Saudi weddings for the bride to be draped with kilos of gold jewelry.

The Form of Gold Can be Easily Altered

Gold's unique characteristics allow its form to be altered. For example, brokers and traders can change gold bars into various forms of jewelry. Moreover, it is not uncommon for gold to be melted or smelted and poured into special molds. In Operation Meltdown[11] in New York City and environs, the proceeds of narcotic sales were used to purchase gold. The gold was then melted or smelted and disguised as machine parts, tools, nuts, and bolts, belt buckles, and other items. Once cast, these fake golden parts require only a coat of black spray paint and grease, making them much easier to smuggle across borders. Similarly, the Jordanian Customs Bureau told me that there have been instances of gold being smuggled in the form of license plates. The smugglers melted the gold, put it in a license plate mold, painted it to resemble a commonly issued vehicular plate, and simply drove it across the border.[12] Although there are some small expenses associated with the schemes, the alteration of the gold is an acceptable cost of doing business for the illicit actors.

Gold also has a myriad of industrial uses that facilitate changing the form of gold and give paper justification for illicit transfers. For example, there are often strict controls on gold exports, particularly in countries that mine their own gold. But in some TBML schemes, the conspirators switch from four-nine gold to gold "scrap" which bypasses controls. While scrap gold theoretically lessens the value of the shipment, the new classification works in the favor of those that want to disguise illegally mined artisan gold. Furthermore, there have been many occasions where gold scrap is actually in-voiced at prices higher than gold bullion![13] Gold scrap is readily susceptible to TBML schemes.

Gold Transactions Can be Easily Layered

As described in Chapter 3, layering is simply a method of disguis-ing a money trail via a series of transactions. In traditional money laundering using financial institutions, this is often accomplished by the use of multiple wire transfers from one location or jurisdiction to another. This tactic can be used with gold as well. For example, criminal organizations involved directly or indirectly in the gold business often have "gold accounts" in banks or trading houses, as well as silver accounts, dollar accounts, and local currency ac-counts. To muddy the trail, they can shift value from one account or institution to another and from one jurisdiction to another. They can even combine this practice with the previous tactic of altering gold's physical form. This type of activity makes it very difficult for criminal investigators to follow the value trail.

Gold is Susceptible to Fraudulent Schemes

Chapter 6 discussed trade fraud and gave examples of fictitious invoicing and related schemes. Although most commodities can be used in such schemes, gold is particularly attractive to trade-based money launderers. Because its high value can be condensed into a comparatively small size, gold can be used to launder or transfer larger amounts of value in a single transaction. Since money launderers generally want the largest return for their efforts, gold's unique properties make it the commodity of choice in various fraudulent schemes.

Gold is Easily Smuggled

Gold smuggling in various forms has been chronicled around the world. Because of its unique characteristics, it can be altered in form to fit a smuggler's needs. As described previously, it can be melted or smelted into various shapes and sizes, disguised, and smuggled across borders. It can also be concealed on a person, within baggage, or hidden in a shipping container. There are special gold smuggling vests outfitted for smugglers that allow them to transport hundreds of thousands of dollars of gold on their person — much more value than actual paper currency. Some gold bars are even manufactured with special rounded corners and edges so as not to rip courier bags (or sensitive body cavities).

In certain areas of the world, illegal gold mines are also a major problem. For example, in Latin America the last decade has seen a tremendous boom in illegal gold mining that in some cases has eclipsed the cocaine trade as the leading source of criminal income (see below on Venezuela for additional examples). Guerilla groups such as the Urabeños and the Revolutionary Armed Forces of Colombia (FARC) have set up their own mining operations or charge miners "fees" to operate in territory they control. The gold is then smuggled out of the country or combined with licit production. Similar schemes involving gold, illegal mining, smuggling, and money laundering have taken place in Mexico and Peru.

Gold smuggling has been curbed in some regions. However, pilfering and smuggling from mines is still a concern in South Africa, Ghana, and other locations. Although the gold trade in the Indian sub-continent was liberalized in the mid-1990s, Dubai still maintains a shadowy reputation as an international gold smuggling center. In fact, the waterway winding through the port of Dubai has been dubbed "Smugglers Creek" because of its multitude of rarely inspected dhows that ply the Arabian Sea, Indian Ocean, and waters of eastern Africa.

In the United States, customs authorities have investigated cases in which drug proceeds are used to purchase gold from American vendors. The gold is then smuggled across the border into Mexico in the same manner as illicit bulk cash.

In most jurisdictions, gold is exempt from traditional cross-border currency reporting requirements. Vietnam, Italy, Saudi Arabia, Jordan, Taiwan, and Ukraine are among the few countries that mandate the declaration of gold as a form of currency. For example, travelers entering or leaving Vietnam must fill out a cross-border currency declaration form if they are transporting the equivalent of more than approximately $5,000 or more than 300 grams of gold.[14] A customs official opined that almost every woman crossing a customs terminal, anywhere in the world, is carrying gold jewelry. He said, "Monitoring this flow of funding can be implemented only through amendments to laws and regulations, including forcing customs declarations for personal precious jewelry. Even then, only a minor portion will be reported."[15]

Gold is Used in Underground Financial Systems

As per the discussions in Chapter 7 on hawala and Chapter 11 on "flying money," gold has long been one of the principal means for brokers dealing in underground finance to balance their books. In fact, a 1998 study by the British Commonwealth Secretariat on the misuse of hawala found that "gold smuggling linked to invoice manipulation plays an important role in the settling of accounts between hawaladars."[16] At the time, the Secretariat concluded that if gold (and silver) smuggling were somehow curtailed, 80 to 90 percent of hawala transactions would cease. Although underground financial systems are increasingly diversified today, TBML and value transfer based on the misuse of the international gold trade are still essential.

According to the U.S. Department of State's 2015 INCSR report, in Taiwan, "Jewelry stores are increasingly being used as a type of underground remittance system. Jewelers convert illicit proceeds into precious metals, stones, and foreign currency, and generally move them using cross-border couriers. The tradition of secrecy in the precious metals and stones trade makes it difficult for law enforcement to detect and deter money laundering in this sector."[17]

Suspicious Supply Chains

The legitimate worldwide gold trade is enormous. From exploration, mining, refining, trading, and final distribution into financial products, jewelry, and industry, the gold industry has steadily grown. According to the World Gold Council, global gold commerce has become larger, stronger and more widely understood.[18] The legitimate trade is professional and the gold supply chain ever more transparent.

However, an invisible, underground and criminally infested supply chain also exists. "An invisible supply chain is a system by which a commodity that is not intrinsically illicit, and for which legitimate markets operate, is criminally sourced or diverted and moved separately from the legitimate supply chain toward illicit sale. An invisible supply chain may extend all the way from extraction or production to the end consumer or for a shorter distance between those points, and it may overlap or intersect with the legitimate supply chain in one or more places. It also may involve processing of raw materials or assembly of products."[19]

It is extremely difficult to counter the criminal golden supply chain. Per money laundering techniques discussed in this book, criminals frequently procure and trade illegal gold in various forms. Sometimes they use illicit shell or front companies using false or incomplete documents. Gold is one of the preferred commodities in trade-based laundering. Gold is often smuggled or routed through multiple countries. Some of this illicit gold is ultimately sold to refineries in the United States.

AML good practices require gold and precious metals dealers to develop and adhere to AML programs. In the United States, the BSA mandates precious metals dealers to establish AML programs with certain minimum requirements under 31 U.S.C. § 5318(h) and 31 C.F.R. § 1027.210. Dealers are required to develop and implement a written AML program "reasonably designed" to prevent dealers "from being used to facilitate money laundering and the financing of terrorist activities" through the purchase and sale of precious metals.[20]

Unfortunately, oversight and ethics sometimes lapse. Greed gets in the way. For example, in 2018 Dallas-based firm, Elemetal, pled guilty to its failure to maintain an adequate AML program. Investigation revealed that some of Elemetal's gold dealers were involved with a $3.6 billion money laundering scheme. The conspiracy involved U.S. imports of illegally mined and smuggled gold from South America Elemetal's Miami subsidiary, NTR Metals. The illegal operations involved deals with drug trafficking organizations based in Peru, Ecuador, Bolivia and Colombia. The criminal supply chain uncovered in the investigation also demonstrated suspect links between South Florida's gold industry and the devastation of wide swaths of South American rainforests where illegal gold mining flourishes under the control of drug traffickers and other criminal groups.[21]

Gold has already become a more lucrative industry for Colombian cartels than drug trafficking.[22] According to research[23] by Dr. David Soud and the Payne Institute, illegal gold mining in Venezuela has also become a lifeline to the failing Maduro regime. The illegal gold trade and illicit supply chain also poses a major security risk to that troubled country's neighbors. As Venezuela collapses, gold has replaced oil as a means to prop up the nearly bankrupt government. The establishment of the Orinoco Mining Arc in 2016, which opened a huge area of southern Venezuela to unchecked exploitation, has brought instability and violence to an area historically difficult to govern. The resulting gold rush, along with Venezuela's economic, political, and social breakdowns, has given rise to a rapidly evolving criminal ecosystem involving the corrupt government and military.

At the bottom of the golden informal supply chain hierarchy are the informal miners, who undertake often dangerous work to extract the ore and perform the initial processing. They often use mercury, which results in enormous human and environmental damage. These groups are often known as sindicatos. These are local gangs that style themselves as labor unions. In addition to illegal mining, the sindicatos follow the organized crime model and use strong-arm tactics to secure contracts and extort gold from other miners. The pranatos are generally larger and more sophisticated outfits, with wider and regional geographic range. Some networks are directed by their leaders from Venezuelan prisons. In addition to the gangs, Colombian insurgent groups, particularly the Ejército de Liberación Nacional or ELN, sometimes coordinate with them but often displace them. The groups have a heavy presence in many of Venezuela's states. The ELN, which dates back to 1964, is a hardened para-military organization with a long history of drawing on drug trafficking and illegal mining as income streams. Finally, at the top of the illicit supply chain hierarchy are the Venezuelan security forces. Miners and other workers routinely pay a "vaccine," a payment in gold, to whichever groups are positioned locally to extort it. The gold, as well as any other funds the security forces are able to extort, are often used to further other criminal schemes such as trafficking in weapons, drugs, and people.

As Dr. Soud explains, the Orinoco Mining Arc has grown from a zone of human and environmental exploitation into a catalyst of regional insecurity. The activities with the Orinoco Arc have extended the chronic lawlessness of the Colombian-Venezuelan border and broadened the base of insurgent groups via their access to rapidly increasing wealth. In addition, transnational organized criminal groups and corrupt officials are entangling Venezuela's neighbors in illicit income streams, invisible supply chains, and money laundering schemes.

There are reports that Venezuela gold is being smuggled to Russia, Turkey, the UAE, and Uganda. In some of these countries, and many more, there are also criminally controlled invisible supply chains. For example, the South African mining industry has long been concerned about "pilfered gold."[24] Many African countries are also alarmed about "conflict gold." Gold has often been a factor in many African civil wars and insurgencies. Today, gold is the primary mineral financing militias and parts of the military in eastern Congo, funding a conflict that has killed millions.

Similar to mining in South America, informal methods of gold production, known in the industry as "artisanal" or small-scale mining, are proliferating in Africa. They have provided a livelihood to millions. But some techniques involved with artisanal mining leak chemicals into the environment. African governments such as those in Ghana, Sudan, Tanzania and Zambia complain that artisan-mined gold is increasingly illegally produced and smuggled out of their countries on a vast scale. These underground supply chains and smuggling networks are sometimes orchestrated via criminal networks.

Burkina Faso is a desperately poor African country in the Sahel. One of its few marketable natural resources is gold. But the gold is literally being stolen. The government identified about 2,200 possible informal gold mines via a government survey of satellite imagery in 2018. About half of them are within 25 km (16 miles) of places where bandits and Islamic militants have carried out attacks. Most of Burkina Faso's informally produced gold is smuggled to neighboring countries, particularly Togo. This is done to avoid export taxes. The gold is then generally flown to refineries before being exported to countries including Saudi Arabia, Turkey, Switzerland and India.[25]

Not everyone in the chain is breaking the law. Some small-scale mining activities are completely legal. The miners sell gold to middlemen. However, some middlemen (many non-African) either fly the gold out directly or trade it across Africa's porous borders, obscuring its origins before couriers carry it out of the continent, often in hand luggage.

Smugglers often carry gold in their hand luggage on planes leaving Africa. Billions of dollars' worth of gold is being smuggled out of Africa every year. The primary destination is Dubai. Gold can be imported to Dubai tax-free with little documentation and oversight. According to analysis of Comtrade data, over the last decade gold from Africa has become increasingly important for Dubai. From 2006 to 2016, the share of African gold in UAE's reported gold imports increased from 18 percent to nearly 50 percent. Customs data shows that the UAE imported $15.1 billion worth of gold from Africa in 2016 - up from $1.3 billion in 2006. And those numbers represent only what is officially imported. Dubai is a gateway to further gold flows into Europe, the Middle East, North America, and South Asia.[26]

Case Examples

Suspect Colombia Gold Sales

The vast majority of Colombia's gold production originates from informal or illegal mines. There are reportedly 3,600 to 6,000 mines that operate without a permit in Colombia. Income from illegal mining is estimated to bring in approximately $2.5 billion per year to Colombia.[27] Colombian officials are well aware of the illicit supply chains and how gold exports are often used in various fraudulent schemes. In one example, an investigation by Colombian law enforcement officials focused on a gold export company. The company reportedly used fake gold sales to launder 2.3 billion pesos or approximately $1 billion at the time of the investigation. Investigators found that many of the thousands of alleged providers of gold that did business with the suspect company didn't even exist or were registered in the names of deceased individuals. Some of the companies were reportedly linked to Colombia's largest criminal group.[28] Another way of analyzing the gold problem with Colombia is to use publicly available trade data which indicates that the United States imports far more gold than Colombia legally produces.[29] Some of the gold is sent via trading companies and bought at inflated prices with drug money. It is a form of TBML.

Cash-for-Gold

In a 2015 investigation centered in Chicago, 32 people from the United States and Mexico were accused of being involved in a "cash-for-gold" conspiracy that laundered more than $100 million in U.S. drug proceeds for Mexico's Sinoloa drug cartel. Individuals used cash from narcotics sales to purchase gold scrap, gold from jewelers and other gold products from pawn shops; they sent it via express mail deliveries to a suspect gold business in South Florida for processing and laundering. Some gold was sent to other metal refineries in Florida and California. The refineries sometimes transferred payments for the gold directly to Mexico.[30]

French and Italian Connections

As noted in the opening of this chapter, I have worked closely with the Italian Guardia di Finanza (GdF) or fiscal police investigating the misuse of the international gold trade. Many years later the GdF is still investigating suspect gold networks. For example, in 2019 Gendarmerie Nationale (the French Gendarmerie) and the GdF jointly targeted suspects across both countries believed to be part of an organized crime group behind a large-scale international money laundering scheme estimated to launder approximately €6 million per month. The two- year investigation resulted in a sting operation. Couriers collected the proceeds of drug trafficking and tax evasion in different cities in France. The illicit funds were then laundered via two different schemes: 1) the hawala system (see Chapter 7), which facilitates the transfer of money without any physical transportation of cash; and 2) via gold laundering, whereby part of the cash collected by the couriers was sent to Italy to buy gold from corrupt business intermediaries. As part of an illicit supply chain, the gold was then transported back to France and Spain in order to be exported by sea to Algeria where the masterminds behind this scheme were based.[31]

Oil for Gold. Largest Money Laundering Case in History?
We began this chapter with a brief explanation of Operation Polar Cap. The investigation ended in 1989. At the time the $1.2 billion case was the largest money laundering case in history. As noted, thirty years later, Polar Cap is still used as a "benchmark" both to compare and contrast money laundering schemes over time and to measure the success and failure of our resultant countermeasures.

Thirty years after Operation Polar Cap, we have a probable "new largest money laundering case in history." It is approximately a $100 billion sanctions busting case. Like Polar Cap, this case revolves around TBML and the misuse of the international gold trade.

The scheme began in 2010 when Iran began to feel the squeeze from U.S. and international sanctions for its quest to develop nuclear weapons. Although there were variations on the theme, the main methodology itself is quite simple. The rogue Iranian regime desperately needed hard currency and access to financial markets. As a result, Iran sold oil and gas to Turkey. Sanctions barred Turkish payment for the petroleum products in dollars or euros. Iran didn't want Turkish lira. There is limited value to the lira in international markets. So, Iran bought lots of Turkish gold with the stockpiled lira. Tens of billions of dollars worth of gold as well as hard currencies were purchased and moved from Turkey to Iran through a complex network of businesses, banks, and front companies. Dubai was often the conduit.

Reza Zarrab, a dual Iranian-Turkish national and gold trader, helped Iran evade sanctions with the help of Turkish banks. He was designated by the U.S. government. Yet during the Obama administration, Iran, the United States, and some European partners negotiated and then signed the Joint Comprehensive Plan of Action (JCPOA); this plan offered Iran sanctions relief (and the release of tens of billions of frozen assets and cash) in an exchange for a promise that Iran would not develop nuclear weapons for a short period of time. Thinking that the JCPOA made his designation and arrest warrant null and void, Zarrab was arrested in 2016 when he and his family made a trip to Disneyworld.

Zarrab initially pleaded not guilty. Nevertheless, he was later flipped and became a U.S. government witness. During his testimony, he identified Turkish banker, Mehmet Hakan Atilla, as a key facilitator in the sanctions busting scheme. Zarrab also implicated former Turkish ministers and even Turkish President, Recep Tayyip Erdogan. In 2018, Atilla was found guilty in a Manhattan courtroom for a range of financial crimes.[32]

Countermeasures

Operation Polar Cap and the Iranian oil for gold case are fitting bookends to a chapter focusing on the misuse of the international gold trade and money laundering. Thirty years apart, both cases lay claim to being the "largest" money laundering case in their respective eras. So, what have we learned? The short answer from an enforcement perspective is not much.

In the early 1990s I was blessed from my unique vantage point in Rome to witness and investigate on four continents the misuse of the international gold trade and its ties to what I called (I believe for the first time) "trade-based money laundering."[33] I used that term in memos, case reports, and other correspondence within the U.S. Customs Service to differentiate money laundering via trade fraud from money laundering via financial institutions. I continued to use the term when I transferred to FinCEN in 1996. During the

90's and in the immediate aftermath of September 11, I constantly promoted the need to be watchful regarding gold and trade-based money laundering during assignments to Customs, Treasury, and the Department of State. I also presented one of the very first methodology reports to a FATF plenary. The report was on gold and trade fraud. I constantly lectured and badgered all that would listen about TBML and the misuse of gold to launder staggering amounts of money. In fact, when I walked down the halls of Customs headquarters, I was sometimes called "Mr. Gold" or "Mr. Dubai" by my colleagues because of my incessant preaching about those two clear and present money laundering dangers. Despite my best efforts (and those of others including Customs Special Agent Lou Bock), nothing was ever done.

Even worse than nothing being done, when I was at FinCEN, the defacto Director — in the presence of others — prohibited me from even talking about the subject of gold! I was forbidden from trying to help my law enforcement colleagues in their efforts to investigate gold-related money laundering cases. This was particularly disheartening because the issue of the misuse of the international gold trade repeatedly surfaced in our examination of threat finance. In all my years in the government service, I had never heard or experienced such a thing. As I said when I wrote about the gag order in Hide & Seek, "How can we fight battles, let alone win a war, when facts and ideas are censored?"[34]

If I have learned anything in the last 30 years of AML work, it is that criminals will continue to use a methodology to launder money until it is not effective anymore or it gets too expensive. Over the last 30 years, criminals have consistently used gold to launder staggering amounts of money. Our countermeasures by almost any measure have been ineffective. Yes, we have occasionally made some big cases in that time frame, but measured against the totality of the international problem, our successes have been insignificant.

However, we know what to do. Gold in all its many forms should be an automatic red flag for customs, law enforcement, intelligence agencies, and bank compliance officers — particularly when the sourcing, destination, or routing is through a problematic area. Trade data for gold in almost all its forms should be collected and analyzed. Anomalies should be identified and the results disseminated. Money laundering via the misuse of the international gold should be made a priority simply because historically gold represents one of the prime risks for laundering large amounts of money or transferring large amounts of value. Also, we know that gold manufacturers and dealers should set up AML/CFT compliance programs.

The challenge is that these common sense countermeasures are not sufficiently implemented. And in areas of the world where the illicit supply chains are active, these measures are often ignored. The situation is exacerbated because of willful blindness or corruption.

So, from my 30-year perspective, the most important countermeasure is awareness. We must continue to educate, advocate, and investigate. Unless we do, in 2050 we will continue to be challenged by the misuse of the international gold trade in international money laundering.

NOTES

1 Information on Operation Polar Cap comes from a variety of sources including the Drug Enforcement Administration, "1985–1990," in A Tradition of Excellence, (Washington, D.C., : DEA Publications), Drug Enforcement, National Institute of Justice, unknown date; https://www.ncjrs.gov/pdffiles1/Digitization/147278NCJRS.pdf; and Robert Powis, The Money Launderers, Probus Publishing, Chicago, 1992, pp. 145–190

2 For a summary of the John of Milan case and my introduction to the misuse of the international gold trade see: John Cassara, Hide & Seek: Intelligence, Law Enforcement, and the Stalled War on Terror Finance, Potomac Books, Inc. Washington, D.C., 1996, pages 57-79.

3 Much of the information taken in this section comes from three previous publications by the author: John A. Cassara, Strategic Financial Intelligence: A Primer on Middle Eastern & South Asian Value Transfer Techniques, Lockheed Martin, March 2009, pages 75 – 86. See also John Cassara, Trade-Based Money Laundering: The Next Frontier in International Money Laundering Enforcement, Wiley, Hoboken, New Jersey, 2016, pages 89 – 110; and John Cassara and Avi Jorisch, On the Trail of Terror Finance: What Law Enforcement and Intelligence Officers Need to Know, Red Cell Publishing, 2010, pages 91 – 112.

4 Veselin Toshkov, "Archaeologists dig up oldest town in Europe," National Post, November 1, 2012; http://news.nationalpost. com/2012/11/01/archaeologists-unearth-oldest-town-in-europe/

5 "Which Countries Consume and Produce the Most Gold," Provident Metals; https://www.providentmetals.com/knowledge-center/pre-cious-metals-resources/world-gold-production-consumption.html

6 The World Gold Council, Gold Facts; https://www.gold.org/ about-gold/gold-facts

7 U.S. State Department, "Introduction," in 2007 International Narcotics Control Strategy Report – Volume II: Money Laundering

and Financial Crimes; http://www.state.gov/j/inl/rls/nrcrpt/2007/
vol2/index.htm

8 "Iran Withdraws $75 Billion from Europe," Reuters, June
16, 2008; http://www.reuters.com/article/2008/06/16/
us-iran-assets-withdrawal-idUSDAH63024720080616

9 Keshia Clukey, "Loot Seized From Pot Ring Goes to Law
Enforcement," Times Union, September 9, 2014; http://www.time-
sunion.com/local/article/8-9M-to-Capital-Region-in-drug-seizure-
case-5741858.php

10 "Which Countries Consume and Produce the Most Gold," Provident
Metals; https://www.providentmetals.com/knowledge-center/pre-
cious-metals-resources/world-gold-production-consumption.html

11 "Operation Meltdown," Immigration and Customs Enforcement;
http://www.ice.gov/doclib/news/library/reports/cornerstone/cor-
nerstone1-3.pdf

12 Author conversation with Jordanian authorities in Amman, 2008

13 Author knowledge and conversations with ICE officials

14 Vietnam Online, Customs Regulations; http://www.vietnamonline.
com/visa/customs-regulations.html

15 Joseph Farah, "Financial Squeeze Pushes al-Qaeda South of the
Border," World Net Daily, March 8, 2004

16 Commonwealth Secretariat, "Money Laundering: Special Problems
of Parallel Economies," paper presented at the Joint Meeting of
Commonwealth Finance and Law Officials on Money Laundering,
London, June 1-2, 1998, p. 16

17 U.S. Department of State, Bureau of International Narcotics and
Law Enforcement Affairs, International Narcotics Control Strategy
Report (INCSR) Volume II, Money Laundering, 2015, Taiwan country
report; http://www.state.gov/j/inl/rls/nrcrpt/2015/vol2/index.htm

18 World Gold Council; https://www.gold.org/about-gold/
market-structure-and-flows

19 Dr. Ian Ralby, Dr. David Soud, and Rohini Ralby, "Defining the Invisible Supply Chain," The Atlantic Council, March 20, 2019; https://www.atlanticcouncil.org/blogs/energysource/defining-the-invisible-supply-chain/

20 Mary Treanor, "Gold and Money Laundering," Money Laundering News, April 245, 2019; https://www.moneylaunderingnews.com/2019/04/gold-and-money-laundering/

21 Jay Weaver, "U.S. company at center of gold racket must pay $15 million fine, Miami judge rules," Miami Herald, May 25, 2018; https://www.miamiherald.com/news/local/article211909529.html

22 "The Nexus of Illegal Gold Mining and Human Trafficking in Global Supply Chains," Verite, July 2016; https://www.verite.org/wp-content/uploads/2016/11/Verite-Report-Illegal_Gold_Mining-2.pdf

23 I am indebted to Dr. David Soud and the Payne Institute for outstanding research into the misuse of supply chains. This section quotes and summarizes sections of Dr. David Soud's article, "The Gold Rush in Venezuela could Destabilize Latin America and the Caribbean," The Payne Institute for Public Policy, May 2019; https://ljp6c3tnea61xd0wz1l33nmf-wpengine.netdna-ssl.com/wp-content/uploads/sites/149/2019/05/Soud-Venezuela_Comment_WDS.pdf

24 2004 author conversations with South African mining officials in Johannesburg.

25 David Lewis and Ryan McNeil, "How Jihadists Struck Gold in Africa's Sahel, Reuters, November 22, 2019; https://www.reuters.com/investigates/special-report/gold-africa-islamists/

26 The primary source for this section on illicit gold production in Africa and using Dubai as an international gateway is: David Lewis, Ryan McNeill, Zandi Shabalala, "Exclusive: Gold worth billions smuggled out of Africa," Reuters, April 24, 2019; https://www.reuters.com/article/us-gold-africa-smuggling-exclusive/exclusive-gold-worth-billions-smuggled-out-of-africa-idUSKCN1S00IT

27 "The Nexus of Illegal Gold Mining," Verite.

28 Elyssa Pachico, "Crime Ring Laundered $1 Billion in Colombia Gold Exports," Insight Crime, January 19,

2015; http://www.insightcrime.org/news-briefs/
crime-ring-laundered-a-billion-in-colombia-gold-exports

29 "The Nexus of Illegal Gold Mining," Verite

30 "Thirty Two Defendants Facing Federal or State Charges Alleging
the Laundering of over $100 Million in Narcotics proceeds Through
Cash-For-Gold Scheme," U.S. Attorney's Office Northern District of
Illinois Press Release, February 11, 2015; http://www.justice.gov/
usao/iln/pr/chicago/2015/pr0211_02.html

31 "19 Arrested in France and Italy in Multi-million Gold Laundering
Operation, " Europol Press Release, February 5, 2019; https://www.
europol.europa.eu/newsroom/news/19-arrested-in-france-and-
italy-in-multi-million-gold-laundering-operation

32 Jonathan Schanzer, "The Biggest Sanctions-Evasion Scheme
in Recent History," The Atlantic, January 4, 2018; https://
www.theatlantic.com/international/archive/2018/01/
iran-turkey-gold-sanctions-nuclear-zarrab-atilla/549665/

33 See John Cassara, Trade Based Money Laundering – The Next
Frontier in International Money Laundering Enforcement, Wiley,
Hobeken, New Jersey, 2016. See page 158 for more information
about how the term "trade-based- money laundering" came about.

34 John Cassara, Hide & Seek, page 174

CHAPTER 11
China:
The Biggest Money
Laundering Threat

IN 1989, WHEN I FIRST started my career investigating international money laundering, the focus was on Colombian narcotic traffickers. The spotlight later shifted to murderous Mexican drug cartels. As a young Customs Special Agent, I recall when a ranking Customs official impolitely but courageously called Mexico "an ongoing criminal enterprise operating as a state."

In the 1990s, I was assigned to the U.S. Embassy in Rome to help fight Italian American organized crime. The mafia was involved with a variety of criminal schemes including narcotics trafficking, extortion and strong arm tactics, fraud of all sorts, racketeering, etc. The Italian mafia was one of the first and most notorious transnational criminal organizations. With the fall of the Soviet Union, Russian-organized crime looted its country, laundered the money, and successfully stretched its criminal tentacles across the Western world. Over the last few decades, Afghanistan's warlords continue to supply the majority of the world's opium.

Today there are still powerful and deadly Colombian, Mexican, and Afghan drug cartels. The Italian and Russian mafias are strong. There are a plethora of other ethnic-based street gangs and organized criminal groups with international ties. But the global crime and the money laundering threat has changed over the decades.

By examining worldwide criminal activity in its varied forms and the illicit proceeds generated and laundered, today China is by far the largest transnational criminal actor and biggest money laundering threat.

More serious still is the ongoing debate of whether or not Chinese global criminality and unethical behavior is done purposefully to achieve China's national ambitions. Is Chinese transnational crime a form of asymmetric warfare? Is an ongoing criminal organization masquerading as a Communist state?

The Chinese government has made no secret of its ambition to surpass the West both militarily and economically by the regime's 100th anniversary in 2049 in the hope that the 21st century will be dominated by China in the same way that the 20th century was dominated by the United States. According to a popular saying in Chinese mythology, "there is only one sun in the sky."

To be sure, as scholar Evan Ellis points out, there is nothing wrong, per se, about China's aspirations for prosperity and security, as expressed by President Xi Jingping's "dream" for the rejuvenation of the great Chinese Nation or his goal for China to be a powerful developed country by the 100th anniversary of Chinese Communist rule. What is worrisome is how China achieves and maintains that wealth and power within the increasingly interdependent global environment and its effects on the security and well-being of the Western democracies.[1]

Michael Collins, the deputy assistant director of the CIA's East Asia Mission Center stated in 2018 that Beijing's tactics to achieve its ambitions fit the definition of a cold war: "I would argue by definition what they're waging against us is fundamentally a cold war . . . A country that exploits all avenues of power licit and illicit, public and private, economic and military, to undermine the standing of your rival relative to your own standing without resorting to conflict."[2]

Indeed, under President Xi the Communist party has moved in the last few years to become more forceful and controlling both internally and globally. For example, Xi's efforts to boost internal control include a continuation of the brutal crackdown on the

Uyghur ethnic group as well as an accelerated civilian surveillance program which includes the use of drones, video monitoring, and a social credit system in which individuals garner credits which help them obtain loans and jobs. Additionally, in 2018 the Communist Party of China (CCP) freed President Xi Jinping from term limits. In 2019 it attempted to exert increasing influence in Hong Kong where it tried institute an extradition law so scofflaws could be tried in mainland China.

China is also increasingly using its power and influence in the international arena. For example, Made in China 2025 and China's Belt and Road initiative have the joint goal of transforming the country into a hi-tech powerhouse that dominates complex industries like robotics, advanced information technology, aviation, and new energy vehicles while simultaneously engaging in infrastructure projects in well over 100 countries. The ability to transform and, indeed, dominate business sectors while concurrently garnering political influence through overseas investment could be the platform on which China's economic dominance is built.

Over the past few decades, to further their influence globally, China has pursued unfair trade practices, intellectual property theft, predatory investment, and other key national economic security imperatives. However, China has pursued one area of economic influence that has received significantly less attention by the West — but is no less important. It's the threat it poses to the international financial system and the licit economy.

There are a number of endemic contributing factors to Chinese financial malfeasance and criminality including corruption, weak rule of law, lack of effective financial oversight and enforcement, weak regulatory controls, entrenched underground financial systems, and government policies that work to facilitate profit, growth, exploitation, and cheating at the expense of international standards and norms. While each of these issue areas may fall in the purview of traditional law enforcement or trade regulation, viewed together they undermine much of the world's efforts over the last twenty years to combat corruption, illicit finance, and money laundering.

Moreover, the illicit finance threats emanating from China pose serious risks to the integrity of the global financial system which is the bedrock of much of the West's economic and political power. This is a risk that is too big to ignore. With China's assumption of the presidency of the FATF in July 2019, its inability or unwillingness to address these risks has been thrown into even sharper focus and causes one to wonder whether Clausewitz's famous dictum should be updated for the 21st Century as "transnational crime is the continuation of war by other means."

This chapter highlights many of the risks China poses to the legitimate world economy and explores ways China is the primary actor in international money laundering and is complicit in illicit financial flows. Available metrics show China has the dubious distinction as being the largest player in almost every major sector of transnational crime. Collectively, the criminal categories outlined below annually generate trillions of dollars of illicit funds that are laundered into the licit economy. In 2019 the State Department included China on its list of "primary countries of concern" for money laundering. [3]

Over the last twenty years criminal activity has seemingly become part of China's strategy to grow its economic and military power. China uses a combination of statecraft, military buildup, espionage, theft, cheating, trade, loans, debt traps, payoffs, investment and other forms of exchanges and engagement to structure a 21st century world order "with Chinese characteristics" in which global trading networks, political relationships, and international institutions support China's expanding wealth and power. "China Inc.", a term[4] that refers to behemoth market-oriented, state-owned enterprises with global commercial reach, also plays a key role in Chinese influence and control.

Chinese growth has relied upon the twin pillars of cheap labor and technology theft from the West. From software to steel, from pharmaceuticals to powerplants, the Chinese are dependent upon both industrial and state espionage. In America and much of the West, this has led directly and indirectly to stagnant wages, a shrinking middle class, loss of manufacturing jobs, dependency on Chinese supply chains and production of vital goods and equipment, and hollowed-out towns and decaying cities. It threatens our national security.

There is no doubt that some activity such as forms of weapons proliferation, identity theft, and intellectual property rights violations are directed by the Government of China. In fact, China's National Intelligence Law from 2017 requires organizations and citizens to "support, assist and cooperate with the state intelligence work." Other suspect activity occurs due to independent actors, lack of capacity by law enforcement and customs, corruption, lack of political will and/or willful blindness. But by identifying the enormous illicit proceeds generated and laundered, the unmistakable picture that develops is that there is a worrisome convergence between the Chinese government/CCP, China Inc. and Chinese-organized crime that directly impacts the United States and order in the world economy.

China's Role in Transnational Crime

There are many components of transnational organized crime (TOC). The adverse effects cross national borders and pose a significant and growing threat to national and international security, with dire implications for public safety, public health, democratic institutions, and economic stability across the globe. Not only are TOC networks expanding, but they also are diversifying their activities. Once mostly distinct, there is a convergence of threats that are increasingly intermingled.

One method of examining TOC is by studying the type and amounts of illicit proceeds generated. As we discussed earlier in this book, criminals, criminal and terrorist organizations, and sometimes even businesses, corporations, and even nation states launder the proceeds of crime. Illicit proceeds originate from various predicate offenses or specified unlawful activities. In 2016 the Organization of Economic Development (OECD) released a report[5] on illicit trade and converging international markets. The report provided an overview of seven sectors or predicate offenses of illicit trade. In 2017, Global Financial Integrity published Transnational Crime and the Developing World [6] in which they examined 11 sectors of transnational crime. In both reports, China is the common denominator. It is the only country that is involved with all major sectors of transnational crime. Chinese illicit proceeds dwarf all others.

The following is a list of transnational crimes and predicate offenses for money laundering where China is a significant actor. It is followed by a section briefly describing Chinese-centric illicit funds methodologies and enablers. Although the numbers are not precise and, in some cases simply do not exist, the bottom line is that a strong argument can be made that China is responsible for introducing and laundering approximately $1.5 to $2 trillion of illicit proceeds into the world's licit economy every year. Another way of looking at the magnitude of the problem is that about one-half of the total amount of money laundered worldwide is of Chinese origin.[7]

Narcotics

According to the China National Narcotics Control Commission, China's economic prosperity has turned recreational drug use into more than an $80 billion of annual domestic business with at least 14 million drug users.[8] The situation is undoubtedly much worse because China is notorious for skewing data and analysis for public consumption. The Government of China does not, as a matter of government policy, encourage illicit drug production or distribution, nor is it involved in laundering the proceeds of the sale of illicit drugs.[9] In fact, in recent years, China has initiated an aggressive campaign of cracking down on narcotics trafficking. Yet there is no doubt that China faces growing and significant domestic illicit drug consumption challenges. Likewise, Chinese-manufactured synthetic drugs are increasingly a source of concern for the Chinese government.

China shares borders with drug-source countries in both Southeast and Southwest Asia and remains a major destination and transit country for heroin produced in these areas. Its numerous coastal cities with high-volume seaports and its vast network of major international airports make China an ideal destination and transit country for illicit drugs, as well as a major source of synthetic drugs, new psychoactive substances (NPS), and precursor chemicals used to produce illicit drugs. Domestic Chinese criminal organizations traffic illicit drugs within China. Additionally, in recent years Chinese authorities have noted the presence of international drug trafficking organizations originating from Africa and Mexico operating within the country.

In addition to domestic drug trafficking, Chinese-organized crime groups increasingly traffic in international markets. China is a major source of NPS and other synthetic drugs, including fentanyl and methamphetamine; China's large chemical and pharmaceutical industries and boutique suppliers provide an ideal environment for the illicit production and export of these drugs. Some are sent directly to the United States via various transport means such as shipping containers, international mail and parcel packages. Other shipments are routed through Mexico and Canada. Fentanyl shipped directly from China is typically seized in smaller quantities but with purities commonly testing above 90 percent.[10] According to Customs and Border Protection data, nearly all fentanyl seized in the United States from international mail and express consignment operations originated in China.[11]

A 2018 report by the Senate Permanent Subcommittee on Investigations found that Chinese websites selling fentanyl and carfentanil rapidly and efficiently respond to online orders for the drugs, and that they are confident in their ability to get drugs into the United States.[12] Data from the Centers for Disease Control reported 72,000 Americans died from drug overdoses in 2017 with approximately 30,000 of these deaths due to fentanyl or its synthetic analogues. Chinese drug sales are responsible for much of the carnage.[13] In 2018, ICE seized enough fentanyl to kill every American citizen twice over.[14]

While the Government of China has promised to crack down on the production of fentanyl and some of its subtypes, or analogues, boutique dealers often tweak the formulas of their drugs to stay ahead of bans or disregard them entirely. They continue to advertise their product online.

Sometimes crypto-currencies such as Bitcoins are used for payment. Investigators found Chinese online merchants in some cases were also willing to accept Western Union, PayPal and even credit cards for their product.[15] China Inc. also has developed its own robust new payment methods that are web and mobile-based. These techniques are also used for the purchase of illicit substances.

According to the DEA, Chinese TOC in the United States plays a key role in both distribution and the laundering of proceeds. They generally transfer funds to and from China and Hong Kong. Chinese-operated cash intensive businesses in the United States are often involved as fronts. Chinese underground banking systems (see below) are also active in the United States and most places where there is a large Chinese presence. Chinese TCOs increasingly contract their services and in some cases work jointly with other Mexican and Latin American criminal groups.[16]

What differentiates China from the U.S. and other large western illegal drug consumer nations is China's direct and indirect involvement in facilitating international narcotics trafficking and laundering the proceeds.[17]

Counterfeit Goods and Intellectual Property Rights Violations

The scourge of international narcotics trafficking is dwarfed by the monetary value of counterfeiting and intellectual property rights violations — also predicate offenses for money laundering. According to a 2019 estimate by the European Union's Intellectual

Property Office and the OECD, global sales of counterfeit and pirated goods have soared to $522 billion a year, amounting to an enormous 3.3 percent of world trade.[18] According to the U.S. Chamber of Commerce, Greater China is the source of 86 percent of the world's counterfeit goods.[19] This includes everything from knock-off Gucci bags, Rolex watches, Marlboro cigarettes, pirated Disney movies, and Nike shoes.

According to a 2019 update to the U.S. IP Commission Report, "the annual cost to the U.S. economy continues to exceed $225 billion in counterfeit goods, pirated software; theft of trade secrets and could be as high as $600 billion."[20]

Furthermore, the non-partisan and independent Commission on the Theft of Intellectual Property states that "IP [intellectual property] theft by thousands of Chinese actors continues to be rampant," and China "remains the world's principal IP infringer."[21] Responding to reports about Chinese intellectual property theft, FBI Director Christopher Wray called China "the broadest, most significant" threat to the nation and said its espionage is active in all 50 states.[22]

The sale of counterfeit goods is not a victimless crime. Law enforcement knows that trafficking in counterfeit consumer goods are high profit and invite the involvement of organized crime and even terrorist financiers. Trafficking in counterfeit goods is ubiquitous; our criminal adversaries always weigh risk versus reward. The penalties for trafficking in counterfeit goods are much less than those for narcotics, but the profits can be just as lucrative. Because victims are often not apparent, in some areas investigating the manufacturing and distribution of counterfeit goods is not a priority.

Related to counterfeit goods is the manufacture and distribution of cheaply Chinese made junk product often in violation of health safety standards. For example, toothpaste was found on the shelves of American stores that is made with poison found in antifreeze. Toxic Chinese drywall has been installed in about 100,000 U.S. homes. The drywall emits such noxious fumes that it destroyed electrical wiring and metal fixtures and sickened homeowners.

Replacement of the drywall, pipes and wiring cost Americans billions of dollars. In 2007, thousands, of American dogs were killed by melamine-laced Chinese dog food.[23] The list of dangerous products goes on including Chinese manufactured toxic toys, fish, pharmaceuticals, milk, and candy. Lest the reader think that the Food and Drug Administration closely monitors the situation, the FDA inspects only about 2 percent of imports.

China also sells poisoned food to its citizens and exports it to the world. Documented toxic foodstuffs include canned mushrooms, produce loaded with pesticides, cabbages sprayed with formaldehyde, honey loaded with antibiotics and pesticides, apple juice with arsenic, milk with melamine, table salt with heavy metals, chicken soaked in salmonella and E.coli, doctored rotten vegetables, and tofu made from garbage.[24]

In trafficking counterfeit goods, perhaps the worst manifestation of greed is Chinese- manufactured and distributed counterfeit medicines, safety air bags, brake linings, and vehicle and aircraft spare parts. Most of these dangerous products are routed to the developing world. Some crucial spare parts have also entered U.S. supply chains including those used by the U.S. military.[25] The Pentagon estimates that approximately 15 percent of all spare and replacement parts for its weapons, vehicles and other equipment are counterfeit.[26] As a result, there have been dangerous malfunctions. For example, in 2015 federal agents arrested three Chinese nationals. They were charged with selling 45 counterfeit Intel microchips to an undercover agent with the understanding the chips would be headed to the U.S. Navy for a project involving submarines.[27] The Justice Department released a report detailing how the U.S. military, government agencies and other purchasers bought more than $20 million worth of Chinese-made counterfeit goods from 2013 to 2018. The goods were designed to look like domestically produced gear. Included in the sales were 200 specialized parkas developed to counter night vision goggles that would have been used by U.S. Air Force personnel stationed in Afghanistan.[28]

According to the World Health Organization (WHO), about 100,000 deaths a year in Africa are linked to the counterfeit drug trade. The International Policy Network, a British think-tank, estimates that fake malaria and tuberculosis drugs causes 700,000 deaths a year globally.[29] The WHO defines counterfeit medicine as "one which is deliberately and fraudulently mislabeled with respect to identity and/or source." Both branded and generic products can be faked and, in some parts of the developing world, more than 30 percent of the medicines on sale are presumed to be fraudulent.[30] While not all of the fake drugs originate from China, enforcement action in Africa revealed that 97 percent of fraudulent pharmaceutical products are shipped from China or India.[31] Counterfeit medicines are also sold in China. There have also been reports of counterfeit medicine and pharmaceuticals entering Western consumer supply chains.

Similar to the marketing of narcotics and designer drugs, the worldwide trade in counterfeit goods is increasingly facilitated online. Chinese websites that peddle counterfeit goods are widespread.[32] It is quite easy for consumers and middlemen around the world to order Chinese counterfeit product, including counterfeit tax stamps, packaging, and holograms to fit the local market. This type of trade fraud is also a predicate offense for money laundering.

Hand-in-hand with the manufacture of counterfeit goods is intellectual property rights (IPR) violations and state-sponsored theft and hacking of critical technologies. China also imposes state-mandated technology transfer requirements on many western companies that wish to do business in China. Every year the United States loses hundreds of billions of dollars via the theft of trade secrets. This does not include all losses due to the infringement of patents. Twenty percent of North American-based corporations on the CNBC Global CFO Council say Chinese companies have stolen their intellectual property within the last year.[33] Most of the theft is perpetrated by Chinese parties or by others on Beijing's behalf. For example, in 2019 U.S. authorities charged a Chinese American engineer and a Chinese businessman with economic espionage and conspiring to steal. The Beijing government also orchestrates the theft of advanced technologies from the European Union and other advanced production centers.[34]

It is estimated that the Chinese government is responsible for 50 to 80 percent of cross-border intellectual property theft worldwide.[35] A 2013 Verizon report claimed China is responsible for 90 percent of cyber-enabled economic espionage in the United States.[36] According to some observers, the profit China derives from stolen commercial secrets is so great that it likely accounts for a large portion of the country's often-touted miraculous economic growth.[37]

There are many examples of this type of theft. American companies excel in research and development. For example, U.S. Steel spent millions of dollars to pioneer a new, lighter, higher-grade steel product. Steel produced domestically is vital for U.S. defense. As is progressively the case, the Chinese hacked the U.S. Steel's computers and stole the advanced procedure. Subsequently, a Chinese firm, Baosteel, sold similar high-tech steel in the U.S. at such discounted prices that U.S. Steel couldn't compete.[38] This type of activity has contributed to loss of American jobs and the current tariff battle and undeclared "trade war."

U.S. technology for nuclear power generators, solar cells, software, and computer hardware was also stolen by China Inc. The technologies were then sold (at prices below the cost of production) in the U.S. and used in China. For example, it's estimated that 20 percent of the wind turbines deployed in China today contain stolen software.[39]

While the Chinese government might not officially back many of the criminal activities outlined in this chapter, regarding the theft of intellectual property, the Chinese Party-State already has an official government program in place to do just that.[40] According to a 2018 White House report coordinated among U.S. agencies and departments, "The Chinese government is implementing a comprehensive, long-term industrial strategy to ensure its global dominance.... Beijing's ultimate goal is for domestic companies to replace foreign companies as designers and manufacturers of key technology and products first at home, then abroad."[41]

Illicit Tobacco

In Chapter 9, we discussed the enormous trade in illicit tobacco. Tobacco trafficking — in varied forms — spans the globe. It occurs in every country. Illicit tobacco is generally considered the best-known and well-documented sector of the word's dark economy.

In 2016, the retail value of cigarette sales worldwide was approximately $683 billion, and over 5.5 trillion cigarettes were sold to more than one billion smokers worldwide.[42] Concurrently, there is an illicit volume of approximately 600 billion sticks (as individual cigarettes are known in the trade) per year.[43] Cigarettes account for about 90 percent of all tobacco products sold worldwide.

In 2017 around one in 10 cigarettes lit globally, excluding China, was illicit, compared to one in 11 in 2012. The annual value of illicit tobacco is more than $60 billion.[44] In 2017 the volume of "duty-not-paid" cigarettes consumed globally was approximately 456 billion sticks. That represents estimated lost tax revenue for governments of about $40 billion.[45] As a percentage of worldwide illicit trade, illicit tobacco trails only narcotics, counterfeiting, and forced labor/human trafficking. Some estimates suggest that the worldwide retail value of illicit tobacco products may be comparable to the size of the international cocaine market.[46] Organized crime is increasingly dominant in the illicit trade of tobacco because the rewards can be high and the penalties minimal. Terrorist organizations and North Korea also traffic in illicit tobacco.

China has about 315 million smokers. It is the world's largest producer and consumer of tobacco products. In 2014, 44 percent of the world's cigarettes were consumed in China.[47] The China National Tobacco Corp., which serves China's 300 million plus smokers, is the largest cigarette maker in the world. In 2013 it manufactured about 2.5 trillion cigarettes. Its next largest competitor, Philip Morris International, produced 880 billion.[48]

China is also the world's largest producer of counterfeit cigarettes. Production currently runs at nearly 200 billion counterfeit
cigarettes annually. Just one 40-foot container of counterfeit cigarettes produced in China could garner approximately $2 million in
profit when sold in Europe. If all 200 billion Chinese counterfeit
cigarettes were exported and sold in Europe, this criminal trade
could be worth up to $40 billion a year.[49]

Most illegal tobacco products are produced in Yunxiao County in
China. Factories are disguised and sometimes hidden underground.
The industry is dominated by organized crime groups. The Chinese
factories producing illicit tobacco products are technically illegal.
But many are so large and employ so many workers that authorities
turn a blind eye. Some attempts by the Chinese government to stop
the trade have been met by street riots and manufacturers armed
with machetes. Every year private investigators are murdered in
retaliation killings.[50]

Chinese websites sell illicit tobacco products and production
equipment including fake holograms and tax stamps with no apparent consequences. Their customer base spans the globe. The
profits generated from the sale of these products are enormous.

Another concern involves Chinese contraband tobacco products
that are legally produced and manufactured but diverted into an
illegal market. No taxes, duties, or fees are paid on the contraband
product. The diversion from manufacturer to retailer occurs in a variety of ways including theft, smuggling, and bootlegging. Chinese
nationals, with the implicit assistance of the Chinese government,
exploit this opportunity in Central America and elsewhere.

For example, Overseas United Inc. (OUI) began its cigarette manufacture operations in 2012 at the Albrook Free Zone in Panama.
The company was owned and operated by Chinese nationals and
obtained a business license from Panama's Ministry of Trade and
Industries which authorized the production of cigarettes exclusively
for export purposes. Authorities in neighboring countries soon
started to notice a significant increase in cigarette smuggling activities originating in Panama, mainly in connection with the brands

produced by OUI. Subsequent investigation by the tobacco industry working with investigators in the region showed that 2.6 billion cigarettes were distributed to 16 countries across Latin America and Canada in violation of health regulations.[51] The cigarettes were sold in high tax/higher price jurisdictions to take advantage of tax arbitrage. This type of tactic is akin to predatory economic business practices such as dumping which damages markets, economies, and lowers tax revenues. [52]

In 2018 the Philippines Bureau of Customs seized P18.5 million (approximately $357,000) worth of cigarettes smuggled from China into the Manila International Container Port. The 40 foot shipping container was declared as 890 cartons of industrial artificial fur texture, but upon examination, it was discovered to contain 914 cartons of Chinese-manufactured cigarette brands.[53] This type of customs fraud is very common and is a predicate offense for money laundering.

Some Chinese counterfeit cigarettes are transshipped through the United States. There are industry reports of counterfeit Marlboro cigarettes manufactured in China that briefly enter the port of Long Beach, California, then continue to Colombia, and lastly are destined for consignees in Belize and Mexico. It is probable that the cigarettes are shipped and distributed by organized crime organizations. While there is no U.S. tax loss, Chinese utilization of a U.S. port and the accompanying documentation help the ship-ment appear legitimate.[54]

According to a 2012 FATF report, the primary international source of counterfeit tobacco products in the United States was China.[55] By 2014 the ATF and U.S law enforcement successfully cur-tailed most of the Chinese counterfeit in the United States. About the same time the Chinese illicit tobacco trafficking model started to shift. Chinese groups on the East Coast are now heavily engaged in purchasing cigarettes in low tax states like Virginia and transport-ing and selling them in high tax states like New York. For example, in New York City, smokers pay a state excise tax of $4.35, a city levy of $1.50, and a federal tax of $1.01 per pack. Retail prices often exceed $13 a pack, or $130 a carton. By contrast, the state tax in Virginia is 30 cents a pack. A vanload of about 600 cartons bought in Virginia and sold without paying New York taxes can produce a profit of $20,000 and an estimated tax loss of over $83,000.[56] While other criminal groups are also involved in this type of trade, Chinese triads and gangs are particularly noteworthy as they cater to the large Chinese and Asian presence in New York City and other East Coast metropolitan areas.

Another growing tactic used by Chinese criminal groups trafficking in illicit tobacco is to satisfy the demands of Chinese smokers in the United States for Chinese-manufactured domestic brand cigarettes and other tobacco products. Since importing shipping containers of the product could be risky, multi-thousands of cartons are sent via commercial mail services every month to mail drops across the United States. International transport of illicit tobacco by mail has proved to be low risk and highly profitable.[57]

Human Trafficking

There are tens of millions of people in various forms of human bondage around the world. According to the U.S. Department of State, China is among the world's worst offenders in human trafficking.

The U.S. Department of State calls China a "source, destination, and transit country for men, women, and children subjected to forced labor and sex trafficking." In the 2017 State Department rankings, "China was downgraded . . . in part, because it has not taken serious steps to address its own complicity in trafficking, including (on) forced laborers from North Korea that are located in China. The North Korean regime receives hundreds of millions of dollars a year from the fruits of forced labor." Former Secretary of State Rex Tillerson affirmed that money from that forced labor in China is used to fund North Korea's nuclear program.[58] In 2018 and 2019, the State Department continued to place China in the lowest tier of its rankings.[59]

There are differences between human trafficking and smuggling of migrants. The issues involve consent, type of border crossing, exploitation and source of profit. Trafficking in persons is linked to a number of other criminal activities including kidnapping, fraud, document forgery, assault, rape, false imprisonment, prostitution, immigration violations, corruption, and money laundering.

Human trafficking earns profits of roughly $150 billion a year for traffickers, according to 2014 estimates by the International Labor Organization.[60] The following is an approximate breakdown of profits, by sector:

- $99 billion from commercial sexual exploitation

- $34 billion in construction, manufacturing, mining and utilities

- $9 billion in agriculture, including forestry and fishing

- $8 billion dollars is saved annually by private households that employ domestic workers under conditions of forced labor

Well-organized criminal syndicates and local gangs traffic Chinese women and girls in China, recruiting victims with fraudulent employment opportunities and consequently forcing them into commercial sex. Chinese men, women, and children are subjected to forced labor and sex trafficking in at least 57 other countries. They are also forced to labor in restaurants, shops, agriculture, and factories in overseas Chinese communities. Despite some recent efforts at reform by the Beijing government, syndicates traffic Chinese men in Africa and South America into forced labor at construction sites, mines, and in other extractive industries. They are subject to the withholding of passports, restrictions on movement, non-payment of wages, and physical abuse. Chinese women and girls are subjected to forced prostitution throughout the world, including in major cities, construction sites, remote mining and logging camps, and areas with high concentrations of Chinese migrant workers. According to the State Department, state-sponsored forced labor continues to be an area of concern.[61]

According to research from the Korea Future Initiative, tens of thousands of North Korean women and girls are trafficked and sold into the sex trade in China where they are forced to endure systemic rape, sexual slavery, forced marriage and cybersex trafficking. In a "complex and interconnected network of criminality," women are treated as mere commodities for the North Korean/Chinese transnational criminal networks.[62]

The Migration Policy Institute estimated that there are multi-hundreds of thousands of illegal Chinese immigrants living in the United States, the most from any nation outside Latin America.[63] Chinese triads are increasingly involved in the smuggling of illegal aliens. A triad is one of many branches of Chinese TCO syndicates. They are based in China, Hong Kong, Taiwan, Macau and in other countries within countries with major Chinese populations including the United States. U.S. officials estimate that up to 100,000 Chinese are illegally smuggled into the country each year.[64] The going rate per Chinese person smuggled into the United States is approximately $50,000 to $70,000; the total value of the trade for the Chinese mafias involved with the trafficking is estimated at $750 million.[65] Some join the influx of Central Americans illegally crossing our southern land border with Mexico. It is far more profitable for human trafficking rings to smuggle Chinese than persons from Latin America. The migrants often labor for years in the United States in a form of endured servitude to pay off their debts to the smuggling organization.

Traffickers in the United States make $2.5 billion a year forcing women to have sex in some 9,000 massage parlors and other locations found along highways and behind storefronts in strip malls across the country. Typical victims are recent Chinese or South Korean immigrant mothers burdened with debt and who speak little or no English.[66] Asian-organized crime groups are involved with the trafficking, servitude, and money laundering. It is believed much of the laundering occurs via Chinese underground financial networks.

Chinese human smuggling groups — some based in the United States — are expanding their ties with counterpart criminal organizations in Latin America and branching out into the trafficking of counterfeit goods and the sale and distribution of narcotics.

In Mexico there is increasing cooperation between Chinese triads and narco-cartels, including those ruled by the ruthless Los Zetas syndicate and the Gulf and Juarez cartels, depending on what routes are used for migrants. Triad groups are believed to operate in the Mexican state of Chiapas. The Red Dragon triad, based in Peru with tentacles in the United States, is involved not only in human smuggling, but also in extortion and drug trafficking. [67]

Wildlife Trafficking

Fueled by cultural traditions, superstitions, and traditional medicine, over the last few decades there has been a growing demand from Asian countries — particularly China and Vietnam — for protected wildlife products like ivory jewelry or rhino horn carvings. Since demand outstrips supply, trafficking in wildlife has become a big business. Asian TCOs are involved at the procurement, smuggling, and transportation levels of the trade. Making matters worse, on the local level in many African countries and elsewhere in the developing world, much of this illegal trade is made up of disorganized, opportunistic local criminals that fulfill orders from Asian procurement syndicates.

The illegal wildlife trade has reached crisis proportions. For example, the insatiable Asian demand for smuggled African ivory has resulted in the slaughter of tens of thousands of African elephants and, according to some experts, the very "survival of the species is in China's hands."[68] Rhinos and other species are also endangered. Wildlife trafficking is facilitated by international criminal networks and gangs — many of them Chinese. Enormous profits are generated and laundered.

A wildlife conservation expert notes that, "There's growing awareness that the illegal wildlife trade is run by international crime syndicates. This $15 to $20 billion a year business is now the fourth largest source of criminal earnings in the world, after guns, drugs, and human trafficking operation. For example, on the black market, rhino horn is worth more per pound than cocaine." [69] Most of these billions of dollars in illegal proceeds are laundered. There are virtually no official investigations or cases being made. These illicit proceeds enter the licit world economy through a variety of techniques corrupting global financial integrity.

Although there is demand in some other Asian countries and several wealthy western collectors, China is the driving force behind wildlife exploitation. China has a voracious appetite for wildlife products including ivory, tiger bone, bear bile, pangolin scales, totoaba bladders, and shark fins. As China's economy and population have grown, so, too, has demand for animals and their parts. "Tiger farms" are common in parts of China. Tigers are bred, and then slaughtered for their bones, meat, fur, teeth, and claws. Particularly in demand are the penises and bones, which are soaked in rice wine and served, usually to men. They're supposed to infuse men with the prowess and sexual energy of the tiger.[70]

While there have been recent reforms in China designed to discourage Chinese demand for wildlife, many of the reforms are for show. Illegal activity of this magnitude cannot continue without some level of corruption (see corruption section below). A common method of introducing illegal African wildlife products into the international market is reusing and counterfeiting government-issued permits.[71] For example, according to Allan Thornton, president of the nonprofit Environmental Investigative Agency (EIA), "North Korean embassy officials in both Zambia and Zimbabwe were known to be prime movers of poached rhino horn out of Africa that was smuggled in diplomatic bags and eventually transited to Guanzhong in China and sold on to the Chinese market."

In another case, Chinese government officials illegally procured ivory during a visit to Tanzania brought it back on President

Xi Jingping's plane.[72] Investigations by conservation groups show that "government officials are some of the most common purchasers of tiger bone wine in China and other Asian countries."[73] Chinese wildlife procurement and smuggling rings are found worldwide. They have strong tentacles in China, Hong Kong, Southeast Asia, Africa, South America and across the world's oceans.[74]

Chinese wildlife trafficking is big criminal business and threatens the very survival of some animal species.

Illegal Logging

According to INTERPOL, the trade in illegally harvested timber is estimated to be worth between $51 and $152 billion annually.[75] In addition to the devastating impact on the environment and bio-diversity, illegal logging and forestry crime fuels transnational crime, corruption, and contributes to billions in lost tax revenues for governments.

China is the world's largest producer and consumer of wood and wood products. Sadly, much of the production comes from illegal timber. Unlike major economies like the United States and the European Union, China has no regulation to keep illegal timber from entering its borders.[76]

For example, Papua New Guinea (PNG) is home to the world's third-largest tropical rainforest. Land and forests belong to the country's indigenous people by law, but many of these ancient rainforests are being razed to supply China — the single largest purchaser of tropical logs.[77]

Over the last few years, China has enacted 'Green Supply Chain' policies that are designed to reduce waste and pollution in its internal manufacturing sectors. Yet these same policies do not yet require commodities sourced from abroad to be legal and sustainable.[78] At the same time, China's Belt and Road Initiative extends its trade and investment partnership ambitions to many dozens of countries including PNG. China is developing the PNG's infrastructure. Nevertheless, the PNG and many other countries that succumb to China's entreaties suffer from corruption and weak governance. The end result is that the PNG is repaying its massive debt to China in part via illegal timber.

Global Witness, the UK-based non-profit organization, conducted a multi-year investigation into the Chinese land grab in PNG and documented how timber logged in the impoverished Pacific nation is exported to manufacturing centers in China before being sent to other countries such as the United States as wooden flooring and other commercial products. According to Global Witness, "U.S. consumers may be unwittingly fueling what is one of the biggest land grabs in modern history."[79]

In the United States, the Lacey Act Amendment of 2008 was enacted to reduce the global demand for illegally obtained timber and timber products, including any tree species illegally acquired in the country of origin and any product containing illegally obtained tree material such as paper or pulp. The U.S. sought to set an example of how importing countries could help discourage illegal logging, with the hope that others would enact similar policies.[80] The E.U. and other developed countries subsequently followed the U.S. lead but problems remain.

The U.S. consumes a relatively small share of wood from countries suspected of having high rates of illegal wood production. But having such material entering global markets affects U.S. producers by depressing wood prices globally.[81] Studies examining the effectiveness of the Lacey Act and similar legislation from other countries show their effectiveness in limiting suspect imports from China. Illegal timber researcher Benjamin Roe notes that because of the influence of timber legality regulations on Chinese and Vietnamese wood product manufacturers, ". . . wood products from suspicious sources are shifting away from regulated markets and towards unregulated markets which are experiencing rapid increases in demand for wood products."[82] In other words, illicit Chinese wood product sales are shifting from regulated to unregulated markets.

According to the United Nations Office on Drugs and Crime, rosewood is the most trafficked form of flora or fauna in the world, measured by value or volume.[83] Most of the rosewood is routed to China where it is manufactured into a variety of furniture, musical instruments, and other items. There is a cultural demand for the product. Chinese buy rosewood furniture as an investment or a gift.

Every year Africa loses approximately $17 billion to illegal logging activities. Madagascar has been particularly hard hit by Chinese illegal timber trading practices. According to international investigations into international smuggling rings and documented by the Environmental Investigation Agency (EIA), Fair Planet, and others, "China [is] at the heart of this trade." China uses the same exploitation, trade fraud, smuggling, and corruption model in the Solomon Islands, Sri Lanka, Peru, Brazil, and elsewhere. The rapacious Chinese appetite for unprocessed timber has left a trail of corruption, destruction and even death.[84]

In 2018, the EIA revealed how 1.4 million illegally harvested rosewood logs in Nigeria with a market value of $300 million were "laundered" into China. The exports were facilitated using irregularly acquired Convention on International Trade in Endangered Species of Wild Fauna and Flora or CITES permits. More than $1 million in bribes were paid to Nigerian government officials.[85]

According to one Chinese timber dealer, "It's a very 'dirty' environment. . . You can't be in this business without corruption." [86] A timber researcher based on the east coast of China stated, "We know that most of the logs are illegally felled, but when they enter China with the 'right' documents, they become legal. Chinese dealers bribe [customs] officials to buy CITES certification."[87]

Generally speaking, illegal logging involves activities such as theft, fraud, corruption and forgery of documents. All of these constitute criminal acts. The illegal activities generate enormous profits. If timber obtained through such criminal activity is procured, traded and sold on world markets, illegal logging is a predicate offense for money laundering. Investigative journalists and non-profit organizations have taken the forefront in exposing illicit logging. Worldwide, there are few government criminal investigations and prosecutions.

Trade Fraud

Perhaps the most pervasive form of Chinese money laundering comes from "trade-misinvoicing." Most forms of trade misinvoicing revolve around invoice fraud and manipulation. Generally speaking, invoice fraud means the contents, description, and/or the value of goods is misrepresented. Sometimes this is done to facilitate simple customs fraud, i.e. minimizing the payment of taxes and duties. As discussed earlier in this book, customs fraud is the most prevalent predicate offense in TBML. Yet it is often overlooked because worldwide customs authorities generally do not have an investigative mandate. Invoice fraud is also sometimes part of value transfer or sending trade goods instead of fund payment transfers from one country or jurisdiction to another. Often this facilitates capital flight. Value transfer is also commonly used in "counter-valuation" or a means of settling accounts between informal value transfer brokers and traders. This is often accomplished in underground financial networks (see below).

For money launderers, transferring value via trade goods is particularly attractive because it generally does not trigger financial transparency reporting requirements. Trade-based value transfer is not closely examined by law enforcement and customs services.

The most common forms of trade misinvoicing are:

- Over-and under-invoicing

- Multiple invoicing

- Falsely described goods

- Misrepresentation of the quantity being shipped

- Misrepresentation of shipment origin to evade customs duties

China and the U.S. are the worlds' two largest general merchandise traders (imports and exports). In 2017, China ranked first in worldwide exports with an export value of about $2.3 trillion.[88] China Inc. completely depends on trade. It is logical that trade is also manipulated and used in ways to facilitate illicit financial flows. This manifests itself in many different ways including underground financial systems and capital flight (see below). Perhaps the most common technique to move money (value) out of China is when companies import goods at overvalued prices or export goods at undervalued prices. To move money (value) into China, companies or fronts import goods at undervalued prices or export goods at overvalued prices.

Despite the China/U.S. trade wars and Chinese coronavirus pandemic and global economic downturn, China remains the United States' largest goods trading partner (two-way). In 2017, the total value of U.S. trade in goods with China amounted to $636 billion; this is composed of a $130.4 billion export value and a $505.6 billion import value.[89] Using the estimates above, it is apparent that multi-tens of billions in trade fraud and TBML value transfer occurs every year between the United States and China. Some of this manifests itself in capital flight and forms of underground banking discussed below.

Global Financial Integrity (GFI) estimates the Chinese economy hemorrhaged $1.08 trillion in illicit financial outflows from 2000 through 2011 — with trends accelerating today.[90] Much of this is in the form of trade misinvoicing. Today China is the largest exporter of illicit capital in the world.[91] In China, the transfer of massive amounts of funds often occurs in contravention of capital controls and the non-payment of applicable taxes. This enormous introduction of Chinese capital (both licit and illicit) has a mixed impact on the global economy including the distortion of market values.

Weapons Proliferation

Of all illicit trades, weapons proliferation has the most direct and damaging impacts on security. Chinese activities in the spread of nuclear weapons, fissionable material, and weapons-applicable nuclear technology and information to nations not recognized as "Nuclear Weapon States" by the Treaty on the Non-Proliferation of Nuclear Weapons or NPT, has long been of concern to Western nations.

Clouded in secrecy, it is very difficult to assess the illicit proceeds generated from the sale of nuclear, biological and chemical technology, weapons, and delivery systems. Apart from China's geopolitical reasoning to engage in proliferation in violation of international norms, without doubt the trade is quite profitable. China's support of Pakistan, Iran, and North Korea and their nuclear programs is particularly alarming.

China is Pakistan's principal military and nuclear supplier. Over the last 25 years the United States has maintained concerns about continued Chinese nuclear cooperation with Pakistan, particularly involving the construction of nuclear power plants. For example, in 1996 the Director of Central Intelligence (DCI) noted that "China was the most significant supplier of WMD-related goods and technology to foreign countries." [92] In 1998, Pakistan tested five nuclear weapons inside shafts bored into the side of a mountain. Much of the technology and nuclear know-how was procured (and stolen) by A.Q. Khan, a Pakistani metallurgical engineer.

In 2004, the DCI confirmed A.Q. Khan's international network of nuclear trade in open testimony to the Senate Intelligence Committee. China's ties to the Khan network was a concern, particularly because China was an early recipient of the uranium enrichment technology using centrifuges that Khan had acquired in Europe. According to Khan, China gave Pakistan materials for the production of bomb-grade uranium, a large quantity of weapons-grade enriched uranium, and a blueprint for a nuclear weapon that China already tested. [93]

Chinese technology transfers have also helped Pakistan to develop and build domestic medium-range ballistic missiles. In September 2001, the George W. Bush Administration imposed sanctions for China's proliferation of missile technology to Pakistan and denied satellite exports to China. As a result, China promised not to transfer missiles. China may have adhered to the specific agreement but later helped Pakistan to develop an indigenous missile capability.[94]

China has also been the key source of goods and technology for the nuclear and missile programs of both Iran and North Korea.[95] A report in 2004 by the U.S.-China Security and Review Commission stated that "Chinese entities continue to assist Iran with dual-use missile-related items, raw materials and chemical weapons-related production equipment and technology" and noted that the transfers took place after the Chinese government pledged in December 2003 to withhold missile technology.[96] In 2013, three leading UK non-proliferation experts concluded that "China continues to be the key source of goods and technology for the prohibited nuclear and missile programs of Iran and North Korea, with some officials estimating that China is used as a transit route for up to 90 percent of goods destined for those programs."[97]

One case during this timeframe involved serial Chinese proliferator Li Fang Wei (aka Karl Lee). Lee controlled a large network of industrial companies based in eastern China. Lee reportedly was able to earn more than $10 million from the sale of missile-related items to Iran, including various metallurgical goods and related components that are banned for transfer to Iran by the United Nations. This continued even after the United States indicted him in 2009 on more than 100 criminal counts of falsifying business records related to illicit trade with subsidiaries of an Iranian military agency.[98]

China plays a particularly duplicitous proliferation game. Much of the Chinese nuclear technology transfer to Iran was accomplished via Pakistan. Later, the same type of trade transshipment scheme expanded to North Korea. For example, in 2011 Reuters obtained a confidential United Nations report that, once again, showed China's double dealing: North Korea and Iran appear to have been regularly exchanging ballistic missile technology in violation of U.N. sanctions. The report said that the illicit technology transfers had "transshipment through a neighboring third country." That country was China.[99]

The type of Chinese entities involved in proliferation and the level of government complicity have changed significantly. In the early years of Chinese proliferation activities, a number of China's large state-owned defense enterprises sold large quantities of conventional arms and missiles, complete nuclear and missile facilities, and dual-use and unfinished technologies. More recently, no doubt because of negative publicity, threats of sanctions, and non-proliferation agreements, involvement of large state-owned strategic and defense companies has largely subsided. Today, the primary source of goods for prohibited nuclear, biological, and chemical programs is China's private sector. In particular, small and medium-sized businesses often act as distributors or middlemen in dual use technology trade with western manufacturers.

China now funnels either dual-use technology or materials at quantities below control-list thresholds that trigger export licensing requirements. [100] In this manner, the Chinese government attempts to set up a plausible deniability defense. China can both benefit from the illicit transactions and appear to uphold nonproliferation agreements.

Methodologies and Enablers

As noted earlier, the three primary methodologies to launder money and introduce illicit funds into the world's licit economy are: 1) via banks; 2) bulk cash smuggling; and 3) trade-based money laundering and value transfer. Illicit funds of Chinese origin are laundered via these methodologies and others we discuss such as the international gold trade, cyber currencies, etc. In this section, we will briefly describe other common techniques and practices used by Chinese actors as well as worrisome enablers of Chinese illicit financial flows.

Underground Banking

According to the 2008 FATF mutual evaluation of China, there are four primary means of laundering money: 1) via banks; 2) via bulk cash; 3) "Proceeds are transferred by importing or exporting over/under priced goods, or falsifying/counterfeiting import/export contracts, shipment bills, customs declarations and other related documents" (i.e. trade-based money laundering); and 4) "Money is laundered through the underground banking system."[101] Points 3 and 4 are intertwined because invoice manipulation and trade fraud are commonly used in underground finance.

It is difficult to determine the magnitude of Chinese underground banking, but there is no doubt it has been used to move vast sums beyond China's borders. For example, in 2015 Chinese authorities seized approximately $130 billion from underground banks operating on the mainland, half through a single illegal operation. Authorities appropriated another $148 billion in the first nine months of 2016.[102] In China, declared confiscated amounts are usually just the tip of an iceberg. According to some anti-corruption specialists, Chinese underground banks are estimated to have over 10,000 clients and are believed to launder over $100 billion every year. [103] These estimates could be on the low side but no one really knows.

Chinese underground financial methods or alternative remittance systems are primarily used to remit wages from the Chinese diaspora back to the homeland. Of course, authorities have no wish to interfere with hard working immigrants sending money "back to the home country" to help support extended family. On the other hand, unfortunately, these low-cost and efficient financial systems are also abused by criminals to move, transfer, and launder illicit proceeds. They are attractive because by their very nature they are opaque. Underground financial systems avoid government scrutiny, taxes, and countermeasures such as the filing of financial intelligence.

It is believed that fei-chien, sometimes known as "flying money," was invented during the T'ang Dynasty (618 to 907 AD).[104] At the time, there was a growing commodity trade within China. Some historians believe it was the rice trade and others the tea trade that were the catalysts for the new financial system. Ironically, as opposed to modern day practice, the transfer schemes were not invented as an underground method of evading the grasp of authorities but rather it was a tool to facilitate taxation.

Merchants sold their goods and then brought their revenues to provincial "memorial offering courts." The government collected taxes. In turn, the merchants were issued certificates for the remaining value of the commodity sales. When the merchants returned to their home provinces, they would present the certificates to the provincial government for payment. Thus the fei-chien system became an efficient way of payment via trade-based value transfer. Completing transactions in this way spared both the merchants and government the risk of transporting large sums of money.

Over the centuries, the system continued to evolve. Chinese workers increasingly began to migrate to other provinces and then overseas. Their families back home needed financial support. Expatriate Chinese businesses began to develop side businesses of remitting money back to China. The international Chinese diaspora spread the indigenous financial system further still. Today, modern Chinese businesses as well as "Chinatowns" and "China shops" are found around the world. So is flying money.

Strong Chinese family bonds are incorporated into "guanxi" which is an overarching social system of rules that govern relationships and social behavior. Guanxi is the guarantor of both secrecy and the integrity of the parties to the transaction. Those who violate its prescriptions find themselves a social outcast, essentially shunned in all circles. Guanxi is an integral component of fei-chien or so-called "flying money." In other words, similar to hawala and other indigenous informal value transfer systems, an essential element of fei-chien is trust. It is very difficult for law enforcement to penetrate the underground financial networks.

In Chapter 7, we discussed alternative remittance systems focusing on hawala. Flying money and hawala are very similar. To illustrate, we will use the same type of money remitting example: Wang in Guangdong province wants to send 200,000 Chinese yuan renminbi RMB to his brother in New York City. As a form of capital flight, Wang wants to protect his hard-earned money by investing in dollars and the United States. Wang gives the Guangdong "flying money" broker the RMB and in turn receives a code number. He trusts the broker as they have a familial relationship. The "flying money" broker in Guangdong directs his counterpart (perhaps a member of the same family) to pay the equivalent in U.S. dollars (approximately $30,000) upon presentation of the code. The code could be transferred in a telephone call or a message contained in an e-mail or the Chinese messaging system, WeChat. Not many years ago, a playing card or a portion of a currency note with a specific chop, marking or seal or other physical sign would be presented to the broker as a sign of authentication. Upon receipt, the New York "flying money" broker pays Wang's brother in New York City. The money did not physically leave China.

Money and value is also sent back to China. Like all immigrant groups, Chinese send money back home to help support their families. The same brokers are involved. Even though "flying money" largely operates on trust, family, clan and community ties, the brokers are in business to make money. Occasionally they have to settle accounts. Transactions go both directions. Using the above example, the New York broker might be running a deficit or a surplus with his counterpart in Guangdong. Various methods are used to settle accounts including banks, cash couriers, online payment services, and trade-based value transfer.

Surplus credits could also be used by a client unrelated to the original transaction(s). For example, credits could be used for the purchase of foreign real estate. For a fee, the client that wants money outside China pays RMB in China to a "flying money broker" and receives credit in the desired foreign location in local currency.

One of the most popular methods of getting yuan out of China involves finding a foreign contact who would like to set up a private exchange for Chinese RMB. "Flying money" networks are sometimes used but so are informal personal networks and business associates. For instance, the overseas person puts their dollars into an account in Hong Kong belonging to the Chinese individual. The Chinese individual in China puts the Chinese RMB in an account in Beijing that is connected with the overseas investor who wants the money in China.[105]

What is often overlooked is that trade continues to be involved with the settling of accounts. This little understood concept was identified in the FATF mutual evaluation quoted above. Most "flying money" brokers are directly involved or associated with trading companies. In our discussion of trade-based money laundering techniques above, invoice fraud and manipulation are employed particularly in over- and under-invoicing.

How do the "flying money" brokers profit? Although commissions are paid to the brokers at both ends of the transaction, the commissions are less than banks or traditional money remitters such as Western Union charge. In comparison to large brick-and-mortar banks and money transfer chains, expenses are small. Often the brokers use legitimate businesses as fronts such as restaurants, "China shops," and trading companies. Of course, in the underground remittance segment of their business they skirt regulations and taxes. In the United States, the flying money brokers are technically classified as a money service business for the purposes of registration, licensing, and reporting financial intelligence. They do not comply.

Another form of Chinese underground banking system sometimes dubbed CUBS is a loose-knit network of money dealers, traders and cryptocurrency brokers who move currencies in and of the economy while sidestepping the country's banking system, currency controls, and capital flight restrictions. According to the 2019 National Drug Assessment, there is an alarming trend of Asian money laundering organizations (MLOs) acting on behalf of Mexican TCOs. "This trend is a result of the imposition of a cap by the Government of China on foreign exchange transactions ($50,000 per year) and overseas withdrawals on Chinese bank-issued credit and debit cards ($15,000 per year). The demand of Chinese nationals to transfer their wealth outside of China and into the United States has fueled the demand for U.S. dollars. Asian MLOs are eager to acquire U.S. dollars (drug proceeds) from Mexican TCOs in exchange for the payment of pesos in Mexico or their equivalent debts in China via a CUBs. Asian MLOs resell the U.S. dollars to customers (Chinese nationals within the United States) for a profit, normally in exchange for RMB payments to China. This demand for foreign exchange, i.e. the U.S. dollar in particular, has provided an outlet for Mexican TCO drug proceeds that is changing the landscape of money laundering within the United States."[106]

There are indications that CUBS is being used in conjunction with the Black Market Peso Exchange System (BMPE) discussed briefly in Chapter 6 and below. In the BMPE, narcotics traffickers sell at a discount the dollar proceeds of U.S. drug sales within the United States to peso brokers. In turn, the brokers place the illicit proceeds into the financial system and use the funds to purchase trade goods that are sent to Colombia or Mexico. No money crosses borders. Only the ownership of the currencies involved change. Increasingly, the purchases, logistics, foreign exchange specialists, and trade intermediaries are Chinese and Chinese-organized crime groups. They arrange for a drug dollar purchase of Chinese merchandise (much of it counterfeit) to be sent to South America including Colombia, Mexico, the Tri-Border Area, and the Colon Free Trade Zone.

Certainly, related to CUBS is the exponential growth of Chinese crypto currencies. For example, there are some reports that Mexican cartels are opting to partner collaborate with the Chinese partners due to their vast crypto currency money laundering networks.[107]

According to the DEA, "CUBS money brokers sell Bitcoin to drug traffickers for cash earned from drug sales in the US, Australia, and Europe. This drug cash is then sold to Chinese nationals in exchange for Bitcoin the Chinese nationals use to transfer the value of their assets outside of China. Many China-based firms manufacturing goods used in TBML schemes now prefer to accept Bitcoin. Bitcoin is widely popular in China because it can be used to anonymously transfer value overseas, circumventing China's capital controls."[108] We will talk more about crypto currencies in Chapter 12.

Capital Flight

According to a former Canadian Ambassador to Beijing, "China is the number one exporter of hot money to the world."[109] The exodus of capital has fueled worries about the Chinese economic outlook. Issues of concern include a China/U.S. trade war, the plummeting Chinese stock market, devaluation of the Chinese currency, fears of a real estate bubble, suspect loans and balance sheets by Chinese banks, the theft of state funds by Chinese officials, paltry returns on savings accounts, the coronavirus pandemic, and other social unrest. Furthermore, as the Chinese government clamps down on corruption, savvy Chinese are transferring wealth out of the country. Many Chinese elites also want "golden visas" and foreign citizenship that are offered for substantial sums of money.

Capital flight also exacerbates the perception of equality in the communist country. "In one generation, China has transitioned from one of the most egalitarian states in the world to one of the most unequal. While Chinese government estimates of income and wealth inequality are state secrets, Forbes reports that there are 400 billionaires in China, second only to the 540 billionaires in the United States. Combined with the country's millionaires, it appears that less than 0.5 percent of the population controls wealth equal to 25 to 33 percent of China's GDP."[110]

As a result, the Chinese government has imposed capital controls on its citizens and has recently begun penalizing severe violators with jail time. Chinese are restricted to sending the equivalent of approximately $50,000 per person out of the country per year. So how does capital flee China? There are a number of methods including:

- Tapping political and personal connections

- Using the transfer quotas of friends and family members to get money out of the country

- Channeling funds through gaming and junkets, particularly via Macau

- Using the special relationship with Hong Kong that serves as a financial conduit to the rest of the world

- Trade-based value transfer

- Underground financial systems

- Obtaining special financial services offered to the elites

Capital flight poses a few important questions and issues regarding illicit financial flows and money laundering: 1) Massive amounts of capital leave China. Is illicit money co-mingled with legitimate money? 2) Does China consider capital flight over the reporting threshold money laundering? If so, is that designation reciprocal in the receiving country? 3) For the U.S. and most other countries, receiving foreign capital is not illegal. In fact, it is often encouraged. However, money laundering could occur if the foreign capital includes the proceeds of crime or it is used to further criminal activity in the destination country. (For example, see the section on real estate below.) Yet the source of Chinese money flooding into the United States and elsewhere is rarely questioned. 4) While the influx of capital can be helpful, it can also distort local markets, cause inflationary pressure, become the catalyst for social disruptions, create undue influence, etc.

Black Market Exchanges

Criminal organizations often use trade-based money laundering and trade fraud techniques to launder the proceeds of crime. The

U.S. Department of Treasury has stated that the Black Market Peso Exchange (BMPE) is one of the largest money laundering methodologies in the Western Hemisphere and responsible for laundering billions of dollars of drug proceeds every year.[111] It is commonly used by both Colombian and Mexican drug cartels which purchase Chinese products to launder the funds.

In the BMPE, drug proceeds, acquired by black market dealers, are used to purchase trade items such as electronics, garments, and toys. Twenty years ago, most of the goods were purchased from U.S. companies. Drug money was used to buy tractors, refrigerators, cigarettes and other business and consumer goods. These products, in turn, were sent by the black market dealers to Colombia. American manufacturers involved in the trade were accused of "willful blindness." They did not ask questions about the source of the money used to purchase their products even though the broker and routing were often suspect.

Over the last decade, the BMPE has evolved. Drug money is increasingly used to purchase Chinese-manufactured merchandise either directly from Chinese vendors or via U.S. importers. Taking advantage of preferential trade policies, imported Chinese goods are sometimes fraudulently presented as made in the United States thus saving the conspirators paying import taxes.[112] This customs fraud is also a predicate offense for money laundering. Once again willful blindness comes into play. The manufacturers and middlemen involved are not practicing due diligence. The technique has still expanded further. Importing cheaply manufactured Chinese goods at overvalued prices gives reason to send criminally derived money directly out Mexico and other drug-producing countries. In some places in the developing world, this trade-based money laundering technique sometimes avoids currency controls.

U.S. law enforcement has seen a spike of BMPE investigations involving Mexican drug cartels and Chinese-manufactured goods. This is a byproduct of burgeoning China/Mexican trade. For example, when China and Mexico established diplomatic relations in

1972, trade between the two countries was approximately $13 million annually. By 2016, trade had exploded to almost $75 billion.[113]

Europe has also been hard-hit with other versions of Chinese trade-based money laundering and black market exchanges. Italy, Poland, Spain and many other countries have seen a flood of cheap Chinese imports and counterfeit goods. Warehouses in industrial parks are found outside major European cities. They offer a vast range of consumer goods such as tools, paper products, electronics, and kitchen supplies. The importers declare only a fraction of each shipment. (The volume of trade is so high customs officials are only able to physically inspect a very small percentage of shipping containers.) The under-valued goods are sold and the proceeds are often laundered back to China. Proceeds rarely stay in the host country. The government loses tax revenue. Billions of euros have been laundered. VAT fraud is sometimes also involved.

There has been a major multi-billion euro TBML investigation in Italy where Chinese authorities actively obstructed justice.[114] In Spain, China's largest bank is accused of facilitating some of the laundering schemes run by "Chinese criminal organizations." Prosecutors say the sums of illicit proceeds are so large that the "damage to the socio-economic order and the national economy is clear."[115]

In addition, black market exchanges are common in the developing world. In Africa, Latin America, and parts of Asia, Chinese cheaply manufactured consumer merchandise (much of it counterfeit and/or smuggled) dominates both the legitimate and black markets. Generally speaking, there is an unfortunate lack of investigations and political interest in cracking down on this type of trade.

Real Estate

As noted in Chapter 8, investment in real estate is one of the most widely used international money laundering methodologies. For criminals and criminal organizations, large property purchases, sometimes paid for using cash and often with no beneficial ownership information, can facilitate the placement, layering, and integration stages of money laundering in a single operation. Real estate represented 30 percent of all criminal assets confiscated worldwide between 2011 and 2013.[116]

Over the last five to ten years, Chinese have gone on an international real estate buying spree. Overseas investment from China includes residential, commercial and industrial property. While residences, hotel, and offices account for the majority of overseas deals, Chinese investors are increasingly interested in industrial parks and logistics centers. Industrial parks are integrated into the "One Belt, One Road" plan to establish infrastructure links with Africa, central Asia, Latin America, and South Asia. The parks will facilitate the operations of Chinese companies and cement Chinese influence in the host countries.[117]

Preferred Chinese targets for residential real estate investment include the United States, the United Kingdom, Europe, Australia, New Zealand, Malaysia, Canada, and Dubai. Chinese are the biggest foreign buyers of U.S. real estate. Completed Chinese deals in the U.S. hit a record $46 billion in 2016. The level dropped to $29 billion in 2017 and then further in 2018.[118] Among Chinese buyers, 65 percent paid cash.[119]

While new Chinese capital controls have somewhat delayed purchases over the last few years, Chinese investors primarily still pay cash for properties. This massive outside placement of foreign capital is an artificial driver that pushes the cost of housing even higher. This fosters resentment from local citizens. It is also a catalyst for residents to leave high cost of living areas.

Responding to concerns about criminals' use of real estate to launder illicit funds, Treasury's FinCEN has used Geographic Targeting Orders (GTOs) that temporarily require U.S. title insurance companies to identify the natural persons behind shell companies used in all-cash purchases of residential real estate. As of 2019, GTOs cover certain counties within the following major U.S. metropolitan areas: Boston, Chicago, Dallas-Fort Worth, Honolulu, Las Vegas, Los Angeles, Miami, New York City, San Antonio, San

Diego, San Francisco, and Seattle.[120] Unfortunately, purchases outside these jurisdictions, or purchases of commercial property, are not covered by the GTO's which creates a loophole that is evaded easily by those who want to launder money through the purchase of real estate.

According to the National Association of Realtors, Chinese buyers have been the top foreign buyers in the United States both in units and dollar volume of residential housing for six years straight. There is also an increasing amount of investment interest by middle class Chinese buyers. California is a favorite market among Chinese buyers as are Texas, Georgia and Florida.[121]

While foreign capital invested in real estate is not illegal (and in fact is encouraged by certain sectors), the primary issue of concern is the origin of the money invested. In the United States there is little if any customer due diligence by real estate agents. Due to the magnitude of the money involved, there is no doubt that some purchases of real estate reflect criminal proceeds that are mixed or co-mingled with invested monies. We also know that Chinese criminal syndicates are directly involved with real estate purchases. In just one example, criminal elements that control chemical factories in China's booming Guangdong province are shipping narcotics, including fentanyl, to Vancouver. Revenue from the drug sales is washed in British Columbia's casinos and high-priced real estate and/or transfers some of the laundered funds back to Chinese factories to repeat the deadly trade cycle.

In 2018, law enforcement seized approximately 100 Northern California houses purchased with money wired to the United States by a Chinese-based crime organization. The property was used to grow massive amounts of marijuana illegally. Much of the marijuana was subsequently shipped to Georgia, Illinois, New York, Ohio and Pennsylvania through Atlanta, Chicago and New York City. Chinese-organized crime in San Francisco and elsewhere helped coordinate the real estate purchases, cultivation of marijuana, sales and distribution. Authorities were able to track 125 wire transfers totaling $6.3 million from Fujian Province in China, all just below the $50,000 limit imposed by the Chinese government. The funds were used to purchase the properties. (See the sections on capital flight above and Chinese organized crime below and the blurring of licit capital mixed with illicit funds.)[122]

Gaming

Historically and culturally Chinese people love to gamble. However, gaming is illegal in mainland China. Illegal gambling in China is still very popular, including unofficial lotteries, betting in games such as mahjong and various card games, and clandestine casinos. The Chinese territory of Macau is the only area where casino gaming is permitted. Millions of tourists flock to the territory each year. Macau's economy is almost entirely dependent on gaming. Despite a recent downturn, the Chinese territory reported gambling revenue of 266 billion patacas (approximately $33 billion) for 2017.[123] In comparison, Las Vegas casinos earned $6.5 billion.[124]

In addition to recreational gaming, Chinese use Macau to evade capital flight restrictions and to launder money. Via junket operators, visitors use RMB to buy casino chips and after playing cash out in foreign currencies, including dollars. To evade currency controls, Chinese high rollers can do one of two things: They can deposit money with junkets in the mainland and use that money in Macau, or they can borrow from junket agents. If they choose to deposit the money, the junket gaming promoters ferry money across borders or simply debit and credit accounts. The gamblers can then use that money in Macau. Once done gambling they can take their winnings in U.S. or Hong Kong dollars and direct it elsewhere. The money is effectively laundered.

Many of the Chinese elite use the above techniques to invest in foreign property or offshore tax havens. For example, there are a number of Canadian investigations into billions of dollars being laundered via integrated networks of underground banking, Chinese TCOs, gaming, and real estate investments. It's called the "Vancouver Model" of transnational crime.[125]

Casinos have long been used to launder money — particularly in areas where there is poor governance, lack of AML safeguards in the gaming sector, and weak law enforcement. For example, countries in South Asia, Africa, the Philippines and other locations have a heavy Chinese gaming presence. The FATF has long recognized casinos and gaming as a major money laundering methodology.

For example, two Chinese/Guatemalan nationals owned and operated two casinos in Guatemala. They used the casinos to launder at least $30 million of illegal drug sales in the U.S. picked up by couriers up and down East Coast of the U.S. The Guatemalan casinos washed the drug money and then routed the funds to Colombian cartels.[126]

Secrecy Jurisdictions

Money launderers and those involved with illicit financial flows use many methods to "layer" and disguise their transactions so that law enforcement authorities have a difficult time "following the money." As we will discuss in Chapter 13, a common tactic is to use offshore shell companies without beneficial ownership information. Most offshore jurisdictions (including those in the United States) are not currently required to list the natural persons who profit from their existence or control their activities — the actual "beneficial owners" of the business. This has made anonymous companies the vehicle of choice for drug cartels, organized crime, corrupt foreign officials, and others who need to launder money. The inability of law enforcement to access beneficial ownership information frustrates police and prosecutors and harms the American public in myriad ways. Investigations into narcotics trafficking, human trafficking, terror financing, sanctions evasion, and many others have all been stymied by the secrecy of offshores.

For example, the British Virgin Islands (BVI) is one of the world's largest offshore destinations for secrecy. It is also one of the favorite destinations for Chinese that want to move businesses and cash offshore. Roughly 40 percent of the BVI's offshore business comes from China and other Asian countries.[127] In Chinese slang, having a "BVI" is shorthand for any offshore company, regardless of where in the world it is located.[128]

Chinese also commonly avail themselves of offshore financial structures in Singapore, Malaysia, Panama, many of the Caribbean islands, the Cook Islands, and other non-transparent havens. The International Consortium of Investigative Journalists traced approximately 22,000 secretive shell companies back to China and Hong Kong. The owners include some of China's richest and most powerful men and women.[129]

According to revelations in the Panama Papers, many clients unmasked in the document that dump and subsequent journalistic investigations include ruling communist Chinese elites and their family members.[130] The documents provide a rare window as to how the Chinese privileged class sends wealth offshore. Other common techniques are to use trade-based value transfer and trade-mispricing techniques, dress up that wealth in offshore secrecy, and then sometimes return it to China disguised as foreign investment which enables special tax and other privileges.

China was Mossack Fonseca's — the subject of the Panama Papers — most important market. The firm's office in Hong Kong was its busiest. The company also has offices in eight other Chinese cities. A review of the company records shows that roughly 30 percent of companies represented by the law firm were Chinese clients.[131]

In 2016, Chinese leaders offered to help bail out a Malaysian government fund at the center of a multibillion-dollar graft scandal involving Malaysia's 1MDB development fund. Monies reportedly would disappear into anonymous companies. In addition, Chinese nationals tried to dissuade U.S. law enforcement from investigating and would harass reporters exposing the scheme.[132]

State-linked Chinese companies and individuals have also used anonymous offshore companies to circumvent U.S. sanctions, most notably in their dealings with North Korea. As well as in 2019, the CFO of Huawei was accused of misleading HSBC executives over the alleged use of a front company in order to do business in Iran. That front company is reportedly owned by an anonymous company registered in Mauritius.[133]

Secrecy jurisdictions are a common denominator in most serious organized crime, money laundering and corruption investigations. The fact that Chinese represent a very large percentage of global offshore users is a serious red flag.

Organized Crime

According to the FBI, "transnational organized crime (TOC) groups are self-perpetuating associations of individuals who operate, wholly or in part, by illegal means and irrespective of geography. They constantly seek to obtain power, influence, and monetary gains."[134]

Chinese TOCs have spread around the globe. They prosper largely due to the globalization of economies, communications technology, and international travel. Generous immigration policies enabled many gang members enter and live undetected.

There are two broad categories of Asian criminal enterprises: Traditional criminal enterprises include the Chinese triads (or underground societies) based in Hong Kong, Taiwan, and Macau. There are also non-traditional criminal enterprises. These include groups such as criminal tongs, triad affiliates, and other ethnic Chinese and Asian street gangs found in several countries with sizable Asian communities.

Chinese TOC groups have been operating in the United States since the early 1900s. The groups evolved from tongs — Chinese social organizations formed by immigrants. Over the years they adapted and branched out into criminality. The enterprises rely on extensive networks of Chinese national and international criminal associates that are fluid and mobile. The FBI notes that they can be "highly sophisticated in their criminal operations, and have extensive financial capabilities. Some enterprises have commercialized their criminal activities and can be considered business firms of various sizes, from small family-run operations to large corporations."[135]

Violence is a defining characteristic of Chinese organized criminal gangs. Disputes over territory and criminal markets among the
gangs are typically resolved using kong so or a process of peaceful
negotiation. When this does not occur, however, the resolution is
usually a violent one.[136] In the United States, the traditional triad
hierarchy has been simplified. Members often switch allegiance if
necessary to improve their financial position. Triads and gangs in
the United States are not unified entities, but rather loose confeder-
ations of independent cells with no identifiable central authority.[137]

According to the FBI, Chinese criminal enterprises conduct traditional racketeering activities normally associated with organized
crime including extortion, murder, kidnapping, illegal gambling,
prostitution, and loansharking. They engage in human trafficking,
traffic heroin and methamphetamine, commit financial frauds, engage in auto theft, deal in illicit tobacco products, trade in counterfeit goods, and other criminal activities. They launder the proceeds
of the crime.

In the U.S., Asian criminal enterprises have been identified
in more than 50 metropolitan areas. They are most prevalent in
Honolulu, Las Vegas, Los Angeles, New Orleans, New York, Newark,
Philadelphia, San Francisco, Seattle, and Washington, D.C.[138] As discussed in Chapter 8, Canada is increasingly concerned about the
presence of Chinese organized crime including involvement in gaming and the purchase of high-end real estate. A recent report also
discussed the explosive increase over the past five years in vehicle
exports to China.[139]

Chinese networks in Canada purchase high-end vehicles with
the proceeds of crime. Sometimes the purchases are made with
bags of cash. (In many countries and jurisdictions, car dealerships
are not required to report large cash or suspicious transactions.)
They then ship the vehicles overseas for resale. In the Canadian
context, organized crime sometimes uses straw buyers who get paid
to purchase the vehicle and then resell it back to the network. The
vehicle is then exported. The provincial sales tax (PST), which can
be 20 percent for vehicles worth $150,000 or more, is then refunded

and deposited to the straw buyer. For example, British Colombia tax law exempts buyers from paying PST on a vehicle if they can prove it is not going to be used in the province.

According to law enforcement officials, Tse Chi Lop, a Canadian national born in China, is suspected of leading an enormous multi-national drug trafficking syndicate formed out of an alliance of five of Asia's triad groups. Its members call it simply "The Company." It is sometimes known as Sam Gor, Cantonese for "Brother Number Three."[140]

There are press reports that the Sam Gor syndicate is funneling tons of methamphetamine, heroin and ketamine to at least a dozen countries from Japan in North Asia to New Zealand in the South Pacific. The United Nations Office on Drugs and Crime (UNODC) estimates the Sam Gor syndicate's meth revenue alone in 2018 at between $8 and approximately $18 billion. The Sam Gor syndicate's tentacles are widespread. It is far more diverse than Latin narco-cartels, cooperating with Japan's Yakuza, Australia's biker gangs and ethnic Chinese gangs across Southeast Asia.

Another form of Chinese organized crime are units of the Chinese military. This is another example of criminal activity ordered by the Government of China. There are many case examples. The following directly affects tens of millions of Americans. Undoubtedly, the same type of Chinese military sponsored criminal activity is happening in other areas of the world.

In 2015, the United States Office of Personnel Management (OPM) announced that it had been the target of a data breach involving the personal information of approximately 21.5 million Americans, including people who had undergone background checks, but who were not necessarily current or former government employees. It was one of the largest breaches of U.S. government data in history. The victims of the data breach lost personal information including Social Security numbers, as well as names, dates and places of birth, medical records, fingerprints, and much more. While the theft is still under investigation, it is believed the Chinese military's Third Department of the General Staff, known as 3PLA, is believed to have carried out the attacks. There are other reports that indicate the Ministry of State Security, the civilian intelligence service, carried out the cyber operation.[141]

In a twisted sort of way, the above can be viewed as a state vs. state espionage operation. This type of thing happens (although the poor security protocols and lack managerial oversight of the OPM that allowed the data breach are scandalous). However, in February 2020, the Department of Justice announced that four members of the People's Liberation Army, an arm of the Chinese military, were charged with breaking into the networks of the Equifax credit reporting agency and stealing the personal information of more than 145 million civilian Americans. The 2017 theft included the loss of individuals' names, addresses, Social Security and driver's license numbers and other personal data stored in the company's databases.[142] The chances are high China has the personal information of the reader of this book.

Corruption

Corruption is the great facilitator for international money laundering. According to Transparency International's Corruption Perception Index, China is ranked 87 out of 180 countries. India, South Africa, Senegal, and Cuba have better scores than China.[143]

Over the last few years, the Chinese government has initiated a sweeping anti-corruption campaign that has led to thousands of arrests. Many of those arrested are the political enemies of Chinese President Xi Jinping and his cronies. The irony is that Chinese CCP leadership is dominated by so-called "red princelings," such as President Xi. The leadership trace their roots to generals and top officials of the initial Maoist regime. The Chinese entrepreneurial class has also been subsumed. Australian political scientist, David Goodman, notes that 90 percent of China's millionaires are the offspring of high-ranking officials.[144] In China about 1,300 individuals control roughly 20 percent of the country's wealth. The top

1 percent has roughly a third of it. This occurs while much of the country, particularly in the countryside, still lives at the brink of poverty.[145]

Unfortunately, corruption continues to negatively influence the business environment inside of China. According to the China Corruption Report, "Companies are likely to experience bribery, political interference or facilitation payments when acquiring public services and dealing with the judicial system. The common practice of guanxi is a custom for building connections and relationships based on gifts, banqueting, or small favors."[146]

International rankings of bribe payers list Chinese managers near the top. When Chinese executives go abroad, they carry on bribing. They undermine good governance in host countries. Some Chinese companies are so unscrupulous that the World Bank has banned them from bidding on contracts in Africa.[147] Beijing routinely uses both a hard and soft a hand around the world that provides quid to extract pro-China quo. Chinese practice various forms of influence, but in most countries around the world corruption and payoffs a predicate offense for money laundering. It is rarely investigated or prosecuted.

Chinese authorities estimate that approximately $2 trillion of funds representing corruption have been laundered out of China since 1995. However, China appears to have stopped sharing data after 2011. It is believed outflows from the proceeds of corruption were severe enough to threaten both its economy and its political stability.[148]

According to the Bank of China, about 16,000 to18,000 officials with ties to the public sector were involved in moving proceeds of corruption illegally from China to other countries. The top recipients of the corrupt funds are the United States, Australia, Canada, and the Netherlands.[149]

In addition to official corruption, there are forms of private and commercial corruption and payoffs which are rampant in Chinese society as well as "grey" income. Grey income is income earned or acquired off the books and not included on income tax reports.

Much of this money also is laundered and enters into the world's licit economy.

Chinese companies also facilitate corruption and crime though the manufacture of fake identification cards and other documents such as birth certificates, passports, test certifications, national identification cards, etc. They advertise their product online, and sales occur around the world including the United States. For example, in November 2019 U.S. Customs and Border Protection seized more than 5,000 fake IDs — or the blank cards used to make them — sent from China. The already-made IDs were headed for various states, including New Jersey, Michigan, Illinois, Missouri, Florida and Ohio. Drivers' licenses and other forms of identification are not just used to obtain liquor for underage students at college campuses; in at least one case, the fraudulent identification was intended for a convicted child rapist.[150]

Predatory Lending and Strong-Arm Tactics

Mercantilism is an economic theory prevalent from the 16th to the 18th century that promoted governmental regulation of a nation's economy for the purpose of augmenting state power at the expense of rival national powers. In 2001, China was admitted to the World Trade Organization (WTO). The U.S. supported China entering WTO with the reduced compliance requirements of a developing nation. This ascension gave China access to world markets, and in particular, the lucrative American market. As China has grown to the second largest global economy, it refuses to give up its predatory advantages. Moreover, China has aggressively pursued developmental policies that revolve around mercantilism. It is ironic because the primary goal of the WTO is to keep mercantilism out of world trade. It is not a coincidence that the rise of China's exploitative trade practices and protectionist investment policies overlap with international criminal activities.

Ironically, today's communist China is arguably both the world's foremost imperialist and mercantilist nation. All but abandoning rigid Marxist ideology, the primary objective of the Beijing government is to maintain control. The Chinese government has developed a comprehensive strategy that uses every tool of government power to achieve its objectives. (Internally, the Chinese communist government is even establishing a vast high tech ranking system that will monitor the behavior of its population and rank and penalize them all based on their "social credit.") Chinese involvement in transnational criminal activity and illicit financial flows can also be seen as an unarticulated means to support China's aspirations.

In 2013, Chinese President Xi Jinping put forward the strategic conception of building the "Silk Road Economic Belt" and the "21st Century Maritime Silk Road," which came to be known as the "One Belt and One Road" (OBOR) initiatives. OBOR plays an integral role in China's massive industrial policy initiative, "Made in China 2025." Initiated in 2015, this policy seeks to make China the world leader in 10 critical categories of the economy that are on the cutting edge of 21st century technology and industry. All of this fits nicely into China's goal of overcoming the United States and becoming the world's preeminent superpower by the 100th anniversary of Chinese Communist rule in 2049.

In order to achieve these goals, China must have ever expanding markets and access to raw materials that are the fuel for its industrial base, secures employment for its large population, and for national security concerns. For example, China aims for a strategic global stranglehold on key resources such as gold, bauxite, copper, nickel, and rare earths. China preys on weak countries by exploiting their natural resources with "debt traps."

It is a strategy that has been used by the unscrupulous for millennia to subjugate others. "It goes as follows: provide loans that are beyond the ability of a distressed or unsophisticated borrower to ever pay back; and when the borrower inevitably falls behind in the required debt-service payments, foreclose and seize the borrower's desirable assets and/or extract wanted concessions. Predators have long used this strategy to turn poor people into indentured servants; payday lenders to get worker's paychecks; monopolies to crush competitors; mafiosos to muscle businesses into their hands; and nations to seize key strategic assets of other nations."[151]

Chinese "investment" has occurred in approximately 152 countries. OBOR has enabled CCP enterprises to gain control of 76 ports and terminals in 34 of these countries.[152] The following are just a few examples:[153]

- Montenegro accepted Chinese loans to build a highway from a port on the Adriatic Sea to Serbia. The highway is less than half built and, in all likelihood, will never be completed. Yet Montenegro has taken on the debt equivalent to 80 percent of its GDP to do so. China now effectively owns the strategically located Montenegro.

- Kenya accepted staggering loans from China to build the Standard Gauge Highway stretching from Mombasa to Nairobi. Kenya is in default. China is about to foreclose and take over Kenya's critically important Mombasa seaport.

- Sri Lanka owes nearly $13 billion, much to China, out of a forecast annual revenue of less than $12 billion. Sri Lanka is so indebt to China that they were forced to give a 99-year lease of the Hambantota sea port to a Chinese company. This is a transparently strategic move that will eventually give China a naval base near its rival India.

- Pakistan embraced the "China-Pakistan Economic Corridor", taking Chinese loans to do so. With its debt to China at $19 billion and rising rapidly, Pakistan will never be able to pay it off. China is seeking an overland link to Pakistan's warm water, deep seaport at Gwadar on the Arabian Sea. A Chinese state-owned enterprise has already taken over operations of Gwadar's port.

- China built an unstable and untenable dam in the heart of Ecuador's jungles. To repay the roughly $20 billion debt to China, Ecuador will give 80 percent of its petroleum exports to China which it can then sell at a profit.

- Somalia is one of the world's poorest countries and is desperate for funds and investments. In return for offering China almost unlimited fishing rights in return for investment, China is rapidly depleting Somalia's fishing stocks. China's demand for fish is utterly out of sync with the sustainability of fish habitats and will further impoverish Somalia.

- Djibouti on Africa's east coast has committed 81 percent of its GDP to servicing Chinese debt. It is not a coincidence that China has a military base on Djibouti soil.

- According to the International Energy Agency (IEA), China is projected to be the world's largest importer of natural gas, with demand rising 60 percent to 376 billion cubic meters from 2017 to 2023. The IEA also projects that Africa's share in the global energy mix is set to soar from 5 percent today to 25 percent by 2040. Over 40 percent of global gas discoveries from 2011 to 2018 have been in Africa: Mozambique, Tanzania, Senegal, Mauritania, Egypt, and South Africa. It is not a coincidence that China has been pouring investment capital into Africa's energy sector and creating debt traps for many of the countries involved.

As noted, China has bought cargo ports throughout the world, including in Latin America, the Indian Ocean and Mediterranean Sea including ports in Greece, Italy, and Spain. In sub-Saharan Africa there are dozens of existing or planned port projects funded or operated by China. China intends to do the same in the United States. In 2012, the Obama administration signed an agreement giving China control of port of Long Beach, California. The Long

Beach port is the most important U.S. gateway for trans-Pacific trade, handling approximately $195 billion in trade annually. In 2018, the port handled more than 8 million container units. The Trump administration instituted a national security review and federal intervention. As a result, a unit of China-based COSCO Shipping Holdings Co. (Orient Overseas Container Line—OOCL) was forced to sell the container terminal business.[154]

The Chinese business model requires corruption and political influence. Chinese payoffs and bribes to corrupt local officials have secured many agreements. No doubt these tainted funds are laundered and parked in a labyrinth of offshores. These payoffs are a predicate offense for money laundering but there are few prosecutions. Particularly in countries with poor governance, law enforcement is hesitant to pursue financial crimes investigations if the money trail leads to the powerful.

To make matters worse, Chinese multinationals sometimes take shortcuts in the developing world. Host countries sometimes turn a blind eye to poor Chinese environmental, health, and safety standards. Cumulatively this has a corrosive effect on the rule of law, good governance, and fosters autocratic behavior in struggling democracies. In some of the Belt and Road sites, special arbitration courts are being introduced where they will promote an "alternative" (read the CCP) legal system.[155]

As part of its efforts to gain dominance, China has directed its state-owned companies to exclusively buy products and services from other Chinese state-owned enterprises. As a result, China International Marine Containers Group is now the world's largest maker of shipping containers. Shanghai Zhenhua Heavy Industries has gained a 70 percent international market share for port cranes. China operates six of the world's ten busiest container ports.[156]

In addition, under President Xi the deepening penetration of the Communist Party into Chinese business has caused Chinese companies to be viewed as extended arms of the CCP. Foreign companies and governments no longer have confidence that a Chinese company — private or not — can resist a CCP directive. China's National

Intelligence Law from 2017 requires organizations and individuals to provide information to the government if asked. For example, this helps explain fears about introducing technology made by China's Huawei into a nation's critical infrastructure.[157] In the United States, the Chinese telecommunications company is banned from 5G network contracts based on suspicion of espionage and sending mined data directly to the Chinese government.

Enforcement and AML Compliance

Generally speaking, China does not cooperate with other countries in pursuing financial crimes and anti-money laundering investigations. This is extremely important because it is imperative to have international cooperation in pursuing international illicit financial flows. The United States and China are parties to the Agreement on Mutual Legal Assistance in Criminal Matters. U.S. agencies consistently seek to expand cooperation with Chinese counterparts on AML/CFT matters and to strengthen both policy- and operational-level cooperation in this area.

Although there have been some recent improvements, particularly in the area of narcotics investigations, U.S. law enforcement agencies note China has not cooperated sufficiently on financial investigations. In addition to the lack of law enforcement-based cooperation, the Chinese government's inability to enforce U.S. court orders or judgments obtained as a result of non-conviction-based forfeiture actions against China-based assets remains a significant barrier to enhanced U.S.-China cooperation in asset freezing and confiscation.[158] It is not clear how diligently, and with what resources, China monitors illegal trading of all sorts by Chinese companies and investigates breaches. Concerns are also heightened by China's weak response to Western requests for interdiction of suspect trade practices.

China boasts the world's second largest economy and a vibrant financial sector. Almost all banks in China are state-owned and the world's top four banks in assets are Chinese.[159] Although in the Chinese banking sector, corruption, lack of honest oversight, high-risk loans, clever valuation techniques, and shadow banking are pervasive.

Shadow banking occurs when banks and non-bank financial institutions lend money outside of lending norms and safeguards. The loans are often packaged into complicated wealth management and other financial products. Banks market these risky loans as a way to increase profits and share debt. Chinese banks keep shadow-banking assets off their balance sheets, thereby sidestepping regulatory constraints on lending.

Shadow banking in China is somewhat analogous to the 2007 and 2008 subprime lending crisis in the United States that triggered a global financial crisis, lost trillions of dollars in wealth, created bankruptcies and foreclosures, and destroyed millions of jobs. Since that time, shadow banking in China has mushroomed into a $10 trillion obscure financial system. It connects thousands of financial institutions with companies, local governments and hundreds of millions of households.[160] A 2016 report from investment bank CLSA said that Chinese shadow banking comprised approximately 57 percent of total bank loans.[161] In other words, Chinese economic activity and financial services are severely distorted. A panic or collapse could pose direct threats both to the GOC and also to the licit global economy.

The Communist Party's Central Commission of Discipline Inspection, Xu Jia'ai, said China's financial system is dogged by a corrupt alliance of "cats and rats."[162] Once again, corruption manifests itself, and the watchdogs and regulators turn a blind eye. Another area where the corrupt alliance manifests itself is in the weak culture of AML/CFT compliance.

For example, in Italy, the Bank of China (BOC) — the largest bank in the world based on assets — facilitated the laundering of billions of euros via a branch of the Bank in Italy. Over a four year period, approximately 4.5 billion euros were illegally transmitted from the greater Florence area to China. The transfers were allegedly facilitated by the Milan branch of the BOC. For years China and the BOC stonewalled the Italian investigation. In 2017, the BOC settled with the government of Italy on the criminal case and later paid a 20 million euro fine to Italian tax authorities.[163]

It was initially reported that when Italian officials tried to appeal to Chinese authorities for help, "they got nowhere." Prosecutors discovered that "Money2Money," an Italian company owned by Chinese immigrants, had been transferring the proceeds of criminal activity. Italian authorities investigating the transactions had encountered the "great legal firewall [that] separates China from the West."[164]

China does not have an independent legal system that is recognizable in the West. The CCP is supreme in legal matters. The Party claims that China is a country ruled by law: the claim is fatally undermined by a 99 percent conviction rate. In 2014, only 1,039 of more than 1.2 million people were found not guilty in the country's Communist Party-controlled courts. The acquittal rate is approximately 0.08 percent.[165] In other words, China is ruled by Party whim, not law.

In February 2016 Spanish police raided the Madrid subsidiary of Industrial and Commercial Bank of China. They arrested five of the bank's local directors on suspicion of money laundering. In this case, Spanish authorities had electronic intercepts of Chinese bank employees conspiring to launder money. The investigation disclosed the bank's complicity in laundering approximately 1.2 billion euros out of Spain to China between 2009 and the end of 2012.[166] There has been a lack of cooperation in the investigation by Chinese authorities with the Spanish investigation.

New York regulators fined the Agricultural Bank of China $215 million for a series of irregularities and apparently deliberate masking of suspicious transactions. Details of originators and counterparties on international payments were concealed through a coding system to hide suspicious sources. The coding was applied to transfers between suspect Chinese and Russian trading companies and transfers enacted on behalf of an Afghan drug trafficker.[167]

Some Chinese banks are also complicit in North Korea's efforts to evade financial sanctions. For example, in September 2016, the U.S. Department of Justice found that from 2009 to 2015, Chinese nationals had used 22 front companies to open accounts in Chinese banks.[168] The laundering facilitated dollar transactions through the U.S. financial system for sales to Pyongyang. Treasury also issued an advisory on North Korea's use of the international financial system, which emphasized the role of Chinese banks.[169]

Agricultural Bank of China and China Construction Bank have been identified as helping North Korea launder its money. Both of these banks, China's second- and third-largest, each have more assets than JPMorgan Chase & Co., America's largest bank. Because of their size, some feel that they are "too large to sanction." [170]

Chinese banks have also been instrumental in providing Iran relief from sanctions. China is Iran's largest trading partner and trade ties between China and Persia have existed for nearly 2,000 years. This close trade relationship has also been boosted of late through China's Belt and Road Initiative. The Export-Import Bank of China and Chinese banks are providing financing and lines of credit in support of Iran's economy. The tens of billions of dollars of loans provided by the Chinese are primarily targeted towards infrastructure projects in the water, energy and transport industries. In return, China is Iran's largest oil customer. China's insatiable appetite for petroleum accounts for a third of Iran's overall trade. [171]

In 2012 the United States sanctioned China's Bank of Kunlun. The Treasury Department singled out the Bank of Kunlun because it provided financial services to designated Iranian banks and facilitated the movement of millions of dollars' worth of international transactions connected to Iran's program of proliferation and/or support for terrorism.[172]

The Bank of Kunlun, a state-owned bank, continued to be one of the main conduits at the heart of China's trade with Iran. However, the Bank of Kunlun recently shifted policy and informed clients that it will no longer process payments that contravene U.S. secondary sanctions on Iran.[173] Chinese commercial banks undoubtedly do not want to risk disconnection from the international banking system by transacting with Iran.

China continues to facilitate Iran's skirting the current round of sanctions. In particular, it is believed imports from China will be facilitated by trade-based value transfer including barter trade. Iranian businessmen and brokers are very active in China. There is also a large Chinese trading presence in Iran. Undoubtedly, these brokers will use smaller transactions to continue the Iranian/Chinese trade. Similar to previous rounds of sanctions, many of the deals will be cleared by Iranian safari or a network of exchange shops. As described in Chapter 7, safari is linked to the hawala (havaleh in Iran) underground financial system. Havaleh has been used for centuries. It operates much the same way as the Chinese fei-chien or flying money system of underground finance. Credits and debits are routinely settled via a trade-based counter-valuation process that is practically immune to outside scrutiny.

Conclusion and Recommendations

All of the above and countless other examples of China's criminal behavior corrupt the world's licit economy and norms. Communist China is the largest, most powerful, wealthiest, and most diverse ongoing criminal enterprise and money laundering threat the world has ever seen.

Unfortunately, China's behavior does not lend itself to traditional AML countermeasures. Its wealth and influence are far too pervasive. Certainly, the FATF, the Asia Pacific Group on Money Laundering, and the Eurasian Group on Money Laundering (China is a member of both the FATF and the two FATF-style regional bodies) should "name and shame" China. Politically, that is not going to happen. (Having participated in numerous U.S. interagency FATF discussions, FATF plenary deliberations as well as acting as an "expert" on FATF and FATF-style regional body mutual evaluations, I assure the reader that double standards and political interests come into play.) The world's media and investigative journalists should focus much more attention on China's criminality. I'm not optimistic that is going to happen either. Parent corporations of the media giants are afraid of losing business in China. Law enforcement and intelligence agencies around the world should step-up scrutiny of Chinese criminal activity and organized crime. However, this also holds little promise because of various factors noted in this book including lack of capacity and resources in certain countries, corruption, and political influence. What about international sanctions and designations targeting China and Chinese bad actors? If we can't get the world to coalesce around implementing and enforcing sanctions against Iran, we certainly will not be able to use these tools against China. Unfortunately, some politicians are beholden to Beijing.

Ultimately, our best hope is a change of government. Communist China will not modify its egregious behavior on so many fronts until it becomes a democracy. That necessary discussion is well beyond the scope of this book. The Chinese coronavirus pandemic could be the catalyst for long overdue policy changes regarding U.S. corporate divestiture from China, bringing critical manufacturing back to the United States, and protecting our vital supply chains from capricious decisions and gamesmanship by the CCP.

In the interim, we can all play a small but vital role in protest. The China brand is tarnished. As individuals, we can register our outrage with product boycotts. If an acquisition choice is available, we should not buy anything made in China. By looking the other way, or trying to save a few dollars on a purchase, we are complicit.

In addition to CCP criminality and money laundering discussed in this chapter, there is also the criminal negligence practiced by Xi and the CCP in dealing with the Chinese coronavirus pandemic. The CCP's mismanagement, untruths, political motivations, and secrecy in handling the outbreak are demonstrable examples of the kind of government it is. The accounting for this unnecessary tragedy will be measured not only in the loss of tens of trillions of dollars in wealth and production around the world, but more importantly in the deaths and sickness of people.

The CCP's handling of the Chinese coronavirus is not isolated. More than three decades after the Tiananmen Square massacre, it reminds the world of the Hong Kong democracy protests, the million-person forced labor and reeducation camps for Uyghur Muslims, the multi-faceted repression China practices at home and seeks to export abroad, internal Chinese Orwellian surveillance, persecution of Christians and the proscribed Falun Gong religious group, organ harvesting from political prisoners, and countless other human rights abuses including enforced abortions, involuntary sterilizations, and the confiscation of children by the authorities. The CCP's responsibility for tens of millions of deaths caused during the Great Leap Forward and further cultural and political upheavals should not be forgotten.

Please understand that I am not pointing my finger at Chinese or Asian people. There is much to admire. China is a great and ancient civilization that has contributed much to the world. But today's Chinese state isn't a race; it's a regime. This chapter isn't culture bashing. It is listing and referencing facts. I have no criticism of Hong Kong, Taiwan, Chinese Americans, etc. But all of us should be concerned about the CCP's political principles and unethical and criminal activity. They are as deadly and perverse as its pandemic.

NOTES

1 Evan Ellis, "China/Latin America and the emerging ideological strug-gle of the 21st Century," Global Americans, June 17, 2018; https://theglobalamericans.org/2018/06/latin-america-and-the-emerging-ideological-struggle-of-the-21st-century/

2 Tom Porter, "China Waging New Cold War to Topple U.S. as World's Leading Superpower, Says CIA Official," Newsweek, July 22, 2018; https://www.newsweek.com/china-waging-new-cold-war-topple-us-worlds-leading-superpower-says-cia-1036226

3 2019 International Narcotics Control Strategy Report (INCSR), Volume 1, U.S. Department of State, March 1, 2019; https://www.state.gov/wp-content/uploads/2019/03/INCSR-Vol-INCSR-Vol.-2-pdf.pdf See the China country report.

4 "China Inc." is a generic term but see Ted Fishman, China, Inc.: How the Rise of the Next Superpower Challenges America and the World, Scribner, 2006

5 "Illicit Trade: Converging Criminal Networks," OECD, 2016; https://read.oecd-ilibrary.org/governance/charting-illicit-trade_9789264251847-en#page3

6 Channing May, "Transnational Crime and the Developing World," Global Financial Integrity, March 2017; https://gfintegrity.org/report/transnational-crime-and-the-developing-world/

7 Note: As discussed in Chapter 2, the FATF has stated that "Due to the illegal nature of the transactions, precise statistics are not available and it is therefore impossible to produce a definitive estimate of the amount of money that is globally laundered every year." With that caveat in mind, the International Monetary Fund (IMF) has estimated that money laundering comprises approximately 2 to 5 percent of the world's gross domestic product (GDP) each year. A good working estimate is roughly $4 trillion. Of course, it all de-pends on what is included in the count. The estimates on individual predicate offenses listed in this report are also not precise. With some estimates there is a high level of confidence and others not.

For example, the magnitude of Chinese trade fraud can only be an educated guess. The data is simply not available. Nevertheless, as detailed in this chapter a rough working number for predicate offenses for money laundering with Chinese culpability approaches $1.5 - $2 trillion annually. Thus a logical argument can be made that approximately half of the money laundered worldwide every year is related to illegal activity by Chinese actors.

8 Shannon Tiezzi, "China's Growing Drug Problem: China's drug problem is getting worse, despite harsh penalties," The Diplomat, March 28, 2015; https://thediplomat.com/2015/05/chinas-growing-drug-problem/

9 2018 International Narcotics Control Strategy Report (INCSR), Volume 1, U.S. Department of State, March 1, 2018; https://www.state.gov/documents/organization/278759.pdf. See the China country report.

10 2018 DEA National Drug Assessment p. 24; https://www.dea.gov/sites/default/files/2018-11/DIR-032-18%202018%20NDTA%20final%20low%20resolution.pdf

11 Ibid, p. 35

12 Bob Portman Press Release, January 30, 2018; https://www.portman.senate.gov/public/index.cfm/2018/1/on-senate-floor-portman-highlights-psi-report-on-drug-traffickers-shipping-fentanyl-into-the-u-s-through-the-postal-service

13 Susan Scutti, "US drug overdose deaths rose 7% in 2017 and doubled over a decade, CDC reports," CNN, August 16, 2018; https://www.cnn.com/2018/08/16/health/us-overdose-death-report-cdc/index.html

14 Melanie Arter, "DHS Secretary: ICE Interdicted Enough Fentanyl Last Year to Kill Every American Twice Over," CNSNews, March 7, 2019; https://www.cnsnews.com/news/article/melanie-arter/dhs-secretary-ice-seized-interdicted-fentanyl-last-year-kill-every

15 Jessica Wehrman, "Drugs by mail: Americans ordering fentanyl online from China, study says," Dayton Daily News, January 4, 2018; https://www.daytondailynews.com/news/state--regional-govt--politics/drugs-mail-americans-ordering-fentanyl-online-from-china/KiO2nNHyainzMox1jU0yhP/

16 2018 DEA National Drug Assessment, p. 104

17 For an overview of Asian organized crime involvement in narcotics trafficking and money laundering in the United States see the 2017 DEA National Drug Threat Assessment, pages 14 – 15; https://www. dea.gov/docs/DIR-040-17_2017-NDTA.pdf

18 "Counterfeit and pirated goods represent 3.3% of global trade: report," France24, March 18, 2019; https://www.france24.com/ en/20190318-counterfeit-pirated-goods-represent-33-global-trade-report

19 Casey Hall, "A Turning Point for China's Stance on Counterfeit Luxury Goods," Business of Fashion, December 11, 2018; https://www. businessoffashion.com/articles/global-currents/a-turning-point-for-chinas-stance-on-counterfeit-luxury-goods#targetText=Accord-ing%20to%20US%20Chamber%20of,at%20a%20 staggering%20%24397%20billion.

20 "Update to the IP Commission Report," 2017, page 1; http://www. ipcommission.org/report/IP_Commission_Report_Update_2017.pdf

21 "The Theft of American Intellectual Property," IP Commission Report Update, February 2017 Pgs . 2 -3; http://www.ipcommission. org/report/IP_Commission_Report_Update_2017.pdf

22 Austin Bay, "China's Communist Dictatorship Targets American Creativity," May 9, 2019; https://townhall.com/columnists/austin-bay/2019/05/09/chinas-communist-dictatorship-targets-american-creativity-n2546066

23 Ann Coulter, "CHEAP TVS, EXPENSIVE FLU," Ann Coulter, March 18, 2020; http://www.anncoulter.com/columns/2020-03-18.html. See the article for the original source references. Also, I suggest the reader do a simple Internet query of "toxic Chinese foods."

24 Andrea Widburg, "It's time to build a Great Wall around China," American Thinker, April 9, 2020; https://www.americanthinker.com/ blog/2020/04/its_time_for_the_world_to_build_a_great_wall_ around_china.html. See the article for original source reporting in Congressional testimony.

25 James Burke, "Fake Electronic Parts From China Infiltrate US Military Supply Chain," Epoch Times, May 22, 2012; https://www.theepoch-times.com/fake-electronic-parts-from-china-infiltrate-us-military-supply-chain_1485178.html

26 Larry Greenemeier, "The Pentagon's Seek-and-Destroy Mission for Counterfeit Electronics," Scientific American, April 28, 2017; https://www.scientificamerican.com/article/the-pentagon-rsquo-s-seek-and-destroy-mission-for-counterfeit-electronics/

27 Ibid

28 Kyle Rempfer, "DoD bought phony military gear made in China, including counter-night vision clothing that didn't actually work," Military Times, May 30, 2019; https://www.militarytimes.com/news/your-air-force/2019/05/30/dod-bought-phony-military-gear-made-in-china-including-counter-night-vision-clothing-that-didnt-actually-work/

29 Jocelyn Sambira, "Counterfeit Drugs Raise Africa's Temperature," Africa Renewal, May 2013; https://www.un.org/africarenewal/magazine/may-2013/counterfeit-drugs-raise-africa%E2%80%99s-temperature

30 Ibid

31 Cécile Barbière, "Counterfeit Chinese and Indian Drugs Invade Africa," EURACTIV, June 24, 2017; https://www.euractiv.com/section/health-consumers/news/counterfeit-chinese-and-indian-drugs-invade-africa/

32 Robert Klara, "Counterfeit Goods Are a $460 Billion Industry, and Most Are Bought and Sold Online," Adweek, February 13, 2017; https://www.adweek.com/brand-marketing/counterfeit-goods-are-a-460-billion-industry-and-most-are-bought-and-sold-online/

33 Eric Rosenbaum, "1 in 5 corporations say China has stolen their IP within the last year: CNBC CFO survey," CNBC, March 1, 2019; https://www.cnbc.com/2019/02/28/1-in-5-companies-say-china-stole-their-ip-within-the-last-year-cnbc.html

34 Numerous sources but see Joe McDonald, "China's technology tactics irk its trading partners," Associated Press, May 20, 2019;

https://www.apnews.com/486e956e6ef54b2bb6c7b627e12230a9
and Cathrin Schaer, "Security: Europe's pushback against Chinese
tech has only just begun," ZDNet, April 15, 2019; https://www.
zdnet.com/article/security-europes-pushback-against-chinese-tech-
has-only-just-begun/

35 Dennis C. Blair and Jon M. Huntsman, Jr., "The Report of the
Commission on the Theft of American Intellectual Property,"
National Bureau of Asian Research, May 2013, page 3

36 "2013 Data Breach Investigations Report," Verizon, 2013, page
21. http://www.verizonenterprise.com/resources/reports/
rp_data-breach-investigations-report-2013_en_xg.pdf

37 James Van de Velde, "Time to Fight Back Against China's Massive
Intellectual Property Theft, "American Thinker, January 18, 2019;
https://www.americanthinker.com/articles/2019/01/time_to_
fight_back_against_chinas_massive_intellectual_property_theft.
html#ixzz5cy0ucOkT

38 "U.S. Steel's costly battle against China's cyber-hacking," The Hill;
https://thehill.com/blogs/pundits-blog/technology/323738-us-
steels-costly-battle-against-chinas-cyber-hacking

39 Zach Mottl, "Trump is right to confront China's high-tech theft,"
Market Watch, June 20, 2018; https://www.marketwatch.com/story/
trump-is-right-to-confront-chinas-high-tech-theft-2018-06-20

40 Stephen W. Mosher, "How does China cheat on trade? Let us count
the ways," FOX News, June 25, 2018; http://www.foxnews.com/
opinion/2018/06/25/how-does-china-cheat-on-trade-let-us-count-
ways.html

41 "How China's Economic Aggression Threatens the Technologies and
Intellectual Property of the United States and the World, "White
House Office of Trade and Manufacturing Policy, June 2018;https://
www.whitehouse.gov/wp-content/uploads/2018/06/FINAL-China-
Technology-Report-6.18.18-PDF.pdf

42 "The Global Cigarette Industry," Tobacco Free Kids. (https://www.
tobaccofreekids.org/assets/global/pdfs/en/Global_Cigarette_
Industry_pdf.pdf)

43 Testimony of Marc Firestone, Senior Vice President and General Counsel, Philip Morris International, United States Commission on Security and Cooperation in Europe, July 19, 2017. (https://www.csce.gov/sites/helsinkicommission.house.gov/files/Firestone%27s%20Testimony.pdf) "The Illicit Tobacco Trade," The FATF

44 "Illicit Trade in Tobacco Products," Euromonitor International, 2018; https://www.euromonitor.com/illicit-trade-in-tobacco-products/report

45 "Illicit Trade in Tobacco Products," Euromonitor International, November, 2018; https://www.euromonitor.com/illicit-trade-in-tobacco-products/report

46 "Countering Illicit Trade in Tobacco Products," Interpol, 2014; https://www.interpol.int/Crime-areas/Trafficking-in-illicit-goods-and-counterfeiting/Legal-assistance/Legal-publications

47 "The Bill China Cannot Afford," The World Health Organization, 2017, p. iv; http://www.wpro.who.int/china/publications/2017_china_tobacco_control_report_en_web_final.pdf

48 Andrew Martin, "The Chinese Government Is Getting Rich Selling Cigarettes," Boomberg, December 12, 2014; https://www.bloomberg.com/news/articles/2014-12-12/the-chinese-government-is-getting-rich-selling-cigarettes

49 "Countering Illicit Trade in Tobacco Products," Interpol

50 Lorraine Kember, "Toxic Black-Market Cigarettes"

51 "Panamanian Cigarette Smuggling," NCFTA, January 8, 2016, page 2

52 Email exchange between John Cassara and Kristin Reif, Director Illicit Trade Prevention at Philip Morris International Washington D.C., March 20, 2019

53 "Customs seizes cigarettes smuggled from China," Rappler, April 16, 2018; https://www.rappler.com/nation/200358-philippines-customs-cigarette-smuggling-china

54 Email exchange between John Cassara and Kristin Reif, Director Illicit Trade Prevention at Philip Morris International Washington D.C., March 20, 2019

55 "The Illicit Tobacco Trade," The FATF

56 John Reid Blackwell, "Altria fights cigarette trafficking from Virginia to New York," Roanoke Times, March 22, 2015. (http://www.roanoke.com/news/virginia/altria-fights-cigarette-trafficking-from-virginia-to-new-york/article_90366994-f636-5cd9-b981-bc7d4eb48c41.html)

57 Telephone conversation between John Cassara and former ATF Special Agent Bart McEntire, March 21, 2019

58 Adam Edelman, "Global Human Trafficking Convictions Rose in 2016," NBC News, June 27, 2017; https://www.nbcnews.com/politics/politics-news/global-human-trafficking-convictions-rose-2016-n777201

59 "Trafficking in Persons Report 2018," U.S. Department of State, see China section; https://www.state.gov/j/tip/rls/tiprpt/2018/

60 "ILO says forced labour generates annual profits of US$ 150 billion," International Labor Organization, May 20, 2014; www.ilo.org/global/about-the-ilo/newsroom/news/WCMS_243201/lang--en/index.htm

61 "Trafficking in Persons Report," U.S. State Department, June, 2018. See China listing; https://www.state.gov/j/tip/rls/tiprpt/2018/index.htm

62 Josh Hammer, "A Huge Number Of North Korean Women Are Sold Into Chinese Sex Slavery, Report Says," The Daily Wire, May 20, 2019; https://www.dailywire.com/news/47469/huge-number-north-korean-women-are-sold-chinese-josh-hammer

63 Jie Zong and Jeanne Batalova, "Chinese Immigrants in the United States," Migration Policy Institute, September 29, 2017; https://www.migrationpolicy.org/article/chinese-immigrants-united-states

64 Mike Brunker, "Asian gangs are brothers in crime," NBC News; August 31, 2018; http://www.nbcnews.com/id/3071662/t/asian-gangs-are-brothers-crime/#.XJN_GyJKiM9

65 Rachael Brown, "The Boom in Chinese Smuggled Across the Southern Border," Newsweek, July 24, 2016; https://www.news-week.com/boom-chinese-smuggled-across-us-border-483262

66 "Sex trafficking in US massage parlours a US$2.5 billion business, study finds," Reuters, July 20, 2018; https://www.scmp.com/news/world/united-states-canada/article/2128742/sex-trafficking-us-massage-parlours-us25-billion. See also the Polaris Project; https://polarisproject.org/

67 Rachael Brown, "Chinese Human Smuggling and the U.S. Border Security Debate," Council on Foreign Relations, July 18, 2016; https://www.cfr.org/blog/chinese-human-smuggling-and-us-border-security-debate

68 Jeffrey Gettleman, "Closing China's Ivory Market: Will It Save Elephants?" New York Times, December 31, 2016; https://www.nytimes.com/2016/12/31/world/africa/africa-ivory-china.html

69 "Wild Laws: China and Its Role in Illicit Wildlife Trade," Wilson Center, June 2, 2016; https://www.wilsoncenter.org/event/wild-laws-china-and-its-role-illicit-wildlife-trade

70 Simon Worrall, "Inside the disturbing world of illegal wild-life trade," National Geographic, November 9, 2018; https://www.nationalgeographic.com/animals/2018/11/poaching-tigers-bears-bile-farming-book-talk/

71 Wilson Center

72 Ibid

73 Worrall, National Geographic

74 Rachel Nuwer, "The Key to Stopping the Illegal Wildlife Trade: China," The New York Times, November 19, 2018; https://www.nytimes.com/2018/11/19/science/wildlife-trafficking-china.html

75 Law Enforcement Assistance for Forests (Project Leaf), INTERPOL; https://www.interpol.int/Crime-areas/Environmental-crime/Projects/Project-Leaf

76 A Major Liability - Illegal logging in Papua New Guinea threatens China's timber sector and global reputation, Global Witness, July 30, 2018; https://www.globalwitness.org/en-gb/campaigns/forests/major-liability-illegal-logging-papua-new-guinea-threatens-chinas-timber-sector-and-global-reputation/?utm_medium=email&utm_sou

77 Ibid

78 Ibid

79 "US firms buying timber from illegal PNG logging: NGO," Phys.Org, August 1, 2017; https://phys.org/news/2017-08-firms-timber-illegal-png-ngo.html

80 Zoe Hoyle, "2008 Lacey Act Amendment Successful in Reducing U.S. Imports of Illegally Logged Wood," USDA Compass Live, "November 20, 2014; https://www.srs.fs.usda.gov/compass/2014/11/20/2008-lacey-act-amendment-successful-in-reducing-u-s-imports-of-illegal-ly-logged-wood/

81 Ibid

82 Benjamin Roe, "The Influence of Timber Legality Regulations on Chinese and Vietnamese Wood Products Manufacturers," University of Washington, 2015, page 4; https://digital.lib.washington.edu/researchworks/bitstream/handle/1773/33936/Roe_washington_0250O_15130.pdf?sequence=1&isAllowed=y

83 Sandy Ong and Edward Carver, "The Rosewood Trade: An Illicit Trail from Forest to Furniture," YaleEnvironment360, January 29, 2019; https://e360.yale.edu/features/the-rosewood-trade-the-illicit-trail-from-forest-to-furniture

84 Bob Koigi, "Illegal Chinese Timber Business is Devastating Africa's Forests," April 5, 2018, Fair Planet; https://www.fairplanet.org/story/illegal-chinese-timber-business-that-is-devastating-african-forest/

85 "Global Wildlife Treaty Bans Massive Illegal Timber Trade from Nigeria," Environmental Investigation Agency, November 1, 2018; https://eia-global.org/press-releases/20181101-immediate-suspension

86 Sandy Ong and Edward Carver

87 Ibid

88 "Top 20 export countries worldwide in 2017 (in billion U.S. dollars," Statista: https://www.statista.com/statistics/264623/leading-export-countries-worldwide/

89 "Total value of U.S. trade in goods (export and import) with China from 2006 to 2017 (in billion U.S. dollars)," Statista; https://www.statista.com/statistics/277679/total-value-of-us-trade-in-goods-with-china-since-2006/

90 Clark Gascoigne, "China's Illicit Outflows Were US$1.08 Trillion from 2002-2011," Global Financial Integrity, September 23, 2014; https://www.gfintegrity.org/chinas-illicit-outflows-2002-2011-us1-08-trillion/

91 Christine Clough, "New Study: Illicit Financial Flows Hit US$1.1 Trillion in 2013," Global Financial Integrity, "December 8, 2015; https://www.gfintegrity.org/press-release/new-study-illicit-financial-flows-hit-us1-1-trillion-in-2013/

92 Shirley Kan, "China and Proliferation of Weapons of Mass Destruction and Missiles: Policy Issues," Congressional Research Service, January 5, 2015, page 2; https://fas.org/sgp/crs/nuke/RL31555.pdf

93 David Sanger and William Broad, "From Rogue Nuclear Programs, Web of Trails Leads to Pakistan," New York Times, January 4, 2004; Simon Henderson, "Investigation: Nuclear Scandal, Dr Abdul Qadeer Khan," Sunday Times, London, September 20, 2009; R. Jeffrey Smith and Joby Warrick, "A Nuclear Power's Act of Proliferation," Washington Post, November 13, 2009

94 Kan, page 6.

95 Wyn Q. Bowen, Ian J. Stewart, Daniel Salisbury, "Engaging China in proliferation prevention," Bulletin of the Atomic Scientists," October 29, 2013; https://thebulletin.org/2013/10/engaging-china-in-proliferation-prevention-2/

96 John Tkacik, "Confront China's Support for Iran's Nuclear Weapons," Heritage Foundations, April 18, 2006; https://www.heritage.org/asia/report/confront-chinas-support-irans-nuclear-weapons

97 Wyn Q. Bowen, Ian J. Stewart, Daniel Salisbury, Bulletin of the Atomic Scientists

98 Kaya Forest and Sierra Rayne, "China Is Still Involved in Iran's Nuclear Weapons Program," American Thinker, July 3, 2018; https://www.americanthinker.com/articles/2018/06/china_is_still_involved_in_irans_nuclear_weapons_program.html. See also, ""Karl Lee" Charged in Manhattan Federal Court with Using a Web of Front Companies to Evade U.S. Sanctions, U.S. Department of Justice Press Release, April 29, 2014

99 Louis Charbonneau, "EXCLUSIVE - N.Korea, Iran trade missile technology - U.N," Reuters, May 14, 2011; https://in.reuters.com/article/idINIndia-57017820110514

100 Forest and Rayne, American Thinker

101 "Mutual Evaluation of China," The Financial Action Task Force, 2007; https://www.fatf-gafi.org/media/fatf/documents/reports/mer/MER%20China%20Annexes.pdf

102 Zhongxia Chen, "Chinese banks are accused of widespread money laundering. What does this mean for China?" January 12, 2017; https://blogs.lse.ac.uk/management/2017/01/12/chinese-banks/

103 "Mexican Narcos Are Using Chinese Crypto Money Laundering Syndicates," Anti-Corruption Digest, January 15, 2019; https://anticorruptiondigest.com/anti-corruption-news/2019/01/15/mexican-narcos-are-using-chinese-crypto-money-laundering-syndicates/#axzz5cmu7JU9N

104 Much of this section is taken from: John A. Cassara, "Flying Money May Land in the U.S.," Banking Exchange, February

21, 2016; http://m.bankingexchange.com/news-feed/
item/6079-flying-money-may-land-in-u-

105 Celia Hatton, "Report reveals offshore dealings of China's
elite," BBC News, January 23, 2014: https://www.bbc.com/news/
world-asia-china-25860494

106 2019 National Drug Threat Assessment, DEA, December 2019;
https://www.dea.gov/sites/default/files/2020-01/2019-NDTA-
final-01-14-2020_Low_Web-DIR-007-20_2019.pdf

107 "Mexican Narcos Are Using Chinese Crypto Money Laundering
Syndicates," Anti-Corruption Digest, January 15, 2019; https://
anticorruptiondigest.com/anti-corruption-news/2019/01/15/
mexican-narcos-are-using-chinese-crypto-money-laundering-
syndicates/#axzz5cmu7JU9N

108 2017 National Drug Threat Assessment, DEA, October, 2017;
https://www.dea.gov/sites/default/files/2018-07/DIR-040-17_2017-
NDTA.pdf

109 Frank O'Brien, "Property sales spike sparks money laundering fear,"
Compliance Alert; http://www.calert.info/details.php?id=105

110 Frank R. Guntner, "Why China Lost About $3.8 Trillion To
Capital Flight In The Last Decade," Forbes, February 22,
2017; https://www.forbes.com/sites/insideasia/2017/02/22/
china-capital-flight-migration/#32a4cbdd4a37

111 2007 National Money Laundering Strategy; https://www.treasury.
gov/resource-center/terrorist-illicit-finance/Documents/nmls.pdf

112 Jamila Trindle, "Drugs, Cash, Luxury Goods, and Maternity
Wear," Foreign Policy, October 13, 2014; https://foreignpolicy.
com/2014/10/13/drugs-cash-luxury-goods-and-maternity-wear/

113 Kaya Forest and Sierra Rayne, "The Sino-Mexican Influence in
America's Backyard," The American Thinker, July 5, 2018; https://
www.americanthinker.com/articles/2018/07/the_sinomexican_in-
fluence_in_americas_backyard.html

114 Mark Hanrahan, "China Obstructed Huge Money Laundering
Investigation By Italy: Report," International Business Times, June

5, 2015; http://www.ibtimes.com/china-obstructed-huge-money-laundering-investigation-italy-report-1953922

115 Angus Berwick and David Lague, "How China's biggest bank became ensnared in a sprawling money laundering probe," Reuters, July 31, 2017; http://www.ibtimes.com/china-obstructed-huge-money-laundering-investigation-italy-report-1953922

116 "Sandcastles: Tracing Sanctions Evasion Through Dubai's Luxury Real Estate Market," C4ADS, 2018; https://static1.squarespace.com/static/566ef8b4d8af107232d5358a/t/5b1fd21d2b6a28e94745ee34/1528812070952/Sandcastles.pdf

117 Gabriel Wildau, "China investment in foreign real estate hits record $33bn," Financial Times, January 29, 2017; https://www.ft.com/content/d8d80b6e-e381-11e6-8405-9e5580d6e5fb

118 Evelyn Cheng, "Chinese investment in the US drops 90% amid political pressure," CNBC, June 20, 2018; https://www.cnbc.com/2018/06/20/chinese-investment-in-the-us-drops-90-percent-amid-political-pressure.html

119 Lam Ka-Sing, "Chinese buying of US residential property hits record high," South China Morning Post, July 19, 2017; https://www.scmp.com/property/hong-kong-china/article/2103314/chinese-buying-us-residential-property-hits-record-high

120 Steve Hudak, "FinCEN Reissues Real Estate Geographic Targeting Orders and Expands Coverage to 12 Metropolitan Areas," FinCEN press release, November 15, 2018; https://www.fincen.gov/news/news-releases/fincen-reissues-real-estate-geographic-targeting-orders-and-expands-coverage-12

121 Diane Olick, "Chinese buyers expand their reach in the US housing market as the middle class gets in on the act," CNBC, January 8, 2019; https://www.cnbc.com/2019/01/08/chinese-middle-class-buying-up-american-residential-real-estate.html

122 Don Thompson, "U.S. Seizes pot-growing houses tied to China-based criminals," Associated Press, April 4, 2018; https://www.apnews.com/60e9e35eeb81482b85acce911a582266

123 "Macau casinos post first annual revenue gain in 3 years," Reuters, January 1, 2018; https://www.reuters.com/article/us-macau-gam-bling-revenues/macau-casinos-post-first-annual-revenue-gain-in-3-years-idUSKBN1EQ0RJ

124 "Move Over Vegas, Macau is Now the Gambling Capital of the World," ValueWalk, October 31, 2017; https://www.valuewalk.com/2017/10/gambling-revenue/

125 Sam Cooper, "How Chinese gangs are laundering drug money through Vancouver real estate," Fresh Radio 103.1, April 19, 2018; https://1031freshradio.ca/news/4149818/vancouver-cautionary-tale-money-laundering-drugs/

126 Adam Rawnsley and Seamus Hughes, "Casino Royale: Feds Say Chinese Drug Barons Laundered U.S. Coke Cash in Guatemalan Casinos," Daily Beast, January 23, 2020; https://www.thedailybeast.com/feds-say-chinese-drug-barons-laundered-us-coke-cash-in-guatemalan-casinos

127 Xie Yu, "China, Hong Kong the biggest source of funds mediated through British Virgin Islands, study says," South China Morning Post, June 25, 2017; http://www.scmp.com/business/banking-finance/article/2099901/china-hong-kong-biggest-source-funds-mediated-through

128 Max de Haldevang, "The secret insider terms used in Chinese money laundering," Quartz, March, 6, 2018; https://qz.com/1223009/corruption-in-china-has-created-new-terms-for-money-laundering/

129 Curtis Ellis, "Exposing China's Financial WMDS," Coalition for a Prosperous America, June 3, 2019; https://www.prosperousameri-ca.org/exposing_china_s_financial_wmds

130 Juliette Garside and David Pegg, "Panama Papers reveal offshore secrets of China's red nobility," The Guardian, April 6, 2016; https://www.theguardian.com/news/2016/apr/06/panama-papers-reveal-offshore-secrets-china-red-nobility-big-business

131 "The Panama papers embarrass China's leaders," The Economist, April 7, 2016; https://www.economist.com/asia/2016/04/07/the-panama-papers-embarrass-chinas-leaders

132 Nate Sibley, "How to fight China's financial abuses: Crack down on anonymous companies," Washington Examiner Opinion, February 5, 2019; https://www.washingtonexaminer.com/opinion/op-eds/how-to-fight-chinas-financial-abuses-crack-down-on-anonymous-companies

133 Ibid

134 Most of the information in this section is found in "Transnational Organized Crime," FBI Website; https://www.fbi.gov/investigate/organized-crime

135 Ibid

136 James O. Finckenauer, Ph.D., "Chinese Transnational Organized Crime," United Nations Activities, page 1; https://www.ncjrs.gov/pdffiles1/nij/218463.pdf

137 "Transnational Activities of Chinese Crime Organizations," Library of Congress, April 2003, page 25; https://www.loc.gov/rr/frd/pdf-files/ChineseOrgCrime.pdf

138 "Transnational Organized Crime," FBI Website

139 Mike Hager, "German Report reveals extensive money-laundering in B.C.'s luxury car market," The Globe and Mail, May 7, 2019; https://www.theglobeandmail.com/canada/british-columbia/article-german-report-reveals-extensive-money-laundering-in-bcs-luxury-car/

140 Tom Allard, "The Hunt for Asia's El Chapo," Reuters, October 14, 2019; https://www.reuters.com/investigates/special-report/meth-syndicate/

141 Bill Gertz, "China Using OPM Records for Spying," Washington Free Beacon, April 11, 2019; https://freebeacon.com/national-security/china-using-opm-records-for-spying/

142 Eric Tucker and Michael Balsamo, "Chinese military stole masses of Americans' data, US says," Associated Press, February 10, 2020; https://apnews.com/05aa58325be0a85d44c637bd891e668f

143 Corruption Perception Index 2018, Transparency International; https://www.transparency.org/cpi2018

144 Joel Kotkin, "A Clash of Values," New Geography, November 14, 2019; http://www.newgeography.com/content/006455-a-clash-values

145 Ibid

146 "China Corruption Report," GAN Business Portal; https://www.business-anti-corruption.com/country-profiles/china/

147 "The Chinese in Africa," The Economist, April 20, 2011; https://www.economist.com/briefing/2011/04/20/trying-to-pull-together

148 Christine Duhaime, "2,000,000,000,000 in Proceeds of Corruption Removed from China and Taken to US, Australia, Canada and Netherlands," Duhaime's Anti-Money Laundering Law in China, January 2, 2017; http://www.antimoneylaunderinglaw.com/2017/01/qa-on-the-2-trillion-in-proceeds-of-corruption-removed-from-china-and-taken-to-us-australia-canada-and-netherlands.html

149 Ibid

150 Stephanie Pagones," CBP finds more than 5,000 fake IDs sent from China," Fox Business, November 29, 2019; https://www.foxbusiness.com/money/cbp-customs-border-fake-id-china

151 George Mullen, "How to Stop China's Debt-Trap March to World Domination," American Thinker, January 13, 2019; https://townhall.com/columnists/georgemullen/2019/01/13/how-to-stop-chinas-debt-trap-march-to-world-domination-n2538969

152 Aaron Sarin, "When the Lion Wakes: The Global Threat of the Chinese Communist Party," Quillette, July 22, 2019; https://quillette.com/2019/07/22/when-the-lion-wakes-the-global-threat-of-the-chinese-communist-party/

153 Ibid; See also: Daniel Holl, "Ecuador's New Dam a Sign of China's Debt Trap Diplomacy," Epoch Times, December 31, 2018; https://www.theepochtimes.com/ecuadors-new-dam-a-sign-of-chinas-dept-trap-diplomacy_2751199.html and Tim Rogan," Why China's fishing habits are a much bigger problem than Japan's," Washington Examiner, December 27, 2018; https://www.washingtonexaminer.com/opinion/why-chinas-fishing-habits-are-a-much-bigger-problem-than-japans and Brad Schaeffer,

"Watch Out For China And What They're Doing In Africa," Daily Wire, December 4, 2019; https://www.dailywire.com/news/schaeffer-watch-out-for-china-and-what-theyre-doing-in-africa

154 "Trump Rids Major U.S. Container Port of Chinese Communist Control," Judicial Watch, October 8, 2019; https://www.judicialwatch.org/corruption-chronicles/trump-rids-major-u-s-container-port-of-chinese-communist-control/

155 Sarin, "When the Lion Wakes"

156 Chris Street, "Trump administration forces China to sell the Port of Long Beach," American Thinker, May 7, 2019; https://www.american-thinker.com/blog/2019/05/trump_administration_forces_china_to_sell_the_port_of_long_beach.html#ixzz5rmiHOYf0

157 Elizabeth Economy, "The Problem With Xi's China Model," Foreign Affairs, March 6, 2019; https://www.foreignaffairs.com/articles/china/2019-03-06/problem-xis-china-model

158 2016 International Narcotics Control Strategy Report, Volume II on Money Laundering, China Section, U.S. Department of State, March 1, 2017; https://www.state.gov/j/inl/rls/nrcrpt/2016/vol2/253391.htm

159 Peter Pham, "How Does China's Banking System Work?" Forbes, March 15, 2018; https://www.forbes.com/sites/peterpham/2018/03/15/how-does-chinas-banking-system-work/#791a86a912d9

160 "A Guide to China's $10 Trillion Shadow-Banking Maze," Bloomberg News, June 7, 2018; https://www.bloomberg.com/news/articles/2018-06-07/a-guide-to-china-s-10-trillion-shadow-banking-maze-quicktake

161 "Shadow Banking Lies at the Core of China's Systemic Financial Risk," China Banking News, December 29, 2017; http://www.chinabankingnews.com/2017/12/29/shadow-banking-lies-core-chinas-systemic-financial-risk/

162 Frank Tang, "China's financial system dogged by a corrupt alliance of cats and rats, central bank discipline chief says," South China Morning Post, February 1, 2018; https://

www.scmp.com/news/china/economy/article/2131629/
chinas-financial-system-dogged-corrupt-alliance-cats-and-rats

163 "Bank of China pays Italy 20 million Euros to Settle Tax Dispute,"
Reuters, June 16, 2017; https://www.reuters.com/article/
bankofchina-italy-tax-idUSI6N1J6005

164 Stanley Lubman, "Dirty Dealing: China and International Money
Laundering," Wall Street Journal, July 13, 2015; Dirty Dealing: China
and International Money Laundering

165 Neil Connor, "Chinese courts convict more than 99.9 percent
of defendants," The Telegraph, March 14, 2016; https://www.
telegraph.co.uk/news/worldnews/asia/china/12193202/Chinese-
courts-convict-more-than-99.9-per-cent-of-defendants.html?utm_
source=dlvr.it&utm_medium=twitter

166 Angus Berwick and David Lague, "How China's biggest bank
became ensnared in a sprawling money laundering probe,"
Reuters, July 31, 2017; https://www.reuters.com/investigates/
special-report/icbc-spain/

167 Zhongxia Chen," Chinese banks are accused of widespread money
laundering. What does this mean for China?" London School of
Economics and Political Science Blog, January 12, 2017; http://
blogs.lse.ac.uk/management/2017/01/12/chinese-banks/

168 Anthony Ruggiero, "Severing China-North Korea Financial Links,"
Center for Strategic and International Studies, April 3, 2017; https://
www.csis.org/analysis/severing-china-north-korea-financial-links

169 U.S. Department of the Treasury, Financial Crimes Enforcement
Network, "Advisory on North Korea's Use of the International
Financial System," November 2, 2017; https://www.fincen.gov/
sites/default/files/advisory/2017-11-02/DPRK%20Advisory%20
FINAL%20508%20C.pdf

170 Christian Berthelsen, "U.S. Considered Blacklisting Two
Chinese Banks Over North Korea Ties," Bloomberg, April 13,
2018; https://www.bloomberg.com/news/articles/2018-04-13/
china-banks-aiding-north-korea-are-said-too-big-to-punish

171 "Chinese Banks Open $35 Billion in New Financing for
    Iran," RWR Advisory Group; https://www.rwradvisory.com/
    chinese-banks-open-35-billion-new-financing-iran/

172 "Treasury Sanctions Kunlun Bank in China and Elaf Bank in Iraq for
    Business with Designated Iranian Banks," Treasury Press Release,
    July 31, 2012; https://www.treasury.gov/press-center/press-releas-
    es/pages/tg1661.aspx

173 "Policy Change at China's Bank of Kunlun Cuts Iran Sanctions
    Lifeline," Bourse & Bazaar, January 2, 2019; https://www.bourse-
    andbazaar.com/articles/2019/1/2/policy-change-at-chinas-bank-of-
    kunlun-cuts-sanctions-lifeline-for-iranian-industry

CHAPTER 12

Technology: Cell Phones and Cyber Laundering

OVER THE LAST 30 YEARS criminals and criminal organizations have concentrated their money laundering efforts in the core three primary categories identified by the FATF; via financial institutions, bulk cash smuggling, and trade-based money laundering. In other words, we continue to be vulnerable to the old-fashioned ways of laundering money. This will hold true unless and until we demonstrate to our adversaries that we can stop them.

Nevertheless, over the last few years there are signs that technology — specifically in the form of new payment methods or NPMs — will be increasingly used to launder money and transfer value.

I am glad I had my career when I did. I frankly don't understand some of the modern methods, and I don't have any personal experience investigating them. Few do. However, this chapter will address two representative and troubling technological money laundering trends: cell phones and cyber laundering. The first I have seen up close and personal in my travels. Its ramifications are not yet fully apparent. Some believe the latter is already a clear and present danger. Together, the technologies they represent present both opportunities and the challenges.

Cell Phones

I have been blessed in my life and career. One of the many opportunities I have enjoyed is traveling and living overseas. Like any good intelligence or law enforcement officer, I took advantage of those experiences by observing, conversing, developing sources of information, and reporting. In my travels during the timeframe after September 11, I was struck by the growing use of cell phones in the developing world. Not tied down by old-fashioned land line infrastructure, countries leapfrogged into 21st century communication. I was intrigued with how people readily embraced the new technology and how they used the ubiquitous cell phone not only for communication, but as a type of mobile wallet. Unfortunately, criminals find new and ingenious ways to use innovations for their own purposes. I began to be concerned that cell phones would eventually evolve into a new kind of money laundering threat.

In 2008, I wrote an essay published by the Department of State titled "Mobile Payments — a Growing Threat."[1] Today, the threat has materialized.

Mobile payments is actually an umbrella term that covers diverse high-tech money transfer systems such as digital precious metals, Internet payment services, prepaid calling cards, and M-payments (i.e., money and e-value transfer via the use of cell phones). Note: I am limiting my remarks in this section to mobile network operators where transactions are generally processed over the operators' wireless network(s). I will not address mobile payment services offered by financial institutions or the mobile payment service provider model where the provider offers mobile payment capabilities to its service users which may include merchants.[2]

The growth of access to cellular devices is breathtaking. In 1990, there were approximately 11 million mobile or cell phones worldwide.[3] In 2016, the number of mobile lines in service surpassed the global population![4] Today more people have cell phones than electricity and running water.[5] The GSMA, an organization that represents the global mobile industry, estimates that the mobile industry is on course to serve almost six billion customers by 2025.[6]

We should applaud these developments. The G-20 included "financial inclusion" on its priority agenda to help over two billion adults around the world who have limited access to financial institutions. [7] For example, only an estimated 4 percent of Mauritanian adults have bank accounts.[8]

I know many readers have traveled extensively in the developing world. Undoubtedly, you have observed how easy access to M-payments via the omnipresent cell phone is transforming lives by providing a much needed link to contemporary financial services at a reasonable price. Users are not required to have a bank account or credit card. For example, in Tanzania only 12 percent of the population is engaged in the formal financial sector. Mobile banking services fill the gap and, as a result, are expanding rapidly. The Central Bank of Tanzania estimates that the equivalent of $650 million is transferred each month through mobile transfers. [9]

In Kenya, using 2016 data, nearly 50 percent of Kenya's GDP flowed through M-Pesa, the country's leading mobile money service provider.[10] Twenty-three million Kenyans use M-Pesa or 90 percent of the adult population. There over 100,000 M-Pesa agents in Kenya.[11] According to the GSMA 2017 State of the Industry Report on Mobile Money, Sub-Saharan Africa has 135 mobile money services processing approximately $20 billion transactions in value per year.[12] In addition, the explosion in mobile banking is similarly occurring in Latin America and Asia.

How it Works

The following is a very simple summary of how money moves via cell phone in a country in the developing world:

1. The subscriber/user gives cash to an M-payment outlet. Sometimes these are nothing more than a small "mom and pop" kiosk or a convenience store in a rural village or city street. The user pays a small fee generally based on the amount of money involved.

2. The M-payment center transfers the money electronically through the phone company to the receiver's cell phone.
3. The recipient receives a text message informing him/her that the transfer to his "electronic-wallet" is complete.
4. The recipient uses the credits.

M-payment credits allow the purchase of products, services, payment of bills, the transfer of money person-to-person (P2P), the facilitation of micropayments for low value repetitive goods such as mass transit, the settlement of utility bills, payment of taxes, school fees, health, and many other services. Salaries and government benefits can be credited to cellular devices. M-payments have empowered small business creation. Remittances from migrant workers are sent home via the use of cell phones. The credits and payments allow for greater user safety and customer empowerment. Corruption at various transaction levels is minimized. Governments benefit from increased and more efficient tax collection. However, I am convinced that this wonderful development in financial services is also going to have increasingly dangerous side effects.

Money Laundering and Terror Finance Dangers

I spent my career traveling the world investigating financial crimes such as fraud, money laundering and terrorist finance. I firmly believe that unless we move quickly to engineer new forms of data collection and analytic tools in M-payment systems and also put in place regulatory and enforcement countermeasures, we will pay a very heavy price. In fact, there are signs that the abuse of the mobile payment industry by criminal elements is already happening.

In Chapter 3 we briefly outlined the three distinct stages of money laundering. Cell phones are being used in all three.

As noted, the first stage of money laundering is "placement" of illicit cash into a financial institution. There are many ways this occurs. One of the most prevalent methods both in the United States and around the world is "structuring," sometimes also known as "smurfing." For example, a professional money launderer takes a large amount of drug dollars and divides it into small amounts. He gives the small sums of money to "runners" or "smurfs" to deposit. The transactions are done in ways that attempt to avoid government mandated financial transparency reporting requirements.

With M-payments criminals now have a new way to "place" the proceeds of crime into financial networks. For example, a professional money launderer recruits a number of runners and gives them the proceeds of criminal activity. Small street sales of drugs, the proceeds of stolen property, street "taxes" (extortion or protection fees), or even suspect charitable or terror financing contributions can be laundered in this manner. The runners then go to M-payment establishments and use the illicit cash to load up their cell phones with money or "e-value" under the maximum threshold level. The runner will be directed to forward the mobile money credit to master accounts or other directed transfers controlled by the money launderer. This technique has been labeled by the Asian Development Bank as "digital smurfing." In contrast to money laundering where cash is placed into traditional financial institutions and sometimes money service businesses (MSBs), these structured M-payment placements are not transparent. With few exceptions, financial intelligence is not generated. And practically speaking, as I describe below, digital smurfing in most countries of concern is immune to law enforcement counter measures.

The second stage of money laundering is "layering." Once the illicit funds are "placed" into a financial institution, the objective is to layer the dirty money by multiple transfers and transactions thereby confusing the paper trail and adding multiple levels of venue and jurisdiction. Layering makes it very difficult for criminal investigators to "follow the money."

With M-payments, layering is taken to new levels. In most jurisdictions, mobile value can be transferred from account to account and then directed to a financial institution or MSB either in the host country or perhaps forwarded to another country or even an offshore haven. Mobile value can even be credited to an online account or perhaps used to purchase virtual currencies in cyber-space. A myriad of formal and informal money transfer systems such as hawala can also be added to the equation to further frustrate criminal investigators trying to follow the money trail. M-payments can also be used in hawala networks as a 21st century means of settling accounts between brokers. In short, layering schemes are only limited by the criminal's imagination.

The third stage of money laundering is defined as "integration." Once the dirty money is placed and layered, fronts for a criminal organization integrate the laundered money back into the economy. They might buy luxury vehicles, palatial homes, invest in shopping centers, the stock markets, and commercial enterprises of all sorts.

For example, the daughter of one of the worst kleptocrats in Africa has a net worth of billions of dollars. The country concerned has tremendous natural resources. The money controlled by the kleptocrat's family could be described as "fruits of corruption." In order to help "integrate" or legitimize the laundered ill-gotten gains, the kleptocrat's daughter has invested in cell phone carriers and M-payment providers in multiple countries.

In another example cited by the U.S. Department of State, in the West African country of Cote d'Ivoire funds are already being laundered via these M-payment techniques. In Uganda, also ac-cording to State Department reporting, "a significant portion of financial transactions . . . take place in the form of 'mobile money' payments and transfers, which could be abused by individuals and entities engaged in money laundering, terrorist financing, or other forms of financial crime. While the AMLA (financial intelligence unit/FIU) requires financial institutions to conduct comprehensive customer due diligence, it does not put the same requirements on mobile money transfers."[13]

According to a 2016 FATF/GIABA 2016 report on money launder-ing in West Africa, "Authorities lack tools to monitor the movement of funds sent via mobile payment platforms. Authorities identified this as an important method of transferring funds across the region, particularly considering the large numbers of the population that do not use regular banking services. There is a lack of available data regarding the potential use of this method to transmitting funds for terrorist purposes, largely due to a lack of adequate oversight of the sector."[14]

While sub-Sahara Africa is the region where mobile money is most widely spread, South Asia, the Caribbean, Latin America, and the Middle East are also rapidly expanding mobile financial services. Per industry sources, some of the most successful introductions of M-payment systems are found in the Philippines, Bangladesh, Pakistan, and Afghanistan.[15] Some of these countries already boast millions of M-payment users.

Unfortunately, these same countries also face terror finance challenges and likewise have extremely weak AML/CFT enforcement. In all of the above examples, due diligence practiced by mandated reporting entities such as banks, MSBs, and designated non-financial businesses and professions is generally very weak. The FIUs are challenged — if not ineffectual — and law enforcement and prosecutors are hampered by a lack of expertise and capacity. To put things in perspective, in 2015 the Philippines had zero convictions for money laundering; Bangladesh had one conviction; Pakistan had zero convictions; in 2014 Afghanistan reported only four money laundering convictions. Over the last few years the situation has not appreciably improved.

Realistically, there are no current tools to help law enforcement and intelligence officers identify and untangle suspicious M-payments in these and other countries where our adversaries operate. As far as I am aware, none are on the horizon. Mobile money transactions present many enforcement challenges because they traverse previously distinct and independent areas of regulation — particularly the telecommunications and financial banking sectors. Jurisdiction often involves multiple ministries and government agencies adding to the complexity of oversight needed. Moreover, there is a lack of understanding of the new M-payment threat and a corresponding lack of resources and financial crimes investigative capacity in most of the countries concerned.

My point is that some skeptics might claim that there are few cases linking mobile payments with money laundering and terror finance. I am convinced that currently there are many incidents and they will increase rapidly in the coming years. Cases are simply not recognized because the necessary technical infrastructures are not in place to trigger "red flags."

There has been a rush by entrepreneurs and mobile payment carriers to develop the technology and deliver services while for the most part ignoring countermeasures that could be engineered into the systems to help thwart money laundering and terror financing.

Some countries are being careful. For example, M-payments in Lesotho are flourishing. So, the Central Bank of Lesotho mandated that mobile money systems such Ecocash and M-Pesa must adhere to the Lesotho Money Laundering and Proceeds of Crime Act. The Central Bank issued guidance that was developed to conform to "international best practices and standards." M-payment providers are mandated to follow AML/CFT compliance programs. All transactions must be local and the amounts transferred have daily and monthly limits. In order to transfer higher amounts, know-your-customer (KYC) rules apply and subscribers are required to present their passport and proof of their sources of income. The system also has unusual behavior triggers which can lead to a suspicious transaction report (STR) being filed with the financial intelligence unit (FIU).[16]

The Lesotho model will help mitigate the digital smurfing risk. It will work for them because the size of the customer base is manageable. Lesotho has a population of two million. The real challenge will be to implement M-payment AML/CFT safeguards for large user communities.

For example, there are more mobile phones in Brazil than people, with approximately 275 million subscribers in a population of approximately 200 million — or approximately 100 times the population of Lesotho. Brazil is the fourth largest mobile market in the world. Despite the extensive mobile device penetration, mobile payments have been relatively slow to catch on. That will soon change.[17]

Action Taken by the United States

What is the United States government doing? The short answer is not much. Twelve years ago, when I first wrote about "the grow-ing threat of M-payments," the idea of money laundering and ter-ror finance via cell phones was mostly theoretical. In the interim, Treasury's Financial Crimes Enforcement Network (FinCEN) was given the mandate to sort out the myriad of legal, regulatory, and enforcement issues. Little was done.

U.S. regulators did make clear that existing financial services regulations apply to mobile banking and mobile payments provid-ers. FinCEN announced "that the acceptance and transmission of currency, funds, or other value that substitutes for currency from one person and the transmission of currency, funds, or other value that substitutes for currency to another person or location, by any means, constitutes money transmission" and is . . . "subject to rel-evant FinCEN regulations for AML/CFT purposes, either as part of the requirements on banks applying to all of their products and services, or as part of the requirements on money transmitters, a subset of regulated 'money services businesses.'" [18] As such, mobile banking and mobile payment providers are required to register with FinCEN, be licensed in most of the states where they operate, and follow traditional financial intelligence reporting norms.

However, it gets complicated. According to the government's own data, FinCEN's MSB registration program has not been suc-cessful.[19] The diversity and accessibility of the MSB sector presents challenges for regulation and oversight.[20] Moreover, most of the businesses involved in the transfer of money through mobile devices aren't financial institutions. Some argue that companies involved in mobile payment systems that don't meet the established definition of providing banking services aren't subject to anti-money launder-ing enforcement scrutiny, regulation, or even consumer protection laws. Undoubtedly, more years will go by while industry pushes back against the requirements.

In addition, there doesn't seem to be a sense of urgency to deal with these issues. While the use of M-payments will continue to grow, we have a social-economic culture that includes very well-established electronic payments systems with numerous existing options to meet consumer needs outside of mobile. Moreover, some observers in the U.S. have voiced concerns about M-payment interoperability, security, availability, consumer protection, etc.

Yet in most jurisdictions overseas, these concerns do not dominate discussion. As noted, many countries are hampered by weak anti-money laundering controls, enforcement, lack of capacity and expertise, corruption, and the lack of political will to seriously confront money laundering. M-payments are thriving in these same areas, and I believe they represent clear and present money laundering and terror finance dangers that will accelerate globally in the near future for the simple reason that criminal networks gravitate towards the weak link.

Cyber Laundering

In the early 1980s, researchers began to assemble the "network of networks" that eventually became the modern Internet. The World Wide Web debuted in 1990. It was the same year that I was sent to Rome to work with the Italian fiscal police to fight Italian American Organized Crime. Since that time, the Internet has revolutionized our lives. Instant communication, information, commerce, finance, and payment systems are at our fingertips. Organized crime and mafias of all sorts remain. However, the development of the Internet has radically changed both crime and law enforcement.

From the beginning of human history, trade has been based on interpersonal, mostly face-to-face dealings. That is changing. Millions of financial transactions take place over the Internet each day. Approximately 7 percent of commerce in United States takes place online and the volume is growing.[21] Both commercial and social relationships are established and maintained online. Unfortunately, commerce on the Internet has devolved into illicit trafficking as well. New technology has also allowed traders in illicit commerce to communicate in encrypted forms and use ever more types of cyber payment methods. It is very difficult — but certainly not impossible — for law enforcement to penetrate the online organizations, intercept online supply chains, and follow the online money and value trails.

The Dark Web is about five hundred times the size of the surface World Wide Web. As a result, massive amounts of information can be stored and accessed by users including criminals and criminal organizations.[22] Cybercriminals and money launderers choose to operate via the World Wide Web or the Dark Web based on the visibility they want for their products and services, sales volume, and level of criminal associated with their products and services. For example, Chinese-manufactured counterfeit goods are readily available on the World Wide Web. Narcotics and weapons are more likely to be found and sold on the Dark Web.[23]

The concurrent rise in cryptocurrencies and the Dark Web have only added to the difficulties for law enforcement. The Dark Web is accessible only via specialized software such as Tor, so that online users are able to browse it anonymously and securely without potential monitoring. This facilitates its use by illicit vendors and buyers. All types of contraband are available on the Dark Web such as narcotics, child pornography, arms, stolen identities, credit cards, and personal information and identification. Services are offered such as coding, prostitution, and even murder for hire. Ransom payments have been made in the Dark Web. Hackers advertise their services. Financial passwords and secure accounts of all sorts are stolen and made available for sale. Illicit proceeds are generated and laundered using cyber currencies.

Malicious products and services on the Dark Web have affected almost all countries around the world.[24] Criminal organizations are laundering illegally acquired funds through covert, anonymous online transactions. The anonymous nature of the Internet, particularly the Dark Web, and ever evolving technologies allow numerous opportunities for online money laundering operations to take place.

Although some cyber criminals rely on payments in traditional currencies and use facilitators such as PayPal, Western Union, and MoneyGram, others are linked to cryptocurrencies such as FBTC Exchange, WebMoney, Bitonic, Bitcoin, and xmlgold.eu. WebMoney works in traditional currencies as well as gold and Bitcoin by means of an e-wallet or digital currency purse. Cryptocurrencies such as Monero or Dash provide more anonymity through changing addresses or automatic mixing. Prepaid cards and vouchers are also used by online criminals.[25]

Bitcoin is the best known cryptocurrency. A 2019 study reported around $76 billion of illegal activities per year involved Bitcoin. About one quarter of Bitcoin users use it for criminal activity.[26] Still, over the years as Bitcoin has evolved, compared some of its competitors it is well understood and better regulated. Perhaps as a result, online investigators have observed that criminals are gravitating towards lesser known cryptocurrencies.

Although there is a lack of hard data, reportedly Mexican drug cartels are increasing their use of Chinese cryptocurrency money laundering networks. As discussed in Chapter 11, the Chinese — Mexican crypto money laundering relationship stems from years of cooperation in procuring precursor chemicals that process drugs such as methamphetamine. Chinese-manufactured fentanyl routed through Mexico to U.S. markets is a very serious concern. There are some reports that Chinese networks have been able to launder illicit funds through the country's banking systems which is then sent back to Mexican shell companies operated by drug cartels. Their crypto money laundering and underground banking networks have impacted the decline of cash seizures related to drug dealing activities in Mexico and the United States.[27]

According to a 2015 Europol report, Bitcoin has featured in high-profile investigations involving payments between criminals. In fact, the cryptocurrency was used in over 40 percent of illicit transactions in the European Union.[28] Similar to the use of hawala in Europe for criminal purposes (see Chapter 7), it is not surprising that terrorists and criminals would use digital currencies for illicit transitions given they offer similar benefits of trust, credibility, and avoid traditional AML countermeasures.

In the 2017 National Drug Threat Assessment Report the DEA stated that "Bitcoin and other virtual currencies enable TCOs [trans-national criminal organizations] to easily transfer illicit proceeds internationally." The DEA continued that TCOs were turning to Bitcoin due to "its longevity and growing acceptance at legitimate businesses and institutions worldwide." [29] However, according to Yaya Fanusie of the Foundation for Defense of Democracies, "The evidence of organized crime using crypto has been sparse." He noted crypto is not replacing "old" methods of money laundering, like cash.[30] Per our earlier brief discussion of crypto currencies in Chapter 3, our AML efforts continue to be defeated by old-fashioned methods such as bulk cash smuggling and TBML. It might be different ten years from now, but overall the percentage of criminal use of cyber currencies is still comparatively small.

Block chain technology is no longer "unhackable." Since 2017, hackers have stolen approximately $2 billion worth of cryptocurrency, mostly from exchanges, and that's just what has been reported publicly. These are not just opportunistic singular attackers; sophisticated cybercrime organizations are now doing it too. We shouldn't be surprised because block chains are particularly attractive to hackers because fraudulent transactions can't be reversed as they often can be in the traditional financial system. Sophisticated techies have long known that just as block chains have unique security features, they have unique vulnerabilities. Just like in the traditional world of criminality where thieves steal from thieves, the same is happening in cyberspace.[31] Some of these vulnerabilities also have allowed law enforcement to follow the cyber money and value including in the Dark Web.

For example, the Silk Road was an early online black market operating in the Dark Web. It was known best as a platform for selling illegal drugs. The website was launched in 2011. Buyers and sellers transacted deals collectively valued at roughly $183 million. In October 2013 the FBI shut down the Silk Road website and arrested Ross Ulbricht under charges of being the site's pseudonymous founder, "Dread Pirate Roberts." Two years later, Silk Road 2.0 came online, run by former administrators of Silk Road. Once again, the operation was shut down by law enforcement. Eventually, Ulbricht was convicted of eight charges related to Silk Road in the U.S. Federal Court in Manhattan. He was sentenced to life in prison without possibility of parole.[32] Law enforcement has had increasing success developing expertise, tracking, and prosecuting these types of cases.

Another crypto currency threat on the not too distant horizon is sanctions busting. Reportedly, U.S. adversaries such as Russia and China are exploring block chain technology projects and contemplating ways to develop national digital currencies. The Maduro regime in Venezuela launched its petro token currency in an effort to sidestep the U.S. dollar and phase in use of its controversial petro token for oil sales.[33] The initiative failed for various reasons, and there was little interest from buyers within or outside Venezuela. Although the Central Bank of Iran has talked a great deal about launching a cryptocurrency perhaps based on gold, the effort remains at the experimental stage. In the short term there are few immediate implications for Iranian sanctions evasion. On the other hand, the initiative does signal Iran's strategic intent to use block chain technology to develop long-term sanctions resistance.[34]

What Should be Done?

I am somewhat optimistic about engineering AML/CFT safeguards into M-payments. As with TBML, M-payments generate big data. Advanced analytics can be applied. For example, current fraud frameworks and security intelligence platforms are agile and can be adapted to various architectures and use cases. They are currently being used by both global banks and telecom companies for financial crime detection, public security and regulatory purposes.

Technology enables identity management capabilities and risk scoring using rules, predictive models, anomaly detection, as well as link and association analysis. In short, "red flags" can be engineered into M-payment systems that could automatically trigger alerts, suspend suspect transactions, and generate the filing of financial intelligence reports with the host country's FIU.

The worldwide growth of mobile money services does necessitate banking and telecom regulators to work together to allow mobile platforms to work. This type of cooperation is challenging. While there will be some costs for the M-payment industry, I believe M-payment providers should welcome robust anti-fraud and AML/CFT safeguards because they cannot afford being labeled as facilitating financial crime.

Overseas, ready markets already exist for M-payment AML/CFT safeguards. I encourage U.S. data and analytics innovators to get involved. If government does not wish to take the lead, I would like to see industry or a neutral and well-respected organization or think-tank convene an open forum where concerned law enforcement representatives, regulators, representatives from mobile carriers, and big data and analytics companies discuss both the challenges and the opportunities of engineering AML/CFT countermeasures into M-Payment systems. Perhaps an analytic solution could be developed and shared with interested mobile operating platforms and host country FIUs in the developing world. The safeguards could be made available in ways similar to the Egmont Group's "secure web" communications network and the United Nations Office on Drugs and Crime (UNODC) standard software system "GoAML" which is made available to FIUs around the world.

In addition, I believe that applicable law enforcement and intelligence agencies should heighten their awareness and reporting on the growing threat of M-payments. It's much easier and less expensive to take proactive steps in the early stages of new financial threats rather than to wait and play "catch-up." We should not wait and react to a crisis if we can identify one in the making.

Regarding cryptocurrencies, regulations are a work in progress in many countries and intergovernmental organizations. The G20 has called for a multilateral response. A conversation is warranted about the feasibility of applying the FATF's AML/CFT 40 recommendations. There must continue to be innovations in technical means to track and trace crypto. Law enforcement must be given increased training in detecting and investigating cybercrime.

M-payments, cybercrime, and crypto laundering are modern challenges. It remains to be seen if these new complex systems will overtake the old-fashioned money laundering methodologies that continue to work so well for criminals.

NOTES

1 2008 International Narcotics Control Strategy Report (INCSR) Volume II on Money Laundering, U.S. Department of State; available online at: http://www.state.gov/j/inl/rls/nrcrpt/2008/vol2/html/101346.htm

2 Note: Much of this section is taken from the author's Congressional testimony; "The Next Terrorist Financiers: Stopping Them before They Start," Before the Task Force to Investigate Terrorism Financing Of the House Financial Services Committee, June 23, 2016; https://financialservices.house.gov/uploaded-files/06.23.2016_john_cassara_testimony.pdf

3 "Electronic Finance: A New Approach to Financial Sector Development?" World Bank Discussion Paper 431

4 David Runde, "M-Pesa and the Rise of the Global Mobile Money Market," August 12, 2015, Forbes; http://www.forbes.com/sites/danielrunde/2015/08/12/m-pesa-and-the-rise-of-the-global-mobile-money-market/#663d74f723f5

5 Roger Cheng, "By 2020, More People will Own a Phone than have Electricity," February 3, 2016, CNET; http://www.cnet.com/news/by-2020-more-people-will-own-a-phone-than-have-electricity/

6 GSMA Annual Review, 2018, page 6; https://annualreport.gsma.com/2018/index.html

7 "Advancing Financial Inclusion to Improve the Lives of the Poor," CGAP; http://www.cgap.org/topics/financial-inclusion

8 2014 International Narcotics Strategy Report (INCSR) Volume II on Money Laundering, U.S. Department of State; see entry under Mauritania

9 2016 State Department International Narcotics Control Strategy Report (INCSR), Volume II on Money Laundering; available online at: http://www.state.gov/documents/organization/258726.pdf

10 Constant Munda, "Transactions through mobile money platforms close to half GDP," Daily Nation, August 2, 2017; https://www.na-tion.co.ke/business/Yearly-mobile-money-deals-close-GDP/996-4041666-dtaks6z/index.html

11 "The Future of Money," 60 Minutes, November 22, 2015; available online via YouTube: https://www.youtube.com/watch?v=AHIgQttKaj c&list=PL55ohbFcgaDMbY-iVxzP6cpJPDVMfDpV3

12 George Bauer and Leonard Kore, "Mobile money transaction fees and utility bill payments in emerging markets," GSMA Online, January 18, 2019; https://www.gsma.com/mobilefordevelopment/programme/mobile-money/mobile-money-transaction-fees-and-utility-bill-payments-in-emerging-markets/

13 2016 INCSR

14 FATF/GIABA, "Terrorist Financing in West and Central Africa," October, 2016, page 32; http://www.fatf-gafi.org/media/fatf/docu-ments/reports/Terrorist-Financing-West-Central-Africa.pdf

15 Runde

16 John Cassara, "Out of Africa – AML Compliance for Mobile Payments," June 12, 2015, Mobile Payments Today; http://www.mobilepaymentstoday.com/articles/out-of-africa-aml-compliance-for-mobile-payments/

17 Bethan Cowper, "Brazil is the Country to Watch for Mobile Payments," Banking 2015; http://www.paymentssource.com/news/paythink/brazil-is-the-country-to-watch-for-mobile-pay-ments-3019867-1.html

18 For more information, see "The Future of Money: Where do Mobile Payments Fit in the Current Regulatory Structure?": Hearing Before the Subcommittee on Financial Institutions and Consumer Credit, 112th Cong. (2012) (statement of James H. Freis, Jr., Director, Fin. Crimes Enforcement Network, U.S. Dept. of Treasury), available online at: http://financialservices.house.gov/uploadedfiles/james_freis_testimony.pdf

19 2007 National Money Laundering Strategy Report; http://www.trea-sury.gov/resource-center/terrorist-illicit-finance/Documents/nmls.pdf

20 Ibid

21 "Trade in Counterfeit and Pirated Goods: Mapping the Economic Impact," OECD, April 18, 2016, page 34; https://euipo.europa.eu/tunnel-web/secure/webdav/guest/document_library/ob-servatory/documents/Mapping_the_Economic_Impact_study/Mapping_the_Economic_Impact_en.pdf

22 Louise Shelley, Dark Commerce, 2018 Princeton University Press, page 141. Shelley's book was particularly helpful in tracking the development of illicit commerce on the Internet

23 Ibid

24 U.S. Department of Justice, "Avalanche Network Dismantled in International Cyber Operation," December 5, 2016; https://www.justice.gov/opa/pr/avalanche-network-dismantled-international-cyber-operation

25 Shelley, page 146

26 Sean Foley, Jonathan R Karlsen, Tālis J Putniņs, "Sex, Drugs, and Bitcoin: How Much Illegal Activity Is Financed through Cryptocurrencies?" Oxford Academic, April 4, 2019; https://academic.oup.com/rfs/article-abstract/32/5/1798/5427781?redirectedFrom=fulltext

27 "Mexican Narcos Are Using Chinese Crypto Money Laundering Syndicates," Anti-Corruption Digest, January 15, 2019; https://anticorruptiondigest.com/anti-corruption-news/2019/01/15/mexican-narcos-are-using-chinese-crypto-money-laundering-syndicates/#ixzz5gB2cvnia

28 Nakita Malik, "How Criminals And Terrorists Use Cryptocurrency: And How To Stop It, " Forbes, August 31, 2018; https://www.forbes.com/sites/nikitamalik/2018/08/31/how-criminals-and-terrorists-use-cryptocurrency-and-how-to-stop-it/#75cc047a3990

29 2017 DEA National Drug Threat Assessment, October 2017; https://
   www.dea.gov/sites/default/files/2018-07/DIR-040-17_2017-NDTA.
   pdf

30 Kevin O'Brien, "Authorities Say Criminal Enterprises Are Using More
   Crypto To Launder Funds," Renovate, December 30, 2018; https://
   www.cryptoglobe.com/latest/2018/12/authorities-say-criminal-
   enterprises-are-using-more-crypto-to-launder-funds/

31 Mike Orcutt, "Once hailed as unhackable, blockchains are
   now getting hacked," MIT Technology Review, February
   19, 2019; https://www.technologyreview.com/s/612974/
   once-hailed-as-unhackable-blockchains-are-now-getting-hacked/

32 Rebecca Campbell, "The Silk Road: A Story of Bitcoin, Drugs, and the
   Dark Web," Block Explorer News, December 1, 2018; https://block-
   explorer.com/news/silk-road-timeline-bitcoin-drugs-dark-web/

33 Yogita Khatri, "Venezuela to Sell Oil for Petro
   Cryptocurrency in 2019, Says Maduro," Coindesk,
   December 7, 2018; https://www.coindesk.com/
   venezuela-to-sell-oil-for-petro-cryptocurrency-in-2019-says-maduro

34 Yaya Fanusie, "Iran faces a long road before using blockchain to
   evade US sanctions," The Hill, February 15, 2019; https://thehill.
   com/opinion/technology/430276-iran-faces-a-long-road-before-
   using-blockchain-to-evade-us-sanctions

CHAPTER 13
Enablers and Facilitators

MONEY LAUNDERING AND ILLICIT FINANCIAL flows have many enablers and facilitators. We have discussed some earlier in the book. This chapter highlights a few more that I believe are particularly troublesome.

Free Trade Zones

Free Trade Zones or FTZs are also sometimes called special economic zones, enterprise zones, free ports, and export processing zones. Together, they are broadly defined as distinct economic areas that benefit from tax and duties exemptions. While located geographically within a country or jurisdiction, they are outside normal customs parameters and essentially exist outside its borders for tax purposes. Generally speaking, companies operating within FTZs can benefit from deferring the payment of taxes until their products are moved elsewhere, or can avoid them altogether if they bring in goods to a store, or manufacture on-site before exporting them again.[1]

FTZs are located in large developed countries such as the U.S. They are also commonly included in economic growth plans for the developing world. They are hubs of manufacturing, trading and transportation. The special economic incentives FTZ offer generate opportunities for growth and employment, support new businesses and attract direct foreign investment. While the exact number of FTZs around the world is a bit of a mystery, in 2015 it was estimated that there were approximately 4,300. Three out of four countries have at least one.[2] Some are enormous. For example, the well-known Colón Free Trade Zone in Panama sees approximately 5 percent of global trade pass through its locks every year. In 2016 the Colon FTZ generated $620 million in re-exports. The U.A.E. boosts 45 FTZs that hosts thousands of multinational and individual trading companies.[3] During my investigative career, I visited the Jebel Ali FTZ outside of Dubai numerous times. Jebel Ali is home to 7,300 international companies and boasts annual non-oil foreign trade worth a whopping $80.2 billion. Jebel Ali Port is a world-class gateway for over 90 weekly services connecting more than 140 ports worldwide.[4] It is the very volume of commerce that makes effective enforcement virtually impossible. In 2018, Djibouti, one of Africa's smallest countries, opened Africa's largest FTZ. The $3.5 billion project was backed by China.[5]

The U.S. leads OECD countries in the use of FTZs. In 2016, 195 active U.S. FTZs were responsible for an estimated $610 billion worth of imports — approximately 22.5 percent of total U.S. imports that year.[6] Today these numbers could be much higher. Unfortunately, not much is known about the zones in the U.S. and elsewhere as a money laundering "methodology." There are few investigations.

We know that FTZs attract criminal activity. Criminals and criminal organizations see them as ideal places to manufacture and transport illicit goods, as controls and checks by authorities are often irregular or absent. The opacity in the zones is a growing security, crime, and fraud challenge. For example, the World Customs Organization found that FTZs play an important role in smuggling tobacco products. The NGO TRAFFIC reported on seizures of illegal wildlife products and timber in FTZs. The FATF has also drawn attention to FTZs, highlighting their money laundering vulnerabilities and identifying 19 forms of predicate offenses frequented in FTZ operations, including such crimes as smuggling narcotics, arms, stolen goods and even humans.[7] The OECD has studied the proliferation of counterfeit and pirated goods trafficked in FTZs and concluded that exports of these fake products rise in parallel with the number and size of free trade zones it hosts.[8] The European Union has declared FTZs are a money laundering threat.[9]

Illegal transactions can be easily disguised as legal, using many of the TBML schemes discussed elsewhere in this book that are notoriously difficult to detect. While enforcement and customs inspection and control vary considerably from zone to zone, in general authorities have little or no oversight of what actually goes on in an FTZ. Goods are rarely ever inspected and companies operating in FTZs tend to benefit from low disclosure and transparency requirements.[10]

FTZs are typically governed by private companies or public-private partnerships that are granted a license to operate the zone. These administrators run the FTZ according to internal policies and regulations. Oftentimes there is little oversight and enforcement by the host government and little attention is given to AML/CFT policies and norms.

The FATF believes that many of the rules and regulations governing FTZs are outdated. The proliferation of FTZs has not kept up with the latest AML/CFT countermeasures and sometimes internationally recognized AML standards and norms do not apply to businesses and transactions within these special economic zones.[11] Currently, there aren't any internationally recognized definitions, typologies, or protocols governing the use of zones. The OECD adopted "Guidance to Counter Illicit Trade, Enhancing Transparency in Free Trade Zones."[12] However, those recommendations are non-binding and have yet to be implemented. While international efforts such as those of the OECD are encouraging and long overdue, global transparency standards need to be enforced by international institutions such as the World Trade Organization (WTO) and the World Customs Organization (WCO) and host customs services must enforce best practices.[13]

I agree with AML/CFT expert Clay Fuller's assessment[14] that the U.S. must take the lead when it comes to FTZ legislation and enforcement. Unfortunately, U.S. authorities do not understand many of the vulnerabilities of our own FTZs. Fuller rightly asks if

"Customs and Border Patrol (CBP) have the resources, workforce, and knowledge base needed to enforce complex due diligence and anti-money laundering laws while deterring increasingly sophisticated customs fraud schemes?" He urges legislation and policies that create a "21st century American zone program that would serve as a model for the rest of the world, standardizing procedures and streamlining trade. Preferably, any changes should be geared toward combating the trade-based money laundering schemes of transnational criminal organizations and terrorist groups."

Offshores

If an FTZ is a haven for illicit trade and associated crimes than an offshore financial center can be thought of as a haven for illicit finance. In mainstream vocabulary the term offshore is too encompassing. The word is an umbrella term and in common AML vernacular commonly covers offshore banking, offshore trusts and company service providers, offshore businesses/IBCs, shell companies, shelf companies, tax havens, offshore jurisdictions and anonymous shell companies, and in the U.S. even the catchall term of "Delaware companies" which we will discuss separately in the section below. Because it is broad, complex, and involves many legal issues that are frankly beyond my expertise, I will address offshores with only a few brief comments. However, brevity does not diminish the fact that offshores are a major enabler for money laundering and other crimes.

The term offshores varies by jurisdiction, but generally speaking it is a company or firm incorporated outside the country where it has its main offices and operations or where its principal investors reside. Commonly used in the layering stage of money laundering or tax evasion, offshores often offer proxies, complicated business structures, lack of transparency, lack of beneficial ownership information, and sometimes remote and inaccessible venues that make it very difficult for investors to follow the paper and money trails.

In short, offshores are like an alternative identity. They make it extremely difficult to link it back to anything or anyone.

Using offshore structures is legal. There are many legitimate reasons for using them. For example, business people in countries where the rule of law is not strong typically put their assets offshore or disguise them via offshore shell companies in order to defend them from criminals or their own government. Offshores are often used in facilitating capital flight and/or to get around currency restrictions. They can be used for reasons of inheritance and estate planning or simply to obscure assets or keep them out of the reach of a spouse or other family member. Offshores pose a number of benefits to the user including privacy, financial and business services, reduced administration fees, low or no taxes or tax deferrals, etc. They often offer low cost services. A simple Internet query will list thousands of offshore specialists that for a few hundred or few thousand dollars set up an offshore. Usually they require minimal or no verified personal information. Offshores can be established in a short period of time. Many can be completed over the Internet. Some business service providers even offer "virtual" office service for spooked customers. For a fee, a company sets up a fake email account and allows clients to communicate via invented names such as Harry Potter and Winnie Pooh.[15]

About 10 percent of world GDP is held in tax havens.[16] While some of it is properly declared to world governments, about 80 percent, or trillions upon trillions of dollars, is never taxed at all.[17] Nobody knows the total amount, but in 2014, the Price of Offshores, Revisited estimates that approximately $21 to $32 trillion[18] in financial assets sit offshore, largely in conditions of secrecy. According to the United Nations, tax havens cost governments between $500 billion and $600 billion a year in lost corporate tax revenue alone.[19] These illicit funds transfers hit the developing world particularly hard. As noted in Chapter 2, Global Financial Integrity estimates that every year, more than $1 trillion flows illegally out of developing and emerging economies due to crime, corruption, and tax evasion — more than these countries receive in foreign direct investment and foreign aid combined.[20] Most of these illicit financial flows avail themselves of offshores and hidden shell companies. Many developing countries do not have a debt problem — they have a hidden asset problem! Kleptocrats in Nigeria, Angola, Haiti, Russia, Ukraine, Philippines, Indonesia and many others have looted their own nations. Money, assets, and resources vanish leaving their impoverished people with nothing. Money that could be used for social welfare, health care, education, roads and infrastructure development are instead deposited in offshore accounts and hidden by an international web of shell companies and proxy owners.

After WWI, many European countries raised taxes to rebuild shattered countries. Modern offshore tax and bank secrecy havens date from the 1920s and 30s when Bermuda and Liechtenstein passed laws for offshore companies and trusts. Individuals were seeking havens from the taxman. Countries and jurisdictions found the advantages of low taxes in attracting money or businesses to their banks. Secrecy laws helped small countries. Countries, jurisdictions, and businesses all benefit from fostering banking, financial, legal, administrative services growth. Offshores provide host country employment. Cash-strapped governments found fees for financial services could prop up their economies.

Offshore financial centers allow companies to incorporate outside their domiciled country (country of residence). They manage companies' assets or personal assets offshore. Directors, shareholders and beneficial owners are offered financial, legal, privacy and tax benefits. The list of offshore financial centers is long and well-known. They range from tropical Caribbean Islands and South Pacific getaways to European "fairylands" such as Liechtenstein, Luxembourg, and Monaco, to more traditional European havens such as the Isle of Mann and Switzerland. Modern developed offshore financial centers include Singapore and the United States. Tax Justice Network's 2018 rankings[21] of the world's worst countries for financial secrecy include some of the same above offshore centers including Panama, the British Virgin Islands, the Cayman Islands, Singapore, and Switzerland. Surprisingly, the United States of America is listed as the second worst country. Much of that is due to U.S. "Delaware corporations" and lack of beneficial ownership information.

U.S. Anonymous Shell Companies

In 2013 I wrote an op-ed published by the *New York Times*.[22] The editor titled it, "Delaware Den of Thieves?" In the op-ed, I explained the reasons for my frustration with anonymous U.S. shell companies:

> As a special agent for the Treasury Department, I investigated financial crimes like money laundering and terrorism financing. I trained foreign police forces to "follow the money" and track the flow of capital across borders. During these training sessions, I'd often hear this: "My agency has a financial crimes investigation. The money trail leads to the American state of Delaware. We can't get any information and don't know what to do. We are going to have to close our investigation. Can you help?" The question embarrassed me. There was nothing I could do.
>
> In the years I was assigned to Treasury's Financial Crimes Enforcement Network, or FinCEN, I observed many formal requests for assistance having to do with companies associated with Delaware, Nevada or Wyoming. These states have a tawdry image: they have become nearly synonymous with underground financing, tax evasion and other bad deeds facilitated by anonymous shell companies — or by companies lacking information on their "beneficial owners," the person or entity that actually controls the company, not the (often meaningless) name under which the company is registered.

Our State and Treasury Departments routinely identify countries that are havens for financial crimes. But,
whether because of shortsightedness or hypocrisy,
we overlook the financial crimes that are abetted in
our own country by lax state laws. While the problem
is concentrated in Delaware, there has been a "race to
the bottom" by other states that have enacted corporate secrecy laws to try to attract incorporation fees.

We have mentioned beneficial ownership and shell companies
elsewhere in this book. So what are they? According to Gary Kalman
of the FACT Coalition, "When people create companies in the United
States, they are not required to disclose who really profits from their
existence or controls their activities — the actual "beneficial owners" of the business. Instead, individuals who benefit can conceal
their identity by using front people, or "nominees," to represent
the company."[23]

The nominee or registered agent can be the real owner's attorney or any other designated individual that has no control or
economic interests in the company. There are companies, easily
located online, whose entire business model is to file paperwork
and represent the real company owners. Some other countries
and jurisdictions do not require any ownership information at all.
Other jurisdictions allow for companies to be listed as the owners
of companies. This is the classic "layering" stage of money laundering making it difficult if not impossible to follow the money and
identify the true owners. Criminals abuse this anonymity to mask
identities, involvement in transactions, and origins of their wealth,
and put up impediments that often prevent law enforcement efforts to identify individuals behind illicit activity.

The forms of shell companies vary, but generally they are non-
publicly traded corporations, limited liability companies (LLCs), or
trusts that have no physical presence beyond a mailing address.
They generate little to no independent economic value. Most shell
companies are formed by individuals and businesses for legitimate

purposes, such as to hold stock or assets of another business entity or to facilitate domestic and international currency trades, asset transfers, and corporate mergers.[24] However, like so many other legal structures, they can and are abused.

In the most recent (2016) FATF mutual evaluation of the United States, the U.S. received failing scores for its efforts to prevent the laundering of criminal proceeds by shell companies. The U.S. was judged to be non-compliant — the lowest possible score — on its ability to determine the true owners of shell companies.[25] The lure of opaque registry is a very important reason why more corporations — anonymous and public — are established in the United States each year than in any other jurisdiction.[26] In fact, a 2014 study by academics at UT-Austin, BYU, and Griffiths University found that the United States is the easiest place in the world for suspect individuals to establish an anonymous company.[27] This was superbly demonstrated by a 2019 report from Global Financial Integrity that showed, on a state-by-state basis, that a person needs to provide far more personal information to a state to obtain a library card than to create a company![28] Spending a few dollars and a few minutes online, one can easily establish their very own Delaware LLC.

Delaware is by no means the only state that fosters easy company registration and does not require beneficial ownership information. Nevertheless, it has become the poster child of unsavory business practices, lack of transparency, and greed. Over a million businesses — more than 50 percent of publicly traded companies in the U.S. and more than 60 percent of Fortune 500 companies — are incorporated in Delaware. Sixty percent of U.S. hedge funds are registered in the state. Approximately two million companies a year are created in Delaware. In 2015, Delaware registered more than 480 companies a day, providing steady business for in-state lawyers, accountants, and registration companies, etc. Over 300,000 companies housed are housed at 1209 N. Orange Street in Wilmington alone. Despite the optics and negative publicity, why is this happening? The short answer is that companies' registration fees provide more than $1 billion or over one quarter of Delaware's annual state revenue.[29]

There are hundreds of U.S. and international investigations that involve anonymous U.S. shell companies. Delaware, and other pre-ferred business-friendly jurisdictions, have facilitated money laun-derers, tax dodgers, embezzlers, drug dealers and arms dealers and many other criminal activities. Here are just a few examples:

- In one of the largest Medicare fraud cases, criminals man-aged to steal over $35 million from the government program by creating at least 118 fake health clinics in around 25 states in the names of anonymous companies incorporated in eight states — Alabama, California, Colorado, Kentucky, Maryland, Nevada, New Mexico and Texas.[30]

- Fraudsters used anonymous shell companies incorporated in Florida, Georgia, North Carolina, South Carolina and Louisiana to steal approximately $70 million that was meant to help HIV and cancer sufferers through Medicare and Medicare Advantage.[31]

- Anonymous companies helped criminals in the United States sell several billion dollars in counterfeited luxury handbags and apparel accessories branded as Burberry, Louis Vuitton, Gucci, Fendi, Coach, and Chanel, as well as sportswear and gear from the NFL, NBA, and MLB including Nike, Adidas, and Under Armour, and many others.[32]

- A corrupt U.S. Lieutenant Colonel passed inside information to a business owner and contractor to create the perfect bid and steal more than $20 million from taxpayers and Afghan commando troops while transferring their illicit loot through anonymous shell companies in Virginia and Massachusetts.[33]

- An anonymous New York company owned part of a Manhattan skyscraper. The office used it as a front for the Iranian government. Millions of dollars in rent were illegally funneled to Iran in violation of U.S. sanctions.[34]

- The son of Teodoro Obiang Nguema Mbasogo, the President of Equatorial Guinea, a small oil-rich country in West Africa where the majority of the population lives on less than $1 a day, used a California shell company to disguise his purchase of a $30 million mansion in Malibu.[35]

Yet for the most part investigators do not work cases such as the above because it is almost impossible to penetrate the maze of shell companies and determine true beneficial ownership. As Manhattan District Attorney Cy Vance said at a Congressional hearing, "Time and again, we find that our international partners are better situated to assist us in thwarting terrorism and financial crime. We can't assist them in taking down U.S.-incorporated terroristic enterprises, because information about the owners of entities formed in our states is beyond our reach."[36]

In my investigations and travels overseas I frequently find that the foreign perception is that if something is registered or incorporated in the United States, it must be "legitimate." Rightly or wrongly, the U.S. benefits from the aura of respectability and good governance. Criminals take advantage of that. They register their shell company/companies in the U.S. and to the unknowing it gives respectability to their operations. Besides using anonymous shell companies, overseas criminals attempt to transfer much of their wealth to the United States and other stable western countries because of the protections afforded by the rule of law. Having accumulated their fortunes illegally, they are cognizant that someone more connected to power could come along and rob them too. Anonymous shell companies facilitate the criminals' schemes. It's embarrassing.

My op-ed in the New York Times that I quoted above continued with an appeal for the U.S. government to enact legislation that requires the disclosure of beneficial ownership information for U.S. companies. Thanks to tremendous work by a number of non-profits such as the FACT Coalition, Global Witness, Global Financial Integrity and other groups progress has been made. Over the last seven or eight years that overlap with both republican and democratic administrations and changing Congressional majorities, Washington is slowly coming to the consensus that something must be done. Support for ending the incorporation of anonymous companies has expanded and now includes "national security experts, police, sheriffs, local prosecutors, state Attorneys General, federal prosecutors, human rights advocates, anti-human trafficking groups faith-based networks, international development NGOs, CEOs, big businesses, small governmental organizations, and scholars at both conservative and liberal think tanks, among others."[37] All companies, large and small, should disclose who ultimately owns and controls them. It should be an expression of business integrity and ethics.

The U.S. should create a national beneficial ownership registry for all legal entities. My preference would be for an "open registry" available to all. If that is politically impossible, the registry should be made accessible to appropriate law enforcement personnel in the same manner as BSA information. The registry should be created, housed, and the information disseminated in a way that does not unduly burden or violate the privacy rights of American businesses, U.S. citizens, or financial institutions.

Corruption

Dante Alighieri, in his timeless masterpiece *The Divine Comedy*, writes: "For pride and avarice and envy are the three fierce sparks that set all hearts ablaze." All of these vices found in the "mountain of purgatory" manifest themselves in corruption. And corruption, in its many and varied forms, is the great facilitator in money laundering. Corruption is a form of greed. For instance, we stated at the beginning of this book, greed or avarice is part of the human condition. As Dante recognized, greed is universal. It is a vice. It is a sin. It is illegal. It is also both an enabler and a predicate offense for money laundering.

There is no comprehensive and universally accepted definition of corruption. It is one of those things one knows when one sees it (or experiences it). Over and over again corruption features prominently in money laundering cases. Corruption can generate or facilitate enormous illicit proceeds that are laundered and given an appearance of legality. There are a multitude of actors. We see corrupt politicians and politically exposed people, influence peddlers, "pay-to-play" charlatans and foundations, businessmen, celebrities and sports stars, bankers and financiers, intermediaries of all sorts including designated businesses and professionals such as attorneys and accountants, corrupt government officials, law enforcement and customs officers, government bureaucrats, that for a price (financial or other benefits) look the other way; they provide the required signature, stamp the necessary document, don't ask questions, use their influence for nefarious purposes, call in favors, cast the requested vote, lobby and facilitate.

Overall, the World Bank estimates $1.5 trillion in bribes[38] are paid every year, squandering business capital, stymying development, destroying good governance, and rotting souls. If corruption were curbed, the IMF estimates about $1 trillion in tax revenues could be realized globally every year.[39]

Corruption has also increasingly become more than a legal and moral issue. It is now a strategic concern and a battleground in great power competition. Corruption helps sustain power.[40] This is certainly apparent in the strategic shenanigans by oligarchs and the interference in democratic regimes by Putin's Russia and the Chinese "Belt and Road" initiative discussed in Chapter 11. They weaponize corruption in weak states to gain influence, win deals, and undermine sovereignty. There are a myriad of tawdry tales involving African kleptocrats content to raid their own countries for personal gain. The slow painful demise of once prosperous Venezuela under the inept socialist Chavez-Maduro regime is a vivid reminder of corrupt states. Across Latin America, corrupted officials are more likely to turn a blind eye at the border, enabling the trafficking of illicit drugs, weapons, and migrants.

Transparency International's Corruption Perception Index was established in 1995 and "has been widely credited with putting the issue of corruption on the international policy agenda." [41] It publishes an annual ranking on how corrupt countries' public sectors are seen to be. I often refer to the index. It is not a coincidence that countries that are ranked as among those most corrupt are the same countries where money laundering, illicit financial flows and other financial crimes are rampant. Countries that score well on the corruption index, similarly have more robust AML/CFT regimes. For a point of reference, in the latest available index the United States is ranked 22 out of 180 countries surveyed; Denmark scored #1 and Somalia was ranked last. [42]

The following are just a few examples[43] of corruption and money laundering:

- Between 2007 and 2015, approximately €200 billion belonging to Russian entities and other former Soviet states flowed through an Estonian branch of Danske Bank, the largest bank in Denmark. Lantana Trade, a limited liability partnership involved in the scandal, held an account. The beneficial owners were alleged to be members of Vladimir Putin's family. Danske Bank is now facing multiple investigations.

- Nicolas Maduro, the authoritarian leader of Venezuela, facilitated the laundering of $1.2 billion stolen from Venezuela's state-owned oil company PDVSA. According to a U.S. federal investigation, at least $200 million generated from the money laundering scheme are believed to have been set aside for Maduro's three stepsons, including 17 properties worth tens of millions were purchased throughout South Florida.

- On March 18, 2009, a French appeals court in Paris fined Dan Etete, Nigeria's former petroleum minister under the presidency of General Abacha, €10.5 for his participation in transactions that laundered the proceeds of passive and active corruption committed in Nigeria, by representatives of ADDAX, a company involved in the exploitation, production and trading of oil. Via a complex financial scheme, helped by Richard Granier Deferre, then one of ADDAX's executives, Etete used the proceeds of corruption in the form of cash to cover personal expenses such as real estate investments including a castle in the French countryside, investments in art, antiques, yachts, and other investments undertaken through the creation of a company. The financial scheme in this case involved transferring the proceeds of corruption to Swiss Bank accounts, either held under fake identities, or held on behalf of off shore companies. The money was then wired to Paris and made available to Etete.

- U.S. Representative William J. Jefferson (D-Louisiana) was investigated by the FBI after an investor alleged $400,000 in bribes was paid through a company maintained in the name of Jefferson's spouse and children. In return for the payment, Jefferson allegedly was to help persuade the U.S. Army to test a company's broadband two-way technology and other products. He was also to influence high-ranking officials in Nigeria, Ghana, and Cameroon and meet with personnel of the Export-Import Bank of the United States in order to facilitate potential financing for business deals in those countries. Jefferson was videotaped by the FBI receiving $100,000 worth of $100 bills in a leather briefcase at the Ritz-Carlton hotel in Arlington, Virginia. A few days later, FBI agents raided Jefferson's home and found $90,000 of the cash in the freezer wrapped in aluminum foil and stuffed inside frozen food containers. He was later found guilty of corruption and other charges.[44]

There are a variety of anti-corruption programs put forward by the U.S. State Department, the World Bank, various non-profits, anti-corruption advocacy groups, and many more. They are necessary and valiant efforts. But we will never fully defeat either foreign or domestic corruption. As noted above it is part of the human condition. Sometimes corruption is rooted in culture. It takes a long time to change those attitudes and ways of doing business. Sometimes corruption is tied poverty. Police officers and customs officials in poor countries can barely support their families on the subsistence salaries they receive. They look the other way or put out their hand because they feel they must. However, we can do much more to prioritize the awareness of the evils of corruption. We can support programs that help alleviate the perceived need for more. The media needs to do much more in shining a light on the problem of corruption. In addition, there is no substitute for successful investigations, prosecutions, and convictions.

Social Media and Secure Communications

The use of social media has exploded. In 2012, the number of Facebook users worldwide surpassed one billion. At the end of 2019, Facebook had approximately 2.5 billion global users.[45] While social media platforms and communications can be a force for good, its long term pernicious effects on the individual and society as a whole have yet to be widely acknowledged. (Full disclosure: I do not participate in social media.) Similarly, many also do not recognize that criminals increasingly exploit social media like Facebook, Twitter, Instagram, and YouTube. They use it for instant communications and organization. For example, television news frequently shows videos of organized shoplifting rings of marauding youth gangs ransacking a department store. The attacks are frequently coordinated via social media.

The above is an example of low level crime. Much more serious crime involving narcotics trafficking, human trafficking, and smuggling involving illicit trade of all kinds is increasingly facilitated by the anonymity of the Internet and by encrypted social media. WhatsApp (over one billion users in 180 countries), WeChat (a Chinese-based service with about one billion users monthly) and Viber (260 monthly users) are just a few examples. Traffickers can communicate and organize in privacy using these free systems and advanced technologies. The companies offering them do not have to maintain records of the calls or text content. Apple and Google have engineered their smartphones to block law enforcement access to this information.[46] And the situation is getting worse.

For example, a criminal money courier brings the illicit proceeds of drug trafficking in the form of bulk cash to a prearranged spot. The courier texts his boss and confirms his arrival. He waits for another individual to arrive and "pick-up" the cash. Later, the person picking up the money confirms via text message that everything went according to plan. He is then given instructions on where to go next. Meanwhile, law enforcement surveilling the pick-up operation intercept their text messages — but only see rows of numbers, letters, and characters that make no sense. The messages are encrypted.

In 2017 former FBI director, James Comey, told the Senate Judiciary Committee that criminal suspects are increasingly using encryption. Of the more than 6,000 phones FBI investigators seized from October 2016 to April 2017, nearly half were encrypted and investigators could not access their content. According to Comey, "That means half of the devices that we encounter in terrorism cases, in counterintelligence cases, in gang cases, in child pornography cases, cannot be opened with any technique. That is a big problem."[47]

In 2019, Vincent Ramos, the chief executive of Canada-based Phantom Secure, was sentenced to nine years in prison for running a criminal enterprise that facilitated the transnational importation and distribution of narcotics through the sale of encrypted communication devices and services.[48] Ramos advertised Phantom Secure's products as impervious to decryption, wiretapping or legal third-party records requests. He offered a much needed service to criminals and criminal organizations and they rewarded him handsomely. As part of his sentence, the court ordered Ramos to forfeit $80 million as proceeds of the crime, as well as international bank accounts, real estate, cryptocurrency accounts, and gold coins.

Owen Hanson, one of Ramos's customers, only used six Phantom Secure devices to coordinate the transportation of more than a ton of cocaine from Mexico into the United States and on to Canada and Australia. Yet it is conservatively estimated there were at least 7,000 Phantom Secure devices in use at the time Ramos was arrested. Law enforcement is unable to calculate the amount of criminal activity facilitated by Phantom Secure encrypted devices.

When I was a criminal investigator, many criminals used "burner phones," or cheap, pre-paid cell phones to limit authorities' ability to track their communications. However, technology changes and today many crime groups keep abreast of developments and are willing to pay for top-of-the-line products like those offered by Phantom Secure. There is a robust trade in custom encrypted phones for organized crime. They often have the microphone and GPS functionality removed, and instead rely on end-to-end encrypted chat programs, making it difficult and sometimes impossible for authorities to intercept criminals' communications.

Phantom Secure offered its products as completely secure and able to block any sort of hacking or third party intrusion. Encrypted platforms are not illegal, and there are many legitimate reasons people use encryption to protect their electronic messages. Likewise, it isn't necessarily illegal to sell a phone installed with encryption technology. But Phantom's entire business model revolved around selling encrypted phones to crime groups. There are many other operations distributing specialized phones through a network of resellers who advertise through social media accounts and the Dark Web. Many of these advertisements feature images such as guns, drugs and cash.

The courts will have to sort out how much cooperation law enforcement can expect to receive from industry that prizes profit over security. One of law enforcement's few remaining advantages over criminal groups is technology. In the area of secure communications, the advantage is disappearing.

NOTES

1 Daniel Neal, "Free trade zones: a Pandora's box for illicit money,"
   Global Financial Integrity, October 7, 2019; https://gfintegrity.org/
   free-trade-zones-a-pandoras-box-for-illicit-money/

2 "Not So Special – Special Economic Zones," The Economist, April
   4, 2015; https://www.economist.com/leaders/2015/04/04/
   not-so-special

3 Neal

4 "Dubai's gem: How Jebel Ali Free Zone has turned the emirate
   into a global trading powerhouse," Gulf News, September 14,
   2017; https://gulfnews.com/business/dubais-gem-how-jebel-ali-
   free-zone-has-turned-the-emirate-into-a-global-trading-power-
   house-1.2089870

5 Abdi Latif Doher, "Thanks to China, Africa's Largest
   FTZ has Launched in Djibouti," Quartz Africa,
   July 9, 2018; https://qz.com/africa/1323666/
   china-and-djibouti-have-launched-africas-biggest-free-trade-zone/

6 Clay R. Fuller, "How Congress can reduce the damage of the White
   House's looming trade war," American Enterprise Institute, June
   6, 2018; https://www.aei.org/economics/international-economics/
   how-congress-can-reduce-damage-of-trade-war/

7 "Online public consultation on the draft OECD Guidance to Counter
   Illicit Trade, Enhancing Transparency in Free Trade Zones," OECD;
   https://www.oecd.org/governance/online-public-consultation-
   draft-guidance-enhancing-transparency-in-free-trade-zones.htm

8 "Free trade zones are being used to traffic counterfeit goods," OECD,
   March 15, 2018;

9 Jennifer Rusken, "Free Zones Favored by Boris Johnson
   are a Money Laundering Threat," The Guardian, July 24,
   2019; https://www.theguardian.com/world/2019/jul/24/
   eu-identifies-free-ports-as-money-laundering-threat

10 "Trade in Counterfeit Goods and Free Trade Zones," OECD, July 7, 2018; https://www.oecd.org/governance/free-trade-zones-are-being-used-to-traffic-counterfeit-goods.htm

11 "Money Laundering Vulnerabilities of Free Trade Zones," FATF, March, 2010; https://www.fatf-gafi.org/media/fatf/documents/reports/ML%20vulnerabilities%20of%20Free%20Trade%20Zones.pdf

12 OECD Guidance

13 Neal

14 Fuller

15 Hans Leyendecker, Frederik Obermaier, Bastian Obermayer and Vanessa Wormer, "Panama Papers – The Secrets of Dirty Money," Suddeutsche Zeitung; https://panamapapers.sueddeutsche.de/articles/56febf8da1bb8d3c3495adec/

16 Gabriel Zucman, "Who Owns the Wealth in Tax Havens? Macro Evidence and Implications for Global Inequality," December 27, 2017, page 2; https://gabriel-zucman.eu/files/AJZ2017b.pdf

17 Libby Nelson, "A top expert on tax havens explains why the Panama Papers barely scratch the surface," Vox, April 8, 2016; https://www.vox.com/2016/4/8/11371712/panama-papers-tax-haven-zucman

18 Nick Shaxon,"The Price of Offshores, Revisited," Tax Justice Network, January 17, 2014; https://www.taxjustice.net/2014/01/17/price-offshore-revisited/

19 "Low-Income Economies Lost More to Illicit Financial Flows than They Receive in Aid, Deputy Secretary-General Tells Dialogue on Development Financing," United Nations, September 26, 2019; https://www.un.org/press/en/2019/dsgsm1350.doc.htm

20 Global Financial Integrity website, "About Us;" https://gfintegrity.org/about/

21 2018 Financial Secrecy Network, Tax Justice Network; https://www.financialsecrecyindex.com/en/introduction/fsi-2018-results

22 John A. Cassara, "Delaware, Den of Thieves," New York Times, November 1, 2013; https://www.nytimes.com/2013/11/02/opinion/delaware-den-of-thieves.html

23 Gary Kalman, ""Outside Perspectives on the Collection of Beneficial Ownership Information," testimony before the United States Senate Committee on Banking, Housing, and Urban Affairs, June 20, 2019; https://thefactcoalition.org/wp-content/uploads/2019/06/Gary-Kalman-SBC-20190620-Written-Testimony-FINAL.pdf

24 "Advisory to Financial Institutions and Real Estate Firms and Professionals," FinCEN Advisory, FIN-2017-A003, August 22, 2017; https://www.fincen.gov/resources/advisories/fincen-advisory-fin-2017-a003

25 "Mutual Evaluation of the United States," Financial Action Task Force, December, 2016, page 13; https://www.fatf-gafi.org/publications/mutualevaluations/documents/mer-united-states-2016.html

26 "The Library Card Project: The Ease of Forming Anonymous Companies in the United States," Global Financial Integrity, March 21, 2019; https://gfintegrity.org/report/the-library-card-project/

27 Kalman

28 "The Library Card Project: The Ease of Forming Anonymous Companies in the United States," Global Financial Integrity, Global Financial Integrity, March, 2019; https://secureservercdn.net/45.40.149.159/34n.8bd.myftpupload.com/wp-content/uploads/2019/03/GFI-Library-Card-Project.pdf?time=1576152230

29 A number of sources including Kalman testimony; Darren Weaver, "This tiny building in Wilmington, Delaware is home to 300,000 businesses," Business Insider, December 27, 2018; https://www.businessinsider.com/building-wilmington-delaware-largest-companies-ct-corporation-2017-4; and David Kocieniewski, "Delaware's $1 Billion Incorporation Machine," Bloomberg, April 27, 2016; https://www.bloomberg.com/news/articles/2016-04-27/delaware-s-1-billion-opacity-industry-gives-u-s-onshore-haven

30 "Hidden Menace," Global Witness, July 2016, page 13; https://www.globalwitness.org/en/reports/hidden-menace/

31 Ibid

32 Kalman testimony

33 "Hidden Menace"

34 "FACT Sheet: Anonymous Shell Companies," FACT Coalition, April 21, 2017; https://thefactcoalition.org/fact-sheet-anony-mous-shell-companies-april-2017?utm_medium=policy-analysis/fact-sheets

35 Ibid

36 Melanie Hicken and Blake Ellis, CNN Money, December 9, 2015; https://money.cnn.com/2015/12/09/news/shell-companies-crime/index.html

37 Kalman testimony

38 Abigail Bellows, "Ten Ways Washington Can Confront Global Corruption," Carnegie Endowment for International Peace, July 25, 2018; https://carnegieendowment.org/2018/07/25/ten-ways-washington-can-confront-global-corruption-pub-76919

39 Rodrigo Campos, "Corruption Costs $1 trillion in Tax Revenue Globally: IMF," Reuters, April 4, 2019; https://www.reuters.com/article/us-imf-corruption/corruption-costs-1-trillion-in-tax-revenue-globally-imf-idUSKCN1RG1R2

40 David Petraeus and Sheldon Whitehouse, "Putin and other authoritarians' corruption is a weapon — and a weakness," Washington Post, March 8, 2019; https://www.washingtonpost.com/opinions/2019/03/08/putin-other-authoritarians-corruption-is-weapon-weakness/

41 Transparency International Corruption Perception Index; transparency.org

42 Ibid, 2018 Corruption Perception Index

43 Two particularly useful sources with many examples are: Clay R. Fuller, "Defeating the Authoritarian-Corruption Nexus," American Enterprise Institute, July 8, 2019; https://www.aei.org/research-products/report/dismantling-authoritarian-corruption-nexus/

and "Corruption and Money Laundering: Concepts and Practical Applications," The World Bank Group; http://pubdocs.worldbank.org/en/887011427730119189/AML-Module-1.pdf

44 Many sources including, "Rooting Out Corruption - A Look Back at the Jefferson Case," The FBI, April 9, 2013; https://www.fbi.gov/news/stories/a-look-back-at-the-william-j-jefferson-corruption-case and William J. Jefferson Corruption Case, Wikipedia; https://en.wikipedia.org/wiki/William_J._Jefferson_corruption_case

45 J. Clement, "Number of Active Facebook Users Worldwide as of 3rd Quarter of 2019," Statista, November 19, 2019; https://www.statista.com/statistics/264810/number-of-monthly-active-facebook-users-worldwide/

46 Louise Shelly, Dark Commerce, Princeton University Press, Princeton, New Jersey, Copyright 2018, page 162.

47 Katarina Sabados, "Encryption: A Godsend to All Who Seek Privacy, Even Criminals," Organized Crime and Corruption Reporting Project, October 31, 2018; https://www.occrp.org/en/61-ccblog/8822-encryption-a-godsend-to-all-who-seek-privacy-even-criminals

48 See: "Chief Executive of Communications Company Sentenced to Prison for Providing Encryption Services and Devices to Criminal Organizations," Department of Justice Press Release, May 28, 2019; https://www.justice.gov/usao-sdca/pr/chief-executive-communications-company-sentenced-prison-providing-encryption-services; Mack Lamareaux and Joseph Cox, "CEO Who Sold Encrypted Phones to the Sinaloa Cartel Sentenced to Nine Years," Vice, May 29, 2019; https://www.vice.com/en_us/article/xwn4vw/ceo-who-sold-encrypted-phones-to-the-sinaloa-cartel-sentenced-to-nine-years; Scott Squires, "Canadian Company Custom-Made Encrypted Phones for Cartels: FBI," Insight Crime, March 14, 2018; https://www.insightcrime.org/news/brief/canadian-company-custom-made-encrypted-phones-cartels-authorities/

CHAPTER 14
More Forward Steps

AS DISCUSSED PREVIOUSLY, IN 1990 I was assigned to the U.S. Embassy in Rome to direct Operation Primo Passo or "First Step." At the time, Italian law enforcement was taking its first baby steps towards combatting international money laundering. The immediate threat was Italian Organized Crime. It took many years and collectively we had a few stumbles but ultimately Italy developed a robust AML/CFT regime.

Certainly, over the last 30 years we have had numerous individual and shared AML/CFT success stories. Yet I remember the lessons of Primo Passo when I think about the sobering statistics or "measureables" we shared in Chapter 2 that show "total failure is only a decimal point away." We have made some mistakes. Certainly, we can do better. In the fight against international money laundering, continued failure is not an option. Throughout this book, after discussions of various methodologies and enablers, I list several countermeasures and recommendations for continued improvement. This last chapter includes a few more suggestions and "forward steps."

I think it is clear we need a re-invigorated AML stratagem. We should begin anew with a holistic perspective. Obviously, we should keep what works but not be afraid to jettison countermeasures that aren't working or that are not cost effective. Band-aids and tinkering around the edges are not going to give us the results we need. It is time for a radical AML paradigm shift.

Really, Truly, Finally Go After the Money

U.S. law enforcement has consistently talked about the importance of "following the money" and taking away the proceeds of crime from criminals and criminal organizations. Yet in practice those self-evident goals have not been emphasized. To take just one notorious example, in our "War on Drugs" our efforts have been concentrated on interdicting the participants and the products. Another strategy the DEA and other law enforcement organizations pursued is to go after the "kingpins" or the leaders or heads of criminal organizations. The strategy is to decapitate the boss of bosses and kill the organization. A further tactic is to go after the low-level participants — the street-level dealers and the mules and follow them to the top of the organizational structure. However, the most common counter measure of all is to go after the product, from bags of cannabis smuggled across the border to tons of cocaine seized on the high seas.

Having been in federal law enforcement, I'll tell you the truth: We go after the participants and the product because it is far easier than going after the money. Also, that product is not just drugs. It similarly holds true for human beings in trafficking networks, counterfeit goods, stolen cars, weapon smuggling, illicit tobacco, wildlife trafficking, etc. All the above and many more are predicate offenses for money laundering. As I wrote in the beginning of this book, criminals do not traffic in drugs for the sake of drugs or any other illegal good or service. They engage in crime for the money. Our emphasis on product and participants has led to failure. In order to change that paradigm, we need to really, truly, finally emphasize money. In order to do that, we have to change the incentives and the culture of the bureaucracies.

Change the Incentives for Law Enforcement

Our AML efforts currently all come down to enforcement. The United States has the best and most robust law enforcement in the world. Yet dated information suggests that, in the United States, money launderers face a less than 5 percent risk of conviction (some plead to lesser charges). Currently, there are about 1,200 money laundering convictions a year at the federal level.[1] That seems like a large number, but — divided into the amount of criminal activity and factoring in the hundreds of billions of illicit proceeds generated — it is not. Yes, I know that many money laundering charges are plea bargained away. But no knowledgeable observer believes that money laundering enforcement is efficient or effective. While every investigation, prosecution, and conviction is important, some are more important than others. Nobody should argue that the conviction of a low-level drug courier rivals that of the head of the criminal organization. But that is the end result of our stat-driven law enforcement culture.

Under the current AML/CFT paradigm, it often takes two years or more for law enforcement to put together a long-term complex money laundering case. They are costly and resource intensive. Many ultimately fail. (Recall my experience with the "John of Milan" investigation I described in Chapter 10). Law enforcement personnel at the federal, state, and local levels are rated and promoted, in large part, by the number of cases they make. Management of a given field office or police department is also rated in large part by case statistics. Agency and departments buttress their appeals for Congressional appropriations by using data that show success. Thus, it is only natural for law enforcement officers and their managers to prioritize shorter-term investigations. In other words, although not part of official policy, emphasis is put on comparatively simple cases and quick arrests that look good statistically but that do not have much of an impact on the entrenched criminal enterprises that are motivated by greed. A common refrain in law enforcement is "big cases mean big problems."

In order to change the current paradigm of failure, priorities must change. Instead of our primary emphasis on intercepting narcotics or seizing stolen vehicles or stopping containers of counterfeit goods, we should finally do what we have been giving lip service to all these years. The new emphasis should be on following the money trail to the criminal hierarchy and taking away the ill-gotten gains.

This will require a massive change in direction, attitude, management, and tactics. It will have to originate from the top. An emphasis on illicit money should be articulated in agency and departmental five-year plans. Budgets and resources should be re-aligned that emphasize following the money and seizing and forfeiting illicit proceeds. We must change the incentives for investigators and their managers. Appropriate directives should be given to promotion boards. Criminal investigators will change their priorities when there are personal incentives to do so. Training programs should be developed that give investigators the knowledge and skill sets required to investigate money laundering. Staffing of investigative squads and groups should reflect the new illicit money priorities. The same directives, incentives, and training should also be carried out in U.S. Attorney offices.

Undoubtedly the first few years of the proposed new paradigm shift will be frustrating. There will be a learning curve that could result in an uptick in criminal behavior. But if adopted and pursued aggressively, we will turn the corner. The paradigm will shift. We will hurt the criminals and criminal organizations where it hurts the most — in their wallets and bank accounts.

The bureaucracies will resist the change in emphasis. Therefore, Congress must change the current incentives. Legislation should be passed that federal law enforcement and prosecutorial budgets will be indexed over time to increases in money laundering investigations, prosecutions, convictions, and seized and forfeited assets. We must really, truly, finally emphasize money.

Take Customs out of ICE and Bring Enforcement Back to Treasury

In the rush to react to September 11, politicians of both parties hurried to create the new Department of Homeland Security. The problems of DHS have been chronicled elsewhere. Thus far few discuss how the merger of Customs and the old Immigration and Naturalization Service (INS) into Immigration and Customs Enforcement (ICE) has negatively impacted our AML efforts. Customs was the oldest enforcement arm of the Department of Treasury. Customs criminal investigators carried badges, guns, and conducted investigations. They had jurisdiction on most crimes dealing with the border. In fact, they enforced more laws than the FBI. Because Treasury was its home, almost by definition Customs enforcement concentrated on money and value — particularly as it relates to trade. In the 1980s and 1990s, almost all of the large, impact, anti-money laundering investigations involved and were initiated by Customs. The forced integration into DHS changed all of that.

The mission of legacy Customs was drastically altered. Over the last 15 years, the attention of politicians and the media has been directed at immigration. Congressional appropriations followed. Legacy customs' jurisdictions suffered by neglect. Expertise departed. Particularly in dealing with trade-based money laundering and value transfer, the FBI and other federal law enforcement agencies are not capable of taking up the slack. They don't have the data, expertise, or mandate.

It makes no sense to me why the FBI and CIA, the law enforcement and intelligence agencies most responsible for the failures surrounding the attacks of September 11 were subsequently rewarded with increased manpower, budgets, and authorities. Treasury had comparatively little to do with the September 11 breakdown. However, it was Treasury that was punished. In the years leading up to September 11, there was a long-running Washington D.C. turf battle between DOJ and Treasury over which department had primacy over money laundering and financial crimes enforcement. DOJ supporters used September 11 to win that bureaucratic battle. In addition to legacy Customs, Treasury's Secret Service and Bureau of Alcohol Tobacco and Firearms were also jettisoned from Treasury's enforcement arm. (The Secret Service was incorporated into DHS and ATF into DOJ). As part of restructuring our federal AML programs, I urge Congress to seriously consider moving Customs and the Secret Service back to Treasury.

Stepped up enforcement of tax laws will equate to more effective enforcement of our anti-money laundering efforts (more on that below). So, I also urge the hire of more Customs and IRS criminal investigators. Many studies have shown that for every dollar spent on Customs and IRS enforcement, many multiples more are returned to the Treasury in the form of tax and duty revenues, seizures, and forfeitures. I am not advocating intrusive policing but better enforcement of laws already on the books.

Develop an Updated Anti-Money Laundering Strategy

Following the completion of the U.S. Money Laundering Threat Assessment in 2005, the U.S. government in 2007 produced an inter-departmental National Anti-Money Laundering (AML) Strategy report. Ten years later, the U.S. government completed a new (disappointing in my view) money laundering risk assessment in 2015. We should follow that threat assessment with an updated strategy to strengthen U.S. anti-money laundering enforcement efforts to counter threats to the financial system. Action items should be included in the report, and Congress should hold the agencies, departments, and bureaus responsible if they fail to implement them. There was no accountability (see below) in the failure to implement action items in our last Anti-Money Laundering Strategy report.[2] Reading the 2007 report years later is eye opening. It is a testament to what we have not done.

Congress Should Get Serious About the Oversight of FinCEN

If there is one federal entity that is more responsible than any other to combat money laundering it is Treasury's FinCEN. In Chapter 3, I briefly discuss the original mission of FinCEN. To recap, 30 years ago FinCEN was created to support law enforcement. Its primary mission was and, in my opinion should still be, the collection, warehousing, analysis, and dissemination of financial intelligence to support law enforcement in their investigations. In the late 1990's a secondary mission was promulgated — regulating and enforcing compliance with the BSA. As demonstrated in Chapter 2, the government's own metrics show that during the timeframe of FinCEN's existence for the most part our AML efforts have failed. While I am certainly not suggesting FinCEN is responsible for the failure, it should be readily apparent that FinCEN has been a major disappointment.

I spent six years of my career at FinCEN. In 2006 I wrote my first book Hide & Seek: Intelligence, Law Enforcement, and the Stalled War on Terror Finance.[3] I included two chapters on FinCEN. The first was titled "Promise and Potential." The concept of FinCEN was brilliant. The world's first FIU, it was the most altruistic initiative I ever saw in my government profession. Ignoring the bureaucratic rule of protecting turf, Treasury gave (with appropriate safeguards) its financial intelligence to federal, state, and local governments in order to help them with their criminal investigations. FinCEN helped create international FIUs. This data sharing occurred long before the bureaucratic post September 11 stove-piping of information was condemned. The next chapter in the book opened the curtain on FinCEN's inner workings and short comings. It is still the only insider account of FinCEN that I am aware of. I felt compelled to write about FinCEN because I knew first-hand that at the time of September 11 FinCEN's BSA analytic systems were flawed, FinCEN management was a mess, and the bureaucracy was fixated on traditional Western-style ways of business and banking. If it did not involve a bank account, wire transfer, check, or the use of an automatic teller machine, they were at a loss.

The emphasis on the BSA was a logical outgrowth of FinCEN's vested bureaucratic interests to preserve its resources and turf. Slow to grasp new and emerging threats, displaying a disdain for non-Western value transfer, reluctant to entertain imaginative

ideas, and bureaucratically wedded to the status quo, FinCEN management could not think of a money laundering or, later terrorist-
finance threat did not have as a solution yet one more financial
reporting requirement.

Of course, our adversaries use banks and all of the financial
accoutrements of the West. But we should not be surprised when
they use them in ways that do not trigger BSA financial intelligence
reporting requirements. Due to my travels in the Middle East and
elsewhere, it also seemed to me that as part of its financial diver-
sification plan, our adversaries in other parts of the world would
use the culturally indigenous, underground, ethnic-based systems
that its members were familiar with, particularly trade-based value
transfer and its various subsets like underground financial systems.
As I describe in the book, these systems and methods were not just
"cracks in the Western financial system" — as Osama bin Laden described them - but rather a Grand Canyon that was easily exploitable.

While I continue to be a strong supporter of the concept of
FinCEN, if the organization is ever going to achieve its original promise and potential the following must be addressed:

1. Without doubt the information originating from the BSA is
    incredibly useful. But FinCEN is fixated on financial intelli-
    gence. There is nothing in FinCEN's name or mission that says
    "Financial Crimes Enforcement Network that solely relies
    on the BSA." Ideally, FinCEN should be one-stop shopping
    for law enforcement that needs help with financial crimes
    enforcement of all sorts. The BSA is a tremendous resource.
    It shouldn't be the only one.

2. Even though FinCEN is fixated on the BSA, its 30-year history
    demonstrates that a variety of their analytic systems to ex-
    ploit the BSA have failed or they do not have the personnel
    expertise to take advantage of some of the systems they do
    have. This analytic malfeasance has to be finally addressed.

We also need to change the analytic paradigm. I'll address that below.

3. FinCEN has slowly moved away from its original mission to support law enforcement. It used to do case support analysis. The analysis had its drawbacks but it did prove helpful on occasion. Because case support was so difficult, FinCEN management moved the organization away from analysis. Increasingly it outsources analysis to its customers. Its main priority now seems to be regulating the BSA. That's fine, but law enforcement support has suffered as a result.

4. With a few notable exceptions, in the federal government FinCEN is synonymous with poor management — particularly in middle management. There are a host of personnel issues that need to be addressed. Over the years, in internal government surveys, FinCEN is consistently rated as one of the worst places to work in the government. The morale is simply bad. (See management above). The result is a constant hemorrhage of talent.

5. Going hand-in-hand with poor management, FinCEN is a timid organization. Nothing has changed since 2006 when I wrote the following: "Before and after September 11, FinCEN's management declined opportunity after opportunity to use its resources and authority, get involved, and make itself relevant. Stan Morris, a former director of FinCEN, had called the tiny organization the 'Little Engine that Could.' It never really was that. But without doubt, FinCEN subsequently became the 'Little Engine that Couldn't.' Its new mantra seemed to be, 'I think I can't, I think I can't, I think I can't, I think I can't.' Simply put, in my opinion, FinCEN was a cowardly organization."[4] There are so many issues where FinCEN could use its authority and get involved to help us strengthen our AML/CFT efforts. If we are to turn the corner in our

AML/CFT efforts, FinCEN's timid and defeatist attitude will
no longer suffice.

Revolving door

A few years ago, a reporter interviewed me for a story he was putting together regarding yet another high-ranking FinCEN official
departing to work for a financial institution.   This was one more
instance of an issue that has concerned me for many years; the revolving door between DOJ, Treasury, and the private sector.

Since September 11, almost all high-ranking Treasury enforcement officials that oversee AML/CFT issues (those heading TFI,
FinCEN, and OFAC) have come from the DOJ. The problem, of
course, is that there used to be healthy competition between the
two departments in the area of financial crimes enforcement. Now
there is collective DOJ inspired "group think." For the most part
the DOJ and Treasury now approach the issues the same way and
offer the same tired solutions. In essence, there has been a defacto
DOJ takeover of Treasury enforcement (or what's left of it after
the creation of DHS).

The lawyers have taken over. Our over-emphasis on sanctions
and designations is but one example. What is even more troubling,
after doing time in Treasury, most of these high-level officials de-
part or retire and are offered jobs in the financial industry sector. They are given high salaries and positions in the very financial
institutions that they were overseeing. While legal, I'm not sure
about the ethics of it all. Insiders don't want to discuss it because
they risk upsetting the "old-boy" network, but I think light needs to
be shed on this issue. The DOJ takeover of Treasury enforcement
must cease. And I would love to see a one-or-two-year moratorium
on Treasury officials exiting the revolving door and entering into the
financial institutions they used to oversee. I don't know whether
this would require legislation or an edict from the Secretary of
Treasury but something needs to be done.

Change the Analytic Paradigm

The Bank Secrecy Act was enacted fifty years ago. The original AML model developed to fight the "War on Drugs" was created in an era with threats much different than the ones we face today. In the intervening years, we have had major AML legislation, enhanced by rules and regulations, which have improved the ability of law enforcement to "follow the money." We have had some enforcement success. There is no doubt we have also disrupted and deterred some criminal activity. But as explained earlier, if we acknowledge the true scale of international money laundering and the enforcement actions that matter —forfeitures and convictions — the current AML paradigm with individual institutions, especially financial institutions (FIs), operating as the designated illicit activity detection agents is having negligible impact on all of this illicit-financing activity. The current paradigm is simply not working.

One of the main limitations is that the detection agents are expected to identify illicit-financing activity by analyzing just their own transaction data. Illicit financiers know that if their financing activity spans multiple financial institutions using a variety of transaction types, there is only a very small chance that their transactions will be identified as illicit, especially if their control of the variety of account holding entities remains hidden.

In 1970, the BSA initiated the collection of financial intelligence by regulated financial institutions. At the time, the financial transactions environment was slow, cumbersome, paper driven, and expensive. Real-time transaction processing was barely feasible. As a consequence, individual financial institutions as the only entities with access to the transaction records, were the only possible choice to be the illicit activity detection agents. Over the years, financial intelligence reporting requirements have dramatically increased and now include many more types of entities, such as money-service businesses and designated businesses and professionals as detection agents. What has not changed is that each designated detection agent is still expected to identify suspected illicit activity primarily from analyzing just its own data.

AML/CFT compliance costs in the United States alone are estimated to be in the billions of dollars every year. If I was in industry, I imagine the costs would be more palatable if I was assured that the data was at least being fully exploited. It's not. To make matters worse, the regulated industry that reports financial intelligence is so afraid of fines for non-compliance that it "defensively" files garbage reports cluttering the system with almost useless data, making it increasingly difficult to identify real and timely suspicious activity. FinCEN analyzes and maintains some 200 million BSA records involving more than 80,000 financial institutions. [5]Approximately 19 million pieces of financial intelligence are filed annually with FinCEN.

I was at Treasury's FinCEN when Suspicious Activity Reports (SARs) were first introduced. SARs were designed to create a "haystack full of needles." [6] Twenty-five years later, there is so much unusable information that we are back to trying to find the "needle in the haystack."

The monumental effort and expense that has been devoted to get the individual FI-based implementation of the current AML/CFT paradigm to produce acceptable results is inefficient and not working. Einstein reportedly defined "insanity" as "doing the same thing over and over again expecting a different result." The evolution of financial transaction processing now enables implementation of a new AML/CFT paradigm that would have been impossible up until fairly recently.

Over the last few years, there has been an explosion in processing speed, efficiency, digitalized data, and advanced analytics. Paper records have been replaced by digital records. Transaction processing is done by computers now connected by networks that enable transactions to be completed in a few seconds almost anywhere. Sophisticated software-based analytical capabilities can access virtually limitless processing capacity to quickly analyze vast amounts of data. Almost instantaneous financial transparency and corresponding alerts are achievable.

The only thing that has not yet been changed is the current AML/CFT paradigm. We need an illicit activity detection capability based on a new AML intelligence collection, analysis, and dissemination paradigm. A new paradigm enables pursuit of two important objectives. First, it will enable adding the objective of preventing illicit access to the financial system in addition to the objectives of detecting and punishment. Second, it will enable a method of accessing multi-FI transaction data that does not require exposure of any private data in detection processing.

Many observers have talked about a public-private "partnership" in the financial intelligence (FININT) world, but nothing of substance has ever materialized. Under the current AML/CFT paradigm, the public/private relationship has become essentially adversarial. While some relationships on the individual level are professional and productive, viewed as a whole there is still mistrust and misunderstanding on both sides. I believe the time is now right for government and industry representatives to work together and design and implement a modern, robust, efficient, effective, and near real-time AML detection system that incorporates the necessary privacy safeguards and oversight.

Technology exists to allow participating institutions to act together in a type of consortium, a new type of detection agent operating on behalf of the individual FIs, to get the collective benefit of analyzing an extract of multi-FI, multi-transaction-type data without any private data being exposed in the detection process. Automated analytics would be applied against transactions to screen sanctioned and suspect parties. Anomaly detection and alerts could be red-flagged on a real-time basis and illicit transaction execution prevented. Cautionary warnings would be provided to participating institutions, relevant authorities, and public and private financial intelligence units. The transaction data extract provided for detection processing could be anonymized to protect customer privacy, while transactions and reports to relevant parties would be provided in real time.

Such a consortium facility would also change the nature of the relationships among the key stakeholders in the struggle to combat illicit financing. The necessarily slow current process of issuing new regulations in response to the discovery of new illicit financing methods would be replaced. There would be no more requirements for FIs to produce a huge volume of financial intelligence or for law enforcement to laboriously shift through those reports to assemble the information and evidence required to support filing cases. Instead, the stakeholders would be positioned to cooperate effectively in combatting illicit financing activity. With access to extracts of comprehensive multi-FI, multi-transaction-type data, the consortium working with its stakeholder partners will be able to uncover new illicit-financing methods, implement the required detection capabilities, and begin limiting the effectiveness of the new illicit method in short order.

This model could be applied on different platforms and involve different parties. A completely revamped FinCEN or another Treasury entity could be at the center of the network, or perhaps a private sector consortium could act as the trusted clearinghouse.[7]

At the financial intelligence consortium, I would like to see law enforcement representatives sit side-by-side with the reporting industry representatives. Responding to the constantly changing enforcement environment, a law enforcement presence at the consortium could continuously tweak reporting tips, provide feedback industry so desperately wants, and directly alert their colleagues in the field with near real-time speed regarding suspicious activity, which is much more useful in thwarting potential criminal activity than it is to react after the fact.[8]

Accountability

Perhaps it is because of my law enforcement background, but I believe the best deterrence is accountability. If somebody breaks the law, he or she should be held accountable. That should apply equally to narcotics traffickers as well as to executives in financial institutions who break the law and facilitate the laundering of illicit proceeds.

In the 1970's and early 1980's, compliance with the BSA was very low. Likewise, the level of scrutiny by federal regulatory agencies overseeing the mandated financial intelligence reporting requirements was minimal. Not until 1985, the year of the watershed case involving noncompliance by the Bank of Boston, did things start to change. The Bank of Boston pled guilty to violating currency reporting requirements and was fined $500,000. Then as now, it was not the amount of the fine that acted as a deterrent. It was the negative publicity. Corporate executives were afraid of headlines linking their bank with narcotics trafficking. As a result, for the most part, the U.S. banking industry provides excellent cooperation with the U.S. government and complies with BSA reporting requirements.

However, there have been notable exceptions. As discussed in Chapter 3, since the end of 2009, U.S. regulators have levied more than $16 billion in fines for AML compliance failings.[9] There is a long list of both U.S. and global banks that have been exposed for noncompliance and sometimes their direct role in money laundering. Perhaps the most egregious example is HSBC. In 2012 HSBC paid a record $1.92 billion in fines to U.S. authorities for allowing itself to be used to launder almost $900 billion of drug money flowing out of Mexico and other banking lapses.[10] According to a former US Deputy Federal Prosecutor who was involved in the HSBC investigation, "Affiliates of drug cartels were literally walking into bank branches with hundreds of thousands, sometimes millions of US cash. "That didn't happen once, it didn't happen twice, it happened systematically over the course of about a decade."[11]

In the HSBC case, and in many others, the malfeasance could have only occurred with corporate executive knowledge. Corporate culture enabled the wrong-doing. The motive was profit. In my mind there is no difference between the greed of narcotics kingpins and the greed of dirty corporate executives. Yet, I don't believe an executive of a financial institution has ever been held personally responsible. None have ever served any jail time or paid a fine out of his or her pocket. There is no accountability.

In the case of HSBC, part of the problem is with the "revolving door" discussed earlier in this chapter. A high ranking official of the Department of Justice transferred to Treasury. That same high level official later "retired" and joined HSBC about the time of the scandal. One of the ostensible reasons for the hire was to help clean up the corporate culture. But could not that former very well-connected government official with experience at both Justice and Treasury turned HSBC executive have used his "old boy network" of contacts and lobby friends and ex-colleagues for a sweetheart deal?

And what about the $1.9 billion settlement fine? Some will say that reflects accountability. No! That money was not paid by the greedy corporate executives. It was paid by HSBC shareholders. And I wouldn't be surprised if a tax-write off was claimed.

As I said at the outset, most U.S. financial institutions are out-standing corporate citizens and do their best to assist with our AML/CFT efforts. But until we have meaningful accountability, we are going to continue to have incidents of non-compliance and financial institution malfeasance. And the real threat lies with overseas banks — particularly with the rise of China in international banking and finance. I urge the Department of Justice to prosecute individual executives for their involvement in money laundering facilitated by their financial institutions.

Initiate a New Money Services Business (MSBs) Registration Effort

In the late 1990s, a study sponsored by FinCEN estimated that there were over 200,000 money services businesses (MSBs) in the United States. MSBs include businesses that cash checks, issue money or-ders, and execute wire transfers. After the September 11th attack and passage of the 2001 USA PATRIOT Act, MSBs were required to register with FinCEN and obtain licenses in the states in which they do business. However, according to the government's own data, the federal registration program has not been successful, with only about one-quarter of the estimated number of MSBs having registered with FinCEN.[12] Moreover, not all states require licensing for companies which do not maintain a physical location in the state, and few states have made MSB licensing a priority. The resulting multiple gaps in federal and state registration and licensing data is of increasing concern because approximately one-half of all suspicious activity reports (SARs) filed with FinCEN every year originate via MSBs. The tens of thousands of MSBs absent from the federal registration and state licensing processes include hawaladars, casas de cambio, and a myriad of informal money-transfer services exploited by money launderers. The diversity and accessibility of the MSB sector also presents ongoing, grave challenges for effective oversight.

For a MSB it is a federal offense to fail to register with FinCEN, to operate a money transmitting business in contravention of any applicable state licensing requirements, or to transport or transmit funds that are known to have been derived from a criminal offense or intended to be used to promote or support unlawful activity. The IRS is responsible for ensuring that MSBs register with FinCEN and for conducting AML/CFT compliance examinations, but it has neither the personnel nor the resources to fulfill those responsibilities.

The IRS should be given additional resources to carry out its MSB duties or it should delegate those duties to FinCEN, which should initiate a new, intensive MSB registration and oversight effort. FinCEN should undertake an aggressive effort to identify unregistered or unlicensed MSBs and ensure they fulfill their registration and licensing requirements. FinCEN should also consider preempting state MSB licensing requirements by issuing a rule establishing uniform licensing requirements applicable to every MSB/money transmitter operating in the United States. Creating uniform, nationwide licensing standards and procedures would reduce the accumulative regulatory burden for interstate MSBs while also providing a more uniform and efficient set of laws for money transmitters to follow.

Promote Usage of the Legal Entity Identifier (LEI)

The LEI is a unique 20-character code that identifies distinct legal entities that engage in financial transactions. The LEI is a global, non-proprietary identification system and freely accessible. Over 435,000 legal entities from more than 195 countries have now been issued LEIs. The LEI will be a linchpin for financial data — the first global and unique entity identifier enabling risk managers and regulators to identify parties to financial transactions instantly and precisely. And, as LEI is adopted, subsequent iterations of the program will begin linking beneficial ownership data to these unique identifiers, thus helping create transparency not only around company structures but around ownership structures as well. The widespread use of LEI will help provide financial transparency, accountability, and assist investigators in following the money trail. Currently, an international collaborative effort between public and private entities is developing the LEI, with the support of the Financial Stability Board (FSB) and the endorsement of the G-20. Legislation should be passed that requires U.S. companies that engage in financial transactions to obtain a LEI.[13]

Close Gatekeeper Loopholes

The U.S. government should close loopholes related to the gatekeepers of the financial system (also known as designated non-financial businesses and professions, or DNFBPs) that enable corrupt individuals and criminals to launder money through the U.S. financial system. DNFBPs include attorneys, accountants, and real estate agents. All appropriate AML/CFT obligations should be applied to these professions as is urged in the 2016 FATF Mutual Evaluation Report of the United States.[14]

Tax Evasion and Money Laundering: Two Sides of the Same Coin

The United States is one of only a small number of industrialized countries that enumerates a list of predicate offenses for money laundering. This contrasts the FATF suggestion to simply designate "all serious crimes" as predicates. Moreover, the FATF also suggests that "tax crimes" are also predicate offenses for money laundering. In the U.S., according to the IRS, money laundering is tax evasion in progress if the underlying conduct violates income tax laws and the Bank Secrecy Act.[15] I suggest legislation that adhere to the FATF suggestions; i.e. all serious crimes including tax crimes should be predicate offenses for money laundering.

For the criminal investigator both in this country and overseas, separating money laundering from tax evasion has become increasingly difficult. The methodologies employed in both crimes are often quite similar. One citizen's tax haven can be the same as a money launderer's hidden offshore account. Financial safe havens, promoted by creative lawyers and accountants and proliferated by modern telecommunications, provide ready tax shelters for corporations and rich citizens eager to escape their tax obligations. The result is an eroding of the tax base, which has to be made up by law-abiding citizens.

In the developing world, the untaxed billions of dollars in illicit financial flows is a gaping hole in the international free-market system. Corrupt kleptocrats and the elites send scarce money offshore, further impoverishing the poor. This has been well documented in Raymond Baker's ground breaking book, Capitalism's Achilles Heel.[16]

As a former criminal investigator, I think it is hypocritical for the American government to talk tough on money laundering while allowing some of its privileged citizens and corporations to dodge their tax obligations and responsibilities via loopholes. As the IRS knows, tax evasion is a form of money laundering often practiced by the rich. White collar laundering creates a huge untaxed economy and promotes a kind of capital flight that harms U.S. economic strength and national interests. While there have been some recent initiatives in this area, I urge Congress to ignore special interests and identify and close tax loopholes.

Compliance Costs and Beltway Bandits

The cost to industry of AML/CFT compliance is staggering. According to the "2019 True Cost of AML Compliance report for the United States," the cost of compliance across U.S. and Canadian financial services firms is approximately $31.5 billion per year.[17] In some financial institutions, one out of every ten employees is dedicated to AML/CFT compliance.[18] Untold additional multi-tens of billions of dollars equivalent of compliance costs are incurred by financial services firms elsewhere around the world. The regulatory burden shows no signs of slowing down. The costs incurred by industry definitely impact the bottom line.

Remember the sobering metrics we discussed in Chapter 2 about criminal proceeds actually forfeited? Clearly, financial institutions spend far more on AML compliance than criminals forfeit as a result of law enforcement action. It is almost insulting that financial institutions are charged for an ineffective process that is an obligation of government. It's another form of regulatory taxation and one that dramatically effects the bottom line.

Yet that is not the whole story. AML/CFT is also a big business. Plenty of companies large and small benefit from the status quo. There are software engineers, analytic service providers, consultants of all sorts, investigators, lobbyists, attorneys, trainers, educators, certified AML "specialists," etc. In candor, since I retired from the government much of my modest income has been from engaging in AML/CFT work.

Some of the worst charlatans are the so-called "beltway bandits." (The beltway is the freeway loop around greater Washington D.C.). These are the large international companies that everyone knows. They offer "consulting services" to both government and business. On the one hand, these consulting companies work with the government to help provide AML software, analytics, design various engineering solutions, and provide contractors to work with the government on various AML/CFT projects. On the other hand, some of these same firms counsel large multi-nationals how to avoid the AML/CFT regulatory burden and engage in tax mitigation strategies such as abusive transfer pricing or the manipulation of the international trading system within the same multinational group to take advantage of lower jurisdictional tax rates. It's nothing less than a form of commercial trade-based money laundering.[19] These consultant service providers have discovered a very profitable recipe to both have their cake and eat it too!

A Panel of Experts

Compliance costs and virtually all of the issues we have discussed are intertwined. To effectively solve one, we must look at the others such as changing the incentives for law enforcement, re-imagining FinCEN, re-designing the AML analytic paradigm, getting back to the basics of enforcement, etc.

The great thing about the issues discussed in this book is that we have 30 years or more of experience. We can judge what works and what doesn't. We have data. But most importantly, we have experience and expertise. I personally am aware of a cadre of people of great intellect and character that have been doing terrific AML work — both in government and industry — for decades. These individuals (and many others) want to do the right things but have been stymied by the "systems" they work for. I would love to see a group like that (no more than 20 people) get together in the same room and hash things out. They could use their imagination, experience, and knowledge of enforcement, industry, technology, regulations, and applicable laws and policies to put forward a package of ideas that would re-imagine the U.S. AML/CFT efforts. Working with Congressional intermediaries, those ideas could then be proposed as legislation or executive action.

The format and politics of Congressional hearings do not allow such a conversation. FinCEN will not take the initiative. Government/

industry partnership isn't functional and is too nebulous. Perhaps the White House could sponsor an AML Commission. But the venue isn't that important. Simply put a group of congenial AML/CFT experts together in the same room and over coffee (or a few beers) I'm confident we could come up with imaginative and effective ideas that would reflect hard-learned lessons from the past and position us to move AML into the future.

Final Thoughts

The truth about following the money and value trails is that for the last 30 years, our targeting of superficial symptoms has not proven sufficient in seriously curtailing transnational crime, international money laundering, and illicit financial flows. Examining the important metrics that matter there is no escaping the conclusion that we have failed. Yet we can't afford to give up. The issues involved are too important. Money remains the root cause of most of our evils. Still, I remain optimistic. The flip side of failure is opportunity. I'm convinced we can put together much more effective, comprehensive, and efficient AML measures. We know many of the ways forward. The big question is whether or not we can muster the will to do so.

Once again, my personal thanks to all of you who have contributed to our AML efforts over the years. I wish success to those who take the next steps and continue this vitally important struggle.

NOTES

1 Financial Action Task Force, "Anti-money laundering and counter-terrorist financing measures: United States: Mutual Evaluation Report," December 2016, page 4; http://www.fatfgafi.org/media/fatf/documents/reports/mer4/MER-United-States-2016.pdf

2 U.S. Government, "2007 National Anti-Money Laundering Strategy," 2007; https://www.justice.gov/sites/default/files/criminal-afmls/legacy/2011/05/12/mlstrategy07.pdf

3 John Cassara, Hide & Seek: Intelligence, Law Enforcement, and the Stalled War on Terror Finance, Potomac Books, 2006, Washington, D.C.

4 Ibid, page 185

5 Steven Dennis and Billy House, "Senate Panel Digs Into 2,000 Financial Documents in Trump Probe," Bloomberg, June 28, 2017; https://www.bloomberg.com/news/articles/2017-06-28/senate-panel-digs-into-2-000financial-documents-in-trump-probe

6 Quote from former FinCEN Director Stanley Morris

7 Conversations with industry representatives; see also: Chip Poncy and Juan Zarate, "Fixing AML: Designing a New AML System," Banking Perspectives, 2016; https://www.theclearinghouse.org/research/2016/2016-q3banking-perspectives/a-new-aml-system

8 Much of the this section was taken from: John Cassara, Senate Judiciary Committee Testimony, "Modernizing AML Laws to Combat Money Laundering and Terrorist Financing," November 28, 2017; https://www.judiciary.senate.gov/imo/media/doc/Cassara%20Testimony.pdf

9 "Senator Warren says U.S. needs to 'rethink' money laundering laws," Reuters, January 9, 2018; https://www.reuters.com/article/us-usa-senate-moneylaundering/senator-warren-says-u-s-needs-to-rethink-money-laundering-laws-idUSKBN1EY28B

10 Aruna Viswanatha and Brett Wolf, "HSBC to pay $1.9 billion U.S. fine in money laundering case," Reuters, December 11, 2012; https://www.reuters.com/article/us-hsbc-probe/hsbc-to-pay-1-9-billion-u-s-fine-in-money-laundering-case-idUSBRE8BA05M20121211

11 "Banksters: the scandalous conduct of a global bank," ABC, May 10, 2018; https://www.abc.net.au/4corners/banksters/9747234

12 "2007 National Anti-Money Laundering Strategy"

13 For further information see: https://www.leiroc.org/lei.htm

14 Financial Action Task Force, "Anti-money laundering and counter-terrorist financing measures: United States: Mutual Evaluation Report," December 2016; http://www.fatf-gafi.org/media/fatf/documents/reports/mer4/MERUnited-States-2016.pdf

15 U.S. Internal Revenue Service, "Overview - Money Laundering," March 2, 2017; https://www.irs.gov/uac/overview-money-laundering

16 Raymond Baker, Capitalism's Achilles Heel, Wiley, Hoboken, New Jersey, 2005

17 "Increase AML compliance efficiencies and lower costs," Lexis-Nexis, 2019; https://risk.lexisnexis.com/insights-resources/research/2019-true-cost-of-aml-compliance-study-for-united-states-and-canada

18 "Almost one in 10 ABN Amro staffers are working on financial crime," Dutch News, February 12, 2020; https://www.dutchnews.nl/news/2020/02/almost-one-in-10-abn-amro-staffers-are-working-on-financial-crime/

19 John Cassara, Trade Based Money Laundering: The Next Frontier in International Money Laundering Enforcement, Wiley, Hoboken, New Jersey, 2016, pages 118-122.

Glossary

Arbitrage
The nearly simultaneous purchase and sale of an asset in order to profit from a difference in the price. It exploits price differences of identical goods in different market locations.

Arm's Length Transaction
If two unrelated companies trade with each other across international boundaries, there is generally negotiation on price, resulting in a fair or market driven charge which is acceptable for tax purposes.

ARS — Alternative Remittance System
See *IVTS*.

AML/CFT — Anti-Money Laundering/Combatting the Financing of Terrorism
Collective term generally used to describe the legal and regulatory framework and other obligations countries must implement. See also *FATF 40*.

APG — Asia Pacific Group
A FATF-style regional body, the APG wrote a comprehensive 2012 TBML typologies report.

ATF — Bureau of Alcohol, Tobacco, and Firearms.
A law enforcement agency responsible for examining violations of Federal laws within the jurisdiction of the United States Department of Justice.

ATT — Afghan Transit Trade
A regional agreement between landlocked Afghanistan and its neighbors that allows goods to be imported into the country with preferential duties. The trade has resulted in massive smuggling and trade fraud, and it continues to facilitate the laundering of narcotics proceeds and contributes to the financing of terrorist groups operating in South Asia.

Beneficial Ownership
In the United States, when people create companies, they are not required to disclose who really profits from their existence or controls their activities — the actual "beneficial owners" of the business. Instead, individuals who benefit can conceal their identity by using front people, or "nominees," to represent the company.

BMPE — Black Market Peso Exchange
One of the most pernicious money laundering schemes in the Western Hemisphere. It is also one of the largest, processing billions of dollars a year from Colombia alone via TBML and other schemes.

BSA — Bank Secrecy Act
Officially known as the "Currency and Foreign Transactions Reporting Act," it requires financial institutions to help various government agencies detect and prevent money laundering. Specifically, the BSA requires banks and other financial institutions to file reports of currency transactions exceeding $10,000, to keep records of cash purchases of negotiable instruments, and to report suspicious activity.

Bulk Cash Smuggling (BCS)

The physical transportation or smuggling of bulk cash currency in order to place it in a jurisdiction with less stringent financial transparency reporting requirements.

Capital Flight

Wealth, capital, and assets are moved from a country when there is a loss of confidence. Generally this is due to an event or policies that have economic consequence such as political instability, monetary uncertainties, increase in taxes, or currency depreciation.

Carousel Fraud

The practice of importing goods from a country where they are not subject to Value Added Tax (see *VAT*), selling them with VAT added, then deliberately not paying the VAT to the government. The fraudster charges VAT on the sale of goods and instead of paying it to the government simply absconds — taking the VAT with him. It is a form of "carousel" or "merry-go-round" when sometimes goods are cycled between companies and jurisdictions collecting ever more fraudulent VAT revenues. Sometimes in TBML, carousel fraud also refers to the process of cycling trade goods (genuine or fictitious) in and out of non-VAT markets in order to justify payment abroad.

CBP — Customs and Border Protection

See *ICE*.

CDD/KYC — Customer Due Diligence/Know Your Customer

The first step financial institutions must take to detect, deter, and prevent money laundering and terrorist financing; i.e., maintain adequate knowledge about their customers and their financial activities.

CMIR — Report of International Transportation of Currency or Monetary Instruments

The United States has established a declaration system that applies to all incoming and outgoing physical transportation of cash and other monetary instruments. It is illegal to transport more than $10,000 (or its foreign equivalent) in cash or other monetary instruments into or out of the country without filing a CMIR, also known as FinCEN Form 105.

Counter-valuation
Often employed in settling debts between traders and those involved with underground finance. For example, a party in a transaction may over- or undervalue a commodity or trade item such as gold, thereby transferring value to another party and/or offsetting debt owed.

Cryptocurrencies
Digital currencies in which encryption techniques are used to regulate the generation of units of currency and verify the transfer of funds. Cryptocurrencies operate independently of a central bank.

CTR — Currency Transaction Report
Financial institutions are required to file a CTR with FinCEN whenever they process a currency transaction exceeding $10,000. These reports include useful identifying information about the transaction. Once FinCEN receives them, they are input into a BSA reporting database that is available to federal banking regulators and —with restrictions — the law enforcement community.

Delaware Corporation
See *shell corporation*.

DNFBPs — Designated Non-Financial Businesses and Professions

Egmont Group
The international standard-setter for financial intelligence units. An organization created with the explicit purpose of serving as a

center to overcome the obstacles preventing the sharing of financial intelligence and other information between member FIUs.

Export Incentives
Tax, legal, and/or regulatory payments or allowances that encourage domestic companies to export goods or services.

FATF — Financial Action Task Force
Also known by the French name *Groupe d'action financiére sur le blanchiment de capitaux* (GAFI), FATF was created by the G-7 leaders in 1989 in order to address increased concerns about money laundering's threat to the international financial system. This intergovernmental policy-making task force was given the mandate of examining money laundering techniques and trends, reviewing domestic and international actions, and setting the international standard for combating money laundering and terrorism financing. FATF-style regional bodies associated with FATF are found throughout the world.

FATF 40
The FATF-issued international standards for preventing, detecting, and suppressing both money laundering and terrorist financing. Although they are technically just "recommendations," they carry the force of "mandates for action" throughout much of the international community and financial sector.

Fei-chien
A very old Chinese underground financial system originally designed to pay taxes. Over the centuries it evolved as an underground money and value transfer system. Today, fei-chien, sometimes also known as "flying money," and other similar indigenous Chinese parallel financial systems are used to fill the needs of both Chinese entrepreneurs and migrants around the world. Skirting official financial restrictions and regulations that impede commercial efficiency,

fei-chien facilitates capital flight, tax evasion, the repatriation of profits, and the remittance of wages.

FinCEN — Financial Crimes Enforcement Network
A bureau with the U.S. Department of Treasury, FinCEN is the U.S. financial intelligence unit.

FININT — Financial Intelligence

FIU — Financial Intelligence Unit
In many countries, a central national agency responsible for receiving, requesting, analyzing, and/or disseminating disclosures of financial information to the competent authorities, primarily concerning suspected proceeds of crime and the potential financing of terrorism. A FIU's mandate is backed up by national legislation or regulation.

Financial Intelligence
Sometimes known as FININT, BSA information, or financial intelligence or financial transparency reporting requirements.

Flying Money
Also known as *fei-chien, hui kuan,* and *chiao hui,* flying money is an ancient Chinese underground financial and alternative remittance system. See *IVTS* and *fei-chien*.

FTZ —FTrade Zone
Designated geographic areas outside of normal customs areas and procedures. FTZs and similar districts such as special economic zones, enterprise zones, free ports, and export processing zones generally offer duty and tax free access and sometimes incorporate a number of other incentives for businesses. They provide a preferential environment for goods and services usually associated with exports.

FSRB — FATF Style Regional Body
These bodies — which are modeled on FATF and are granted certain rights by that organization — serve as regional centers for matters relating to AML/CFT. Their primary purpose is to promote a country's implementation of comprehensive AML/CFT regimes and implement the FATF 40 recommendations.

GFI - Global Financial Integrity
A Washington D.C. based non-profit that analyzes illicit financial flows and abusive trade misinvoicing particularly from the developing world.

GTO — Geographic Targeting Order
An order issued by the Financial Crimes Enforcement Unit (FinCEN) of the United States Secretary of Treasury requiring any United States designated domestic financial or non-financial institution within a geographic area to report on transactions any greater than a specified value.

HS — Harmonized Tariff Schedule
Developed by the World Customs Organization, the HS comprises about 5,000 commodity groups, each identified by a common six-digit code. The HS is supported by well-defined rules to achieve uniform classification. The system is used by more than 200 countries as a basis for their customs tariffs.

Hawala
A very simple and centuries-old broker system based on trust, found throughout South Asia, the Middle East Africa, and the Americas. It allows customers and brokers (*"hawaladars"*) to transfer money or value without physically moving it, often in areas of the world where banks and other financial institutions have little or no presence. Historically and culturally, trade is often used to settle accounts between hawaladars. Hawala-like systems are used by many different cultures but under different names.

Hawaladar
A broker in a hawala or hawala-type network.

Hundi
In Pakistan and Bangladesh, hundi is the term used to describe hawala.

HSI — Homeland Security Investigations
An investigative arm of the Department of Homeland Security active in combating criminal organizations illegally exploiting America's travel, trade, financial, and immigration systems. HSI is a part of ICE that employs special agents to do investigations. ICE has other divisions.

ICE — Immigration and Customs Enforcement
Part of the Department of Homeland Security, ICE executes its mission through the enforcement of more than 400 federal statutes, and focuses on immigration enforcement, preventing terrorism and combating the illegal movement of people and trade.

INCSR — International Narcotics Control Strategy Report
A congressionally mandated report released annually in March by the U.S. State Department Bureau of International Narcotics and Law Enforcement Affairs. Volume I describes international narcotics production, and Volume II describes money laundering and related financial crimes in countries around the world.

IVTS — Informal Value Transfer Systems
Sometimes known as *parallel banking, underground banking, or alternative remittance systems*, IVTS refers to any system, mechanism, or network that transfers money for the purpose of making an equivalent amount of funds payable to a third party in another geographic location, whether or not in the same form. The transfers often take place outside of conventional banking systems and often use trade-based value transfer systems to settle accounts between brokers.

IFFs — Illicit Financial Flows
IFFs generally refers to cross-border movement of capital associated with illegal activity or more explicitly, money that is illegally earned, transferred or used that crosses borders.

Integration
This is the last stage of the money laundering process. The laundered money is introduced into the economy so that it appears to be normal business earnings, making it very difficult for law enforcement to detect. Some methods of integration include real estate purchases, buying luxury vehicles, investing in the stock market, and investment in trade goods. See also *placement* and *layering*.

IPR — Intellectual Property Rights

IRS /CI — Internal Revenue Service/Criminal Investigations
This U.S. law enforcement agency investigates potential criminal violations of the Internal Revenue Code, Bank Secrecy Act and related financial crimes.

KYC — Know Your Customer
KYC is the process of a bank or business knowing the true identity and activity of a client or customer. (See *CDD*.)

LLC — Limited Liability Corporation
Is a corporate structure in the United States whereby the owners are not personally liable for the company's debts or liabilities. Limited liability companies are hybrid entities that combine the characteristics of a corporation with those of a partnership or sole proprietorship.

Layering
This is the second stage of the money laundering process. The purpose of this stage is to make it more difficult for law enforcement to detect or follow the trail of illegal proceeds. Methods include

converting cash into monetary instruments and moving money between bank accounts. See also *integration* and *placement.*

MSB — Money Service Business

Any individual or business that engages in accepting and transmitting funds by any means through a financial agency or institution. All informal financial operators in the United States, including hawaladars, are legally categorized as MSBs. Examples include currency dealers, check cashers, and issuers of travelers' checks, money orders, or stored value.

M-Payments — Mobile Payments

An umbrella term that covers diverse high-tech money transfer systems such as digital precious metals, Internet payment services, prepaid calling cards, and M-payments (i.e., money and e-value transfer via the use of cell phones).

NGO — Non-Governmental Organization

NPM — New Payment Methods

OCDETF — Organized Crime Drug Enforcement Task Force

The multiagency/departmental OCDETF Program was established in 1982 to mount a comprehensive attack and reduce the supply of illegal drugs in the United States and diminish the violence and other criminal activity associated with the drug trade.

OFAC — Office of Foreign Assets Control

An office of the U.S. Treasury that enforces economic and trade sanctions against countries and groups of individuals involved in terrorism, narcotics and other disreputable activities.

Offshore

A broad term, but generally it is a company or firm incorporated outside the country where it has its main offices and operations or where its principal investors reside.

Over-invoicing

When money launderers and those involved with value transfer, trade fraud, and illicit finance misrepresent goods or services on an invoice by indicating that they cost more than what they are actually worth. This allows one party in the illicit transaction to transfer money to the other under the guise of legitimate trade.

Parallel banking

See *IVTS*.

Placement

This is the first stage of the money laundering process. Illicit money is disguised or misrepresented, then placed into circulation through financial institutions, casinos, shops, and other businesses, both local and abroad. A variety of methods can be used for this purpose including currency smuggling, bank complicity, currency exchanges, securities brokers, blending of funds, asset purchase, and so forth. See also *integration* and *layering*.

Remittance Code

In underground money and value transfers such as hawala and fei-chien, brokers sometimes provide the customer with a code when they receive the money to be remitted. The customer, in turn, communicates this code to the intended recipient of the money. When the money is actually delivered, the recipient presents the code to the courier or partner hawaladar to complete the transaction.

SAR/STR — Suspicious Activity Report/Suspicious Transaction Report

If a financial institution suspects or has reasonable grounds to suspect that the funds involved in a given transaction derive from criminal or terrorist activity, it is obligated to file a report with its national FIU containing key information about the transaction. In the United States, SAR is the most common term for such a report, though STR is used in many other jurisdictions.

Service-based Laundering

Instead of laundering money or transferring value through trade goods, services are used. Similar to TBML, service-based laundering revolves around invoice fraud and manipulation.

Shadow Banking

Shadow banking occurs when banks and non-bank financial institutions lend money outside of lending norms and safeguards. The loans are often packaged into complicated wealth management and other financial products. Banks market these risky loans as a way to increase profits and share debt.

Shell Company

An incorporated company with no significant operations, established with the sole purpose of holding or transferring funds, often for money laundering purposes. As the name implies, shell companies have only a name, address, and bank accounts; clever money launderers often attempt to make them look more like real businesses by maintaining fake financial records and other elements. Generally, there is a lack of beneficial ownership information.

Smurfing/Structuring

A money laundering technique that involves splitting a large bank deposit into smaller deposits to evade the U.S. government's CTR and SAR requirements for financial institutions.

Supply Chain
A network between a production company and its suppliers to produce and distribute a specific product to the final buyer or end user.

Task Force
In the United States, a task force is a collaborative effort between federal, state, and local law enforcement designed to target a particular criminal activity, and often in a particular geographical area. Resources, expertise, and jurisdictions are combined. The task force has proven to be an effective way to combat crime. There have also been international law enforcement task forces. The FATF is an international policy-making task force. See *FATF*.

TCO — Transnational Criminal Organization

TFI — Terrorism and Financial Intelligence
An office within the Department of Treasury that develops and implements U.S. government strategies to combat terrorist financing domestically and internationally, develops and implements the National Money Laundering Strategy as well as other policies and programs to fight financial crimes.

TBML — Trade-based Money Laundering
The process of disguising the proceeds of crime and moving value via trade transactions in an attempt to legitimize their illicit origin.

Trade Diversion
In an international trade situation, a business or broker that offers a lower-cost product for importation into a particular country tends to create a trade diversion away from another importer or local producers whose prices are higher for a similar product.

Transfer Pricing
In the context of TBML, transfer pricing is what subsidiaries of the same multinational charge each other for goods and services. It is generally done to shift tax liability to tax-free or low-tax haven.

Tri-Border Area
The frontier junction of Paraguay, Argentina, and Brazil. This area is known for its illicit activity, including TBML, terrorism financing, customs fraud, drug smuggling, intellectual property rights viola-tions, and tax evasion. The geography of the region makes it very difficult to monitor, facilitating and promoting organized crime and related activities.

TTU — Trade Transparency Unit
TTUs examine trade between countries by comparing, for example, the export records from Country A and the corresponding import records from Country B. Allowing for some recognized variables, the data should match. Any wide discrepancies could be indicative of trade fraud (including TBML). Anomalies could also be the back door to underground remittance and informal value transfer systems that are based on trade such as hawala. The first TTU was established in the United States and is currently directed by Homeland Security Investigations. TTUs have since been established around the world.

UNODC — United Nations Office on Drugs and Crime

Underground Banking
See *IVTS*.

Under-invoicing
When money launderers and those involved with value transfer, trade fraud, and illicit finance misrepresent goods or services on an invoice by indicating that they cost less than the form of goods or services.

VAT — Value Added Tax
A type of consumption tax by which the value of an article is increased at each stage of its production or distribution.

WCO — World Customs Organization
Established in 1952 as the Customs Co-operation Council (CCC), the WCO is an independent intergovernmental body whose mission is to enhance the effectiveness and efficiency of 180 Customs administrations across the globe that collectively process approximately 98 percent of world trade.

Made in the USA
Coppell, TX
28 September 2023

22154498R00203